Nothing Abstract

Nothing Abstract

INVESTIGATIONS IN

THE AMERICAN

LITERARY IMAGINATION

TOM QUIRK

University of Missouri Press

Columbia and London

Library of Congress Cataloging-in-Publication Data

Quirk, Tom, 1946–
    Nothing abstract : investigations in the American literary imagination / Tom Quirk.
        p.   cm.
    Includes bibliographical references and index.
    ISBN 0-8262-1364-2 (alk. paper)
        1. American literature—History and criticism.   2. Imagination.   I. Title.
PS121 .Q57   2001
810.9′384—dc21

                                                                    2001041581

Designer: Stephanie Foley
Typesetter: The Composing Room of Michigan, Inc.
Printer and binder: The Maple-Vail Book Manufacturing Group
Typefaces: Sabon and Gill Sans Light

For credits for previously published material, see p. ix.

C O N T E N T S

ACKNOWLEDGMENTS

Most of these essays have been published previously. I wish to thank the following journals and publishers for permission to reprint these pieces. "Authors, Intentions, and Texts," *Essays in Arts and Sciences* 28 (October 1999): 1–15. Grateful acknowledgment is made to the American Humor Studies Association for permission to reprint, in slightly modified form, "What If Poe's Humorous Tales Were Funny?: Poe's 'X-ing a Paragrab' and Twain's 'Journalism in Tennessee,'" *Studies in American Humor* n.s. 3, no. 2 (1995): 36–48. "Sources, Influences, and Intertexts," *Resources for American Literary Study* 21, no. 2 (1995): 65–82. "'In the Shallow Light of the Present': The Moral Geography of *Death Comes for the Archbishop*," *Essays in Arts and Sciences* 24 (October 1995): 1–20. "The Judge Dragged to the Bar: Lemuel Shaw, Herman Melville, and the Webster Murder Case," *Melville Society Extracts* no. 84 (February 1991): 1–8. "Realism, the 'Real,' and the Poet of Reality: Some Reflections on American Realists and the Poetry of Wallace Stevens," *American Literary Realism* 21, no. 2 (winter 1989): 34–53. "Justice on the Reservation: Hillerman's Novels and the Conflict Between Federal and Tribal Jurisdiction," *The Armchair Detective* 18, no. 4 (fall 1985): 364–70. "Hawthorne's Last Tales and 'The Custom House,'" *ESQ: A Journal of the American Renaissance* 30, no. 4 (4th quarter, 1984): 183–94, (c) Board of Regents of Washington State University. "Cather and Fitzgerald: *The Great Gatsby*," *American Literature* 54, no. 4 (December 1982): 576–91. "A Source for 'Where Are You Going? Where Have You Been?'" *Studies in Short Fiction* 18, no. 4 (fall 1981): 413–19. "The Short Stories of Ambrose Bierce," introduction to Ambrose Bierce, *Tales of Soldiers and Civilians and Other Stories*, ed. Tom Quirk, New York: Penguin Publishers, 2000. "Mark Twain in His Short Works," introduction to Mark Twain, *Selected Tales, Essays, Speeches, and Sketches of Mark Twain*, ed. Tom Quirk, New York: Penguin Publishers, 1994.

Nothing Abstract

I

Introduction

On my office door I have taped several Glen Baxter cartoons. It is my way of introducing myself to the student who might want to know in advance what sort of professor lurks within. I find that I can identify with the feisty bewilderment of his comic characters and am particularly fond of his cowboy series. There is one of a ranch hand standing before a large blank canvas dumbstruck, as though he has just been bested in this showdown. The caption reads: "It was Tom's first brush with modernism." Another is a sketch of an unshaven, slightly puzzled cowboy carrying his carbine and eyeing rather suspiciously the heavy drapery in the corner of his otherwise rustic cabin. The caption reads: "A wind of change was sweeping through the old bunkhouse, and Zeke didn't care for it one little bit." But my favorite is the picture of a man standing alone in the desert, his hat pushed back and eagerly holding up a very small sign. The caption reads: "Jed had organized another of his mini-protests"; the sign reads: "MAYBE NOT."

Perhaps because of my western upbringing, I rather enjoy adopting this sort of persona (in person and in print) because it frees me up to do what I most like to do (in person and in print), sometimes in a boisterous way, sometimes with artificial bravado. But one is responsible for the masks one wears, nonetheless, and in a sense, this selection of essays, written at various times during the last twenty years, may be seen as my own mini-protest. At the time I wrote most of them, however, I hardly thought of them in that way. Far from it. I was simply doing what I was trained to do in graduate school—to proceed in my inquiries with a certain scholarly rigor, to base my conclusions on sound evidence, and to disclose my findings in as straightforward and readable prose as I could muster. If I could make my own essays provocative or interesting, so much the better; at the very least, I could try to avoid being tedious. These were ordinary ambitions and anything but protests. Instead, they were timid forms of application into the scholarly community; there was nothing rebellious, or even antisocial, about them. But circumstances have a way of altering cases, and yesterday's orthodoxy becomes today's heresy.

I was, and am, principally interested in the study of the creative imagination as it is enacted in seemingly endless ways by original and gifted writers who for one reason or another have caught my fancy. There were, and are, certain familiar ways to inquire into the mysterious nature of the literary imagination. A blanket term for those methods is literary geneticism. Geneticism is an inductive method and includes such forms of inquiry as biographical and textual criticism, literary history, and source and influence study. Those once familiar and respectable activities have sometimes been succinctly dismissed by critical theorists, however: Biographical criticism— *"The author is dead."* Source and influence study—*"Banal," "tedious," "narrow," "positivistic."* Contextual, especially historical, study—*"There is nothing outside the text."*[1] Research into authorial intention and the establishment of texts—*"Our language thinks us."* Inquiry into the shape of an author's career and his or her originality—*"We are socially constructed."* Faced with such confident rebuttals over the years, I began to feel like Mark Twain's Scotty Briggs, who could neither understand nor make himself understood to the parson: "Why, you're most too many for me, you know. When you get in with your left I hunt grass every time. Every time you draw, you fill; but I don't seem to have any luck. Let's have a new deal."

Well, no new deal was forthcoming. After a while, I started to bark back, though mostly in antic ways. So far as I know, nobody heard me, or if they did, they didn't care. My younger colleagues in the profession have an exalted calling—they do "cultural work." I'm just an English teacher. But it isn't so bad being considered a dinosaur by younger folk; after all, who, a hundred years from now, will be able to distinguish between a structuralist and a poststructuralist fossil? However, when some of my senior colleagues started calling me a "provincial" and a "throwback," I winced. I winced, and then, like Jed in Baxter's cartoon, I did a little theorizing of my own, as if to prove, perhaps only to myself, that I knew what I was about. Hence, the first two essays in this volume—my timid *maybe not*s put up against uncompromising *undoubtedly so*s.

Though they are among the most recently composed and therefore real-

---

1. Interestingly, for many who have rebelled against this deconstructionist dictum (new historicists, neo-Marxists, cultural materialists, etc.) now, or so it seems to me, there is nothing inside the text either.

ly afterthoughts, the essays "Sources, Influences, and Intertexts" and "Authors, Intentions, and Texts" provide a lens through which to view the subsequent essays. Those essays, in their turn, provide evidence by example for my quasi-theoretical assertions. The first two essays, then, are forms of proof; the remaining essays are the pudding, and I forgive in advance the reader who wishes to avoid polemics and go straight for the pudding. Taken together, however, all these essays have quite fortuitously become my mini-protest after years of bullheadedly practicing a kind of scholarship that, in some minds, is reductionist, unfashionable, and not very sophisticated.

But the winds of doctrine may be shifting. Genetic studies may or may not be making a comeback, but the term does seem to crop up every once in a while these days. My meditations on sources, influences, and intertexts, on authors, intentions, and texts, at any rate, were written with a certain playful irony but were also meant to convey a sense of feeling beleaguered. However, even the ironist sometimes finds an unanticipated and happy irony once in a while. As I indicate in the final essay, a rekindled interest in genetic scholarship seems to be taking place, though its partisans occasionally appear unaware that they are working within a long and distinguished scholarly tradition. If history is cyclical, and if you stand still long enough, sooner or later you wind up at the head of the line after all.

But what, precisely, was I protesting? It is true that I have gathered these essays together for a purpose, but this book is not meant to be a pale imitation of Allan Bloom's *The Closing of the American Mind*, E. D. Hirsch's *Cultural Literacy,* or John Ellis's *Literature Lost.* I may be disgruntled, but I very much doubt the republic of letters is in any real danger. And I am no reactionary; if anything, I find the new left a little too exclusionary and inflexible for my tastes. Nor is this collection some latter-day version of *The Scholar Adventurers;* I am too shy and too lazy to embark on the sorts of heroic scholarly feats Richard Altick described in that book. Actually, Kenneth Burke's collection of essays, *Counter-Statement* (1931), though quite different in approach and substance from this book, comes closer to the model I have in mind. At any rate, his defense of the critical position he occupied in that volume will, with some qualification, serve as a statement of my own present purposes quite nicely: "These essays, read in their present order, should serve to elucidate a point of view. This point of view is somewhat apologetic, negativistic, and even antinomian, as regards everything but art. It is not antinomian as regards art because of a feeling that art is naturally antinomian. Art's very accumulation (its discordant voices arising out of many systems) serves to undermine any one rigid scheme of living—and herein lies 'wickedness' enough."[2]

In rereading these essays, I realize how often I have relied on Kenneth Burke, along with William James, to make a point. As an unembarrassed Jamesian pluralist, I subscribe to the view that a rigid scheme of living is dangerous, but I have never had a desire to be "wicked" or even mischievous. More often than not, I have been motivated by simple curiosity. Sometimes that curiosity was prompted by an odd detail—a curious Melvillean phrase, perhaps: "Who's to doom, when the judge himself is dragged to the bar"; or the fact that Joyce Carol Oates's fiendish character Arnold Friend appears to have on mascara and to wobble in his boots. At other times, I became fascinated by a curious lapse of judgment in otherwise shrewd and gifted writers. Why, for example, did Poe believe he could write humorous fiction, and what imp of the ridiculous possessed him to make him think "X-ing a Paragrab" was funny? More curious still, why did F. Scott Fitzgerald contemplate making Tom Buchanan the main character in *The Great Gatsby*?

And why did Willa Cather interrupt the composition of *Death Comes for the Archbishop*, a book that she said was written in a mood of relative ease and contentment, to make a difficult two-thousand-mile trip from New York City to Canyon de Chelly on the Navajo Reservation? Why, when he believed that he was living in the midst of the true "madmen" of the nineteenth century, should Hawthorne write the story "The Great Stone Face," which on the surface looks all the world like a transcendentalist tale? And why, when one inspects his short fiction written just before and just after the composition of *The Scarlet Letter,* do we find Hawthorne's tales so slight compared not only to his masterpiece but also to any number of tales he had written much earlier? This discrepancy is made all the more curious because Hawthorne displays, at least tonally, an earnest and significant interest in those stories.

Wallace Stevens appears a weary iconoclast when he records that "One cannot spend one's time in being modern when there are so many more important things to be."[3] But he was nonetheless eager and excited to write

2. Kenneth Burke, *Counter-Statement* (Berkeley and Los Angeles: University of California Press, 1968), viii.
3. Wallace Stevens, *Opus Posthumous: Poems, Plays, Prose,* ed. Samuel French Morse (New York: Vintage, 1982), 175.

a "poetry of the earth" and to be a (perhaps *the*) "poet of reality." In his repeated emphasis on the terms *reality* and *life* and *imagination,* was Stevens, just maybe, both modifying and continuing the realist literary tradition inherited from William Dean Howells instead of making some irreconcilable break with his predecessors? If so, the answer might go a long way in explaining why, different as they are, both Howells and Stevens thought that literature should serve the uses of life.

Those more or less accidental artists, Mark Twain and Ambrose Bierce, claimed they would (and for a brief time did) give up the writing game if something more profitable came along. How, then, did they acquire the audacity and genius that marked them as distinctive voices in American literature? What redemptive claims did the imagination have on Bierce so that, when his private life was falling apart, he was able to write his best short fiction? As for Mark Twain, he once confessed his surprise that, at the age of thirty-seven, he woke up to discover he was a "literary person." How did this casual occupation allow him to master so many literary forms and, at the same time, equip and motivate him to lampoon them?

Questions such as these, though no doubt in half-articulated ways, occurred to me in writing these essays. Simple curiosity may have prompted my inquiries, but that is surely not sufficient justification for the essays themselves. My willingness to indulge in the sorts of speculations I found provocative, to make the cross-connections and comparisons I had, or to draw the inferences and conclusions that I did stemmed from a simple desire to write an essay. I am not so egotistical or obtuse to believe that the satisfying of my own curiosity is a warrant to write, still less to be read. Rather, these are essays, and essays ought to have a form, a texture, and a point; in a word, they ought to be interesting. And I think they are. They are interesting not because I am, but because writers and writing, especially good writers and good writing, are always fundamentally interesting to anyone intrigued by the mysterious operations of the literary imagination.

There are many profitable ways to study how the imagination works in a particular writer, but there is only one bad way—in the abstract. There is no antiseptic high road that will explain the resources of art. If one is tempted to chase to their dens the intricate origins of texts, one also has to become involved in the messy and often incompatible details of inspiration and expression, composition and publication, ambition and achievement. One may trace the genesis of a poem or review the revisions of a novel. One may look into the history of publication and reception. One may place an author in context—in the social and political contexts to be sure, but also in the contexts of recorded experience and imaginative transformation, of petty personal annoyances and grand schemes, of calculated interest and generous sympathy, of unintended plagiarisms alongside deliberate departures from established fashion or recorded fact. One can locate the author in the context of other writers, and, just as important, one can study a text in the context of other writings by the same author. One can perform all these contextualizing acts and many more, but William James provides a cautionary word about this process. I quote the passage elsewhere in this volume, but it is worth repeating here: "Let the q be fragrance, let it be toothache, or let it be a more complex kind of feeling, like that of the full-moon swimming in her blue abyss, it must first come in that simple shape, and be held fast in that first intention, before any knowledge *about* it can be attained. The knowledge *about* it is *it* with a context added. Undo *it*, and what is added cannot be *context*."[4]

In other words, context should be an enhancement, not a corrosive agent that dissolves the object of analysis and contemplation in the very process of studying it. Naturalistic philosophers and scientists were making this sort of mistake a hundred years ago; humanists should not be so anxious to repeat the error. In the words of a now obscure detractor of the then current scientific method, the typical chemist isolates the organism he proposes to study in altogether suspect ways: He "resorts to crystallization, precipitation, filtration, evaporation, and congelation; he utilises temperatures ranging far above the 30–40° C of living beings, and solvents such as pure alcohol, petrol, benzol, ether, which are deadly to the organism."[5] It comes as no surprise, then, that such a chemist would discover that "life" is the result of certain predictable mechanical operations, that, lo and behold, his experiments have confirmed his theory; for he has systematically eliminated the living principle from his observations.

I don't say that literature is a living organism in the biological sense, but it just may be, as Wallace Stevens said a poem is, the "cry of its occasion." And if this is so, it is prudent to look into the occasion and the cry as well. Besides, contexts can be pretty complicated in themselves. Perhaps Herman

4. William James, *Pragmatism, and Four Essays from "The Meaning of Truth"* (New York: Meridian Books, 1955), 211.
5. Marcus Hartog, *Problems of Life and Reproduction* (London: John Murray, 1913), 234.

Melville's father-in-law epitomized the Victorian Boston Brahmin and was therefore a man Melville might hold in contempt, but Judge Lemuel Shaw was also a very intelligent man and, as fathers-in-law go, a pretty indulgent and sympathetic one. Melville seems to have wrestled with his own ambivalent feelings toward Shaw when the judge was publicly vilified for his instructions to the jury in a notorious murder case and to have expressed those feelings in fictional terms in both *Moby-Dick* and *Billy Budd.* F. Scott Fitzgerald may well have suffered from the anxiety of influence when he distinguished his Middle West from that of Willa Cather. But he also apologized to her for writing a passage that struck him as too reminiscent of one from *A Lost Lady,* and he was so delighted by her written approval of *The Great Gatsby* that he woke up Christian Gauss in the middle of the night to show him the letter.

Perhaps Tony Hillerman's tribal policeman becomes more vividly interesting when one knows that Joe Leaphorn, as the product of a matriarchal Navajo culture, is forced to labor under largely patriarchal and paternalistic federal restrictions placed upon tribal jurisdiction. And it may be that Joyce Carol Oates's story, "Where Are You Going, Where Have You Been?" is an allegorical tale concerning freshly scrubbed innocence and seductive evil. But if this is so, the principal source for that story nevertheless reveals something more sinister at work in the tale than a latter-day Satan out cruising and looking for kicks.

From time to time in the following essays, sometimes only in passing, I supply contexts for otherwise perplexing elements in writers or in their texts. In the final pages of *Death Comes for the Archbishop,* for example, Willa Cather risks subverting the reader's sympathy for her archbishop. Why should this be? And why wasn't Mark Twain able to "fix" his play *Colonel Sellers* in ways that reflected his felt intentions? The complicated history of that play provides some explanation, as well as shedding some light on the vexed question of authorial intention. Both Jack London and Robert Frost read and responded to Henri Bergson's *Creative Evolution,* but their very different reactions to it point concretely to their differences as artists as well. What disruptive social circumstances should move Henry James from the realist's belief that the real "represents to my perception the things we cannot possibly *not* know" to a modernist dread that one's perceptions are in perpetual risk of being "impaled on the naturalist's pin"?

I will say in advance that there are no definite answers to these questions, since by its very nature genetic inquiry requires that one be tentative and speculative in such matters. The scholar's faith cannot exceed the facts, and a new set of facts (in the form of manuscripts, diaries, letters, and the like) may appear at any moment. Sometimes a new deal is forthcoming whether you want it or not. But, to adopt the language of Henry James, the devil of it is not so much that "the hostile fact crops up as that the friendly fact breaks down." Still, the essays I have selected here have held up pretty well, so far as factual accuracy is concerned.

With the exception of the Postscript, all of these essays have been published before. They are arranged here more or less according to the dates of publication of the works under consideration, however. I have lightly revised several of them and in one instance ("Authors, Intentions, and Texts") augmented the argument a bit. Some of them were accidental by-products of my research. When I was in the Library of Congress looking into proposed legislation for a tax on "old bachelors" in the early nineteenth century, I was coming up short. For no particular reason that I can now recall, I thought I would glance at the Lemuel Shaw papers there and discovered the story that would eventuate in "The Judge Dragged to the Bar." Once, I was working on Willa Cather and was reading *Alexander's Bridge* when Jay Gatsby's green light jumped out at me, and I was suddenly off chasing down a source and an influence.

The first time I read Joyce Carol Oates's "Where Are You Going, Where Have You Been?" the fear the story generated in me was out of proportion to the merits of the tale, considerable though they are. In a subconscious way, I suppose, I was both reading and remembering this story at the same time. For in 1965 I was a freshman in college in Arizona when the news of the bizarre murders Charles Schmid and his accomplices had committed in Tucson came out. My own experience came into play once again when I first read Tony Hillerman's *Dance Hall of the Dead*. I had been living on the Navajo Reservation a few years before I picked up the novel and already knew something of the complications that surround law enforcement on an Indian nation. The essays on Twain and Bierce and Stevens, on the other hand, were written for a specific occasion. The first two were introductions to collections I put together, but, with minor adjustments, they seemed to me to serve as essays that trace the contours of at least a portion of Twain's and Bierce's writing careers and therefore are genetic inquiries as well. "Realism, the 'Real,' and the Poet of Reality" was written for a special issue of *American Literary Realism* on the theory of realism, but it was not theoretical in the usual sense. All I wanted to do was to account for the movement from literary realism to literary modernism as it was evident in the poetic aspirations of Wallace Stevens. Nevertheless, I found it necessary to engage in philosophical and historical speculations in order to follow the evolution of one sort of artistic credo to another.

All of these essays have at least this in common—they study writers and writings in transit, so to speak. That is the chief preoccupation of those interested in literary geneticism. The essays trace the evolution of a literary era, of an individual attitude, of a single text; they follow the transformation of yesterday's news into memorable literature or the complicated influence that one writer might have upon another. By bringing them together, the common quality that runs throughout is more obvious. In that sense, these essays may be taken as the embodiment of a certain point of view and may be judged as of a piece. However, for many, I suspect, this collection will likely be considered merely a period piece. For those unfriendly to the sorts of questions I put to literature, to authors, and to texts, and the provisional answers I hope to achieve, these essay will seem quaint and curious. Perhaps they will be right, but, then, maybe not.

The Proof

II

Sources, Influences, and Intertexts

When I read Owen Miller's announcement of the "demise of source-influence studies" as corresponding to the need to "replace the author as the authenticating source of identity [of a text] . . . by the reader as the agent who confers identity on the text"; when I learn from Michael Worton and Judith Still that traditional source criticism, by virtue of its focus on the "original" text, is therefore "blind to the workings of contemporary, vernacular intertextuality"; when I am told by Jonathan Culler that source study is positivistic and narrow and that the concept of the intertext was designed to "transcend" that narrowness, or by Julia Kristeva that intertextuality is not so "banal" a concept as the source or influence; when I observe that in Udo J. Hebel's 2,033-item bibliography, *Intertextuality, Allusion, and Quotation,* there is not listed a single essay devoted to the relation of sources and influences to the intertext; when I learn these things, I must confess that I feel threatened.[1] I suppose I should be consoled to find that I am myself included in the bibliography of intertextuality, but I am not. I feel rather like the man in the cartoon one used to see in cheap diners—a bucktoothed man with a wart on his nose saying, "6 munths ago, I cudn't

---

1. See respectively, Owen Miller, preface to *Identity of the Literary Text,* ed. Owen Miller and Mario J. Valdés (Toronto: University of Toronto Press, 1985), xviii; Michael Worton and Judith Still, introduction to *Intertextuality: Theories and Practices* (Manchester: University of Manchester Press, 1990), 8; Jonathan Culler, *The Pursuit of Signs: Semiotics, Literature, Deconstruction* (Ithaca: Cornell University Press, 1981), 109; and Julia Kristeva, *The Kristeva Reader,* ed. Toril Moi (New York: Columbia University Press, 1986), 111. In fairness, I should add that Laurent Jenny, in "The Strategy of Form" in *French Literary Theory Today,* ed. Tzvetan Todorov (Cambridge University Press, 1982), 34–63, writes: "Contrary to what Kristeva says, intertextuality in the strict sense is not unrelated to source criticism: it designates not a confused, mysterious accumulation of influences, but the work of transformation and assimilation of various texts that is accomplished by a focal text which keeps control over the meaning. It is not hard to see that what threatens this definition with vagueness is the notion of a 'text' and the position to be adopted with respect to metaphorical uses of the term" (39–40).

even spel SUPERVIZER, and now I R one." For source-influence study is, in the main, what I do. It is my professional life, so to speak, and reading of its demise is like stumbling upon my own obituary in the evening paper.

What is it that has so convincingly contributed to the demise of source-influence study? It is the death of the author and the attendant birth of the intertext. Now, I am not exactly sure what an intertext is. Julia Kristeva may help me to understand it: "Each word (text)," she writes, "is an intersection of words (texts) where at least one other word (text) can be read." And thus it is that "any text is constructed as a mosaic of quotations; any text is the absorption and transformation of another."[2]

I confess that intertextuality remains obscure to me, and Michael Riffaterre's collateral clarifications in his essay "Syllepsis" only systematize my confusion. Riffaterre discerns three distinct types of intertextuality: the complementary type (the obverse side of any word or text, as in a pun); the mediated type (in which a reference to an intertext is effected by the intercession of a third text); and the intertextual type ("where the intertext is partly encoded within the text and conflicts with it because of stylistic or semantic incompatibilities"). The examples Riffaterre offers of these three types of intertextuality are almost exclusively Derridean and are far too elaborate to go into here. But Riffaterre does make a statement that is pertinent to this essay: "These three distinctions should help check the tendency, now all too general, to see intertextuality as nothing more than a newfangled name for source or influence. Influence from text to text, or the linkup of text with source, is a 'vertical' relationship of recurrence and sameness, whereas the intertext is related to the text 'laterally': there is a simultaneity and otherness, a contiguity, a mutual solidarity, so that the text functions as a literary artifact only insofar as it complements another text."[3]

Seemingly, this statement should foreclose any future discussion of the matter, but so far as I can see, it only proves that Riffaterre is as much in the dark about sources and influences as I am about the intertext. As I think will become self-evident, the source and the influence establish not the relations of sameness or recurrence, but the relations of complementarity, me-

2. Julia Kristeva, *Desire in Language: A Semiotic Approach to Literature and Art,* ed. Léon Roudiez, trans. Alice Jardine, Thomas A. Gora, and Léon Roudiez (New York: Columbia University Press, 1980), 6.

3. Michael Riffaterre, "Syllepsis," *Critical Inquiry* 6 (summer 1980): 625–38.

diation, and supplementarity. And if by a "vertical" relation, Riffaterre means hierarchy (whether that be aesthetic or historical privileging), then he misunderstands the genetic method, which has nothing whatsoever to do with the aesthetic. And he misunderstands the historical and biographical method, which links fact to fact, text to text, on the basis of probable sequence, not consequence, and forever stands ready for amendment or augmentation. And though the source hunter never, or hardly ever, announces the ground for such linkages, he or she perfectly recognizes that evidence, as well as the focal text itself, always exists in the present, else how would the scholar (who, whatever else one might say, is no time traveler) ever come by evidence at all?

Let us suppose, nevertheless, that it may be true that every text is a quoted text, every word an unlabeled citation. And Ralph Waldo Emerson stands ready to assist in the supposition: "All minds quote. Old and new make the warp and woof of every moment. There is no thread that is not a twist of these two strands. By necessity, by proclivity, and by delight, we all quote." The passage, from "Quotation and Originality," has a nice and special tang to it. Its cutting edge has long since been blunted, however, and its steel is rusted from disuse, but the title indicates that Emerson would not deny the possibility of originality (which surely has to do with the much discredited notion of authorial intention). Perhaps one ought to add a less familiar observation by another American romantic, Herman Melville: "No one great book must ever be separately regarded and permitted to domineer with its own uniqueness upon the creative mind, but that all existing great works must be federated in fancy."[4] Melville's creative strategies are notable for such federations.

If I sound sardonic, I should say that I find the notion of the intertext (even though I doubt that I fully understand it) quite useful if, like most useful notions, it is used well. Even those who so casually announce the demise of source and influence study recognize the interpretive dangers of intertextuality. The intertext, like the analogue, is in danger of being too flexible to be coherent. Since anything at all can be analogous to virtually anything at all, analogy is typically regarded as a specious form of reason-

---

4. Ralph Waldo Emerson, *The Oxford Authors: Ralph Waldo Emerson*, ed. Richard Poirier (New York: Oxford University Press, 1990), 427; Herman Melville, *Pierre; or, The Ambiguities* (Evanston and Chicago: Northwestern University Press and the Newberry Library, 1970), 284.

ing. The intertext, by analogy, is likewise specious (at least potentially so) since virtually any text can serve as an intertext to yet another text. For that reason, some theorists have sought to distinguish between the aleatory intertext and the obligatory intertext, the latter derived not from an open and ranging possibility of intertexts, but from procedures constrained and restricted. It is thought that some systematic approach to intertextuality will eliminate the danger of its excessive accommodation. Thus is hypothesized an idealized intertext that relates specifically to the text in question, or a particular interpretive problem of the text. Such an animal may not be possible, theorists confess; the search for an intertext that is truly explanatory of a focal text may be a mythic quest. But so far as I can see, this hippogriff is in fact a camelopard. The intertext they seek does in fact exist, though under another name—it is called criticism.

Nonetheless, I share their concern. How does one avoid the incipient randomness of intertextuality? How can we construct the "mosaic" Kristeva speaks of and still avoid the gravel pit of free association? The problem is real enough. Kenneth Burke once responded to R. P. Blackmur's charge that "[Burke's] method could be applied with equal fruitfulness to Shakespeare, Dashiell Hammet, or Marie Corelli" by accepting the criticism (after he was done wincing) and going Blackmur one better: "As a matter of fact, I'll go a step further and maintain: You can't properly put Marie Corelli and Shakespeare apart until you have put them together. First genus, then differentia."[5] The trick (for history as well as hermeneutics), of course, is finding a way of putting things together, if only to be able to tell them apart.

The option (and the problem) that the notion of the intertext introduces is by implication epistemological—for it invites, and perhaps is thus inviting on just this score, the sort of literary discourse one is apt to hear at cocktail parties and in faculty lounges: "That reminds me of . . . " It is an epistemology that may be variously characterized as associationism, spon-

5. Kenneth Burke, "Literature as Equipment for Living," in *The Philosophy of Literary Form,* rev. ed. (New York: Vintage, 1957), 261. It goes without saying that there are all sorts of grounds for putting things together—semantic, rhetorical, semiotic, mythic, etc. The scholar typically proceeds on the basis of biographical and historical evidence. As with most conflicts, the opposition between opposing parties, if pushed far enough, is usually recognized to be a difference about what, in truth, constitutes evidence. For Freud the unconscious is a fact, for Kant the transcendental ego is a fact—though both facts, it is recognized, are logical inferences that enable one to account for other sorts of facts (psychological, epistemological, etc.).

taneous memory, stream of consciousness, and so forth. And it encourages rather than discourages literary one-upmanship. Worse still, it ventures toward solipsism: *Tess*-reminds-me-of-*War and Peace*-reminds-me-of-*Beowulf*-reminds-me-of-Raymond Chandler-reminds-me-of-Eudora Welty—which, in the long run, is but a way of saying "I remind me of myself."

What is needed, I believe, is a principle of *thrift.* I borrow the term from Michel Foucault, and I accept his diagnosis of the problem in "What Is an Author?" That is, so says Foucault, we must find some way to halt the "cancerous and dangerous proliferation of significations" in the modern world.[6] Foucault, with special qualifications, accepts and reconstitutes what so many blithely discard—the concept of the author. And I do not mean the author as "the authenticating source of the identity of a text," whatever that may mean. Anyone with the slightest acquaintance with the problems of textual editing—the commercial obligations and interests of editors and publishers; the scruples and tastes (real or imagined) of readers (of the present or the past); the unreliability of transcriptions; the truly dreadful hand that many important writers write or wrote in; the numbskull inattention of printers and printer's devils; the fateful glitch, typo, or erratum—will know that there is no text, that textuality (never mind intertextuality) has, at best, only a negotiable existence, and no "identity" at all.

The vexed question of authorial intention need not concern us here. It is enough to say that the author stands in relation to his or her work, if only hypothetically, as the creative cause of the text. Now we know, because logicians tell us so, that (1) a cause, creative or other, can but rarely "explain" its effects and that (2) the effect, except in very restrictive cases, is always logically prior to the cause. Strictly speaking, it is only by virtue of *Bleak House* that Charles Dickens, as "author" of that text, comes into being. I have strayed considerably from what Foucault has to say about the author, and may indeed have managed his argument to suit my purpose, but I can hardly find any ground at all lest I preserve at least the Foucauldian notion of the "author function," if not the author himself or herself. Source-influence study cannot exist unless one assumes that something or someone has been influenced.[7] And I would add that biographers and literary historians are

6. Michel Foucault, "What Is an Author?" trans. Donald F. Bouchard and Sherry Simon, in *Contemporary Literary Criticism: Literary and Cultural Studies*, ed. Robert Con Davis and Ronald Schleifer (New York: Longman, 1989), 274.

7. Louis A. Renza, in "Influence," in *Critical Terms for Literary Study*, ed. Frank Lentriccia and Thomas McLaughlin (Chicago: University of Chicago Press, 1990), 186–

perfectly aware that authors, like meanings, are constructed, not discovered. The principle whereby that construction takes place is, again, thrift, and, I would submit, has little to do with—as so many poststructuralists would have it—a naive celebration of genius or even self, much less some supersensual ground or center for the distribution of meanings and form.

And let us suppose, for the sake of contemplating the problem I have described, that the author function is useful in applying the principle of thrift to the principle of the intertext. Let us further suppose that if it can be proved, through the careful scrutiny of existing evidence, that author X read, responded to, and was influenced by text Y, then text Y can be shown to be the sort of intertext we designate as a source or an influence for the literary text under consideration, that is, text Z. And why should we not suppose it? Does not Owen Chase's *Narrative of the Most Extraordinary and Distressing Shipwreck of the Whale-Ship Essex, of Nantucket* (1821), which Melville acquired and read while and because he was writing *Moby-Dick*, does not this book, which Melville did read, have as much (in fact, a greater) right to be considered an intertext as, say, Frederich Nietzsche's *Beyond Good and Evil*, which the poststructuralist has probably read but which Melville obviously did not?

"Clearly not," says the intertextualist, "because Chase is not a likely part of the 'reader's' literary repertoire, and the reader is the agent who supplies identity to a text." "And this 'reader,'" I ask, "hypothesize or homogenize him or her as you will, is to know only what you are to determine as the right, the good, the true, the beautiful?" "But the superficial historicization of the text that you are recommending denies that meanings are constructed not extracted and likewise denies the contemporaneous experience of the reader," is the reply. My answer is, once again, that "Owen Chase's text (insofar as readers are made conscious of it) exists in the present just as much as does, say, *Of Grammatology* or today's newspaper."

202, undertakes to place this concept in contemporary critical discourse. Perhaps he is right to say that after Harold Bloom's studies of the "anxiety of influence" the term *influence* is most often used by critics "to designate the affiliative relations between past and present literary texts and/or their authors" (186). Nevertheless, while most scholars might relish the stature of Bloom, the fact remains that the great bulk of the work of source and influence study is still performed by a typically unvisionary but by no means unintelligent company of scholars and bibliographers, neither diverted by nor very interested in Oedipal struggles for authority and originality.

Let me further suppose that the enterprise of source and influence study is in no way "positivistic"—a charge so often leveled at scholars that we sometimes come to believe it. With Walt Whitman, I find that "facts are useful, and yet they are not my dwelling, I but enter by them to an area of my dwelling." Anyway, let me describe a few examples of source-influence study that serve as well as intertexts. These examples are meant to demonstrate that conventional source and influence study is not so narrow or reductive an activity as some theorists suppose. They are not meant to serve as refutation of the theory of intertextuality itself so much as to disclose that one may indulge in the analysis of focal texts in relation to other texts without likewise contributing to what Umberto Eco once called "interpretive drift." To forestall the deadly and tiresome complaint of "positivism," I'll not describe these examples as causal or factual, biographical or historical, methodological or ideological. They are neither criticism nor interpretation as such. Instead, they are symptomatic of interpretation (and biography and history, too, for that matter), and the examples introduce problems of their own. For the moment, let me call them symptoms.

The Single-Source/Double-Reaction Source-Influence Symptom

Except for the fact that both were born in San Francisco at around the same time, Jack London and Robert Frost have virtually nothing in common. The first is an out-and-out naturalist who took his cues from Karl Marx, Charles Darwin, Herbert Spencer, and Ernst Haeckel; the second reclaimed the romantic tradition of Emerson while at the same time showing a fervid if ambivalent interest in the modern-day physics of Arthur Stanley Eddington and Werner Heisenberg and the philosophy of William James and John Dewey. We have scant reason to put these two figures together—they so convincingly exclude one another, intellectually and aesthetically. Indeed, the authors may not have known of, or, at least, cared about, each other's existence. They never corresponded; one wrote highly didactic and often clumsy fiction, the other seemingly simple but quite subtle poetry; one looked back over the materialism of the nineteenth century and exalted it, and the other seemed to outlive the very future he so anxiously foresaw. By the time London died at the age of forty, his career was already in decline; Frost's career was just getting under way by the time he was the same age.

Nevertheless, there may be good reason to find a way to put these two figures together because they so epitomize differing casts of mind and different eras.

"Matter and motion of matter make up the sum total of existence," London wrote to his friend Cloudsley John in 1902.[8] For a man, such as London, who wanted his materialism "straight," Henri Bergson's diluted vi-
talism as it appeared in *Creative Evolution* (1907; English trans., 1911),
which London read in 1912, proved to be something of a test. In any event,
the record of Jack London's reading of this book (as it is preserved in the
margins of his copy) reveals a reader (who is also a writer) coming to grips
with an emergent new reality. London's reading begins in skeptical curiosity, but it soon becomes dismissive. (He penciled next to a statement that
probably struck him as smacking of the romantically transcendental, "Same
old story.") Later in the text (actually a book, since we are here referring
to the "thing" London owned and quite literally inscribed), the materialist
becomes quarrelsome—next to the statement "Life had to enter thus into
the habits of inert matter," he writes, "Why not grow out of the habits of
matter? Why not an impetus of matter?—Remember radium."[9] By degrees,
however (by page 102 to be exact), London is attempting to reconcile the
positions of Herbert Spencer and Bergson at the level of diction rather than
thought. He begins to underline words and phrases such as "dangerous,"
"lay in wait," or "voracious." By about halfway through, all marginalia
(and perhaps London's reading also) ceased.

How different is the recorded reaction of Robert Frost to the same
book.[10] Frost told Lawrance Thompson that he began reading *Creative
Evolution* a few days after Christmas 1911 and he found in the book an
inspiration that had its inevitable if residual effect on his poetry. Though

8. *Letters from Jack London,* ed. King Hendricks and Irving Shepard (New York:
Odyssey Press, 1965), 425.

9. It is ironic that the discovery of radium was itself to help erode the reigning notions of the immutability of matter and the conservation of force.

10. London's copy of *Creative Evolution* is in the Huntington Museum and Library.
The annotations are discussed by David Mike Hamilton in *"The Tools of My Trade":
The Annotated Books in Jack London's Library* (Seattle: University of Washington Press,
1986), 60–61. Frost's reaction to *Creative Evolution* and a record of the marginalia are
presented in Ronald Bieganowski's "Sense of Time in Robert Frost's Poetic: A Particular Influence of Henri Bergson," *Resources for American Literary Study* 13 (autumn
1983): 184–94.

London was two years younger than Frost, he belonged intellectually to an era that was passing, if, in fact, it had not already passed. Frost saw in the same text a basis for a new aesthetic, and his marginalia indicate a manifold influence upon his thinking about evolution and science generally, history, religious faith, and, of course, poetry. Frost read the following passage, for example, in the opening chapter: "Evolution implies a real persistence of the past in the present, a duration which is, as it were, a hyphen, a connecting link. In other words, to know a living being or *natural system* is to get at the very interval of duration, while the knowledge of an *artificial* or *mathematical system* applies only to the extremity." Frost underlined "to get at" and "interval" and wrote alongside the passage three statements:

> The writer's greatest wonder is at how he got from here to there.
>
> All that counts.
> This is poetry.
>
> Some writing is like a series of dots as close together that they almost make a line. The best writing of the young authors flows like a line, a real line.

Together, these statements prefigure much of what Frost would have to say in such familiar essays as "The Figure a Poem Makes" (1939) or "The Constant Symbol" (1946)—as, for example, his observation that the "word" is "a point of many departures"; or "the line will have the more charm for not being mechanically straight. We enjoy the straight crookedness of a good walking stick."[11] But more to the point, what one can see from these dramatically different reactions to Bergson's *Creative Evolution* is, if nothing more, that the source or influence is not at all to be regarded as causal or reductionist; on the contrary, this "intertext," if you will, opens up a text (whether that text is a novel, a poem, a letter, a life, or a moment in history) at the same time that it focuses any discussion of it. Also, the above example demonstrates that the methodology of source-influence study presupposes that there are multiple readings of a

11. See *Selected Prose of Robert Frost,* ed. Hyde Cox and Edward Connery Lathem (New York: Collier, 1966), "A Romantic Chasm," 78, and "The Figure a Poem Makes," 19.

text, and often undertakes to show the how and why of divergent readings.

The Chain-Letter Source-Influence Symptom

Here is a more complicated example:

Nathaniel Hawthorne published a story called "Wakefield" in 1835. The story is an ingenious narrative digression on an old magazine or newspaper clipping (as yet unidentified) that describes a man who abandoned his wife for many years and took up residence just a few blocks away. The man returns home after so long an absence and crosses the threshold, about to be face-to-face with his (presumably) dumbstruck wife. The story ends with Wakefield being described as "the Outcast of the Universe."

In 1852 Herman Melville recited a story and sent along a letter sent to him by a John Clifford about a woman abandoned by her sailor husband. Melville urged Hawthorne to write the tale of Agatha Hatch and supposed it was right up Hawthorne's alley because it is so much like Hawthorne's story of the "London husband" (that is, like "Wakefield").

Hawthorne politely declined the urging and evidently responded that Melville himself should undertake to write this story. He did. We now know that Melville in fact wrote a novel about this woman titled *Isle of the Cross* that was completed by spring 1853 and was rejected by Harper and Brothers that June. Apparently Melville was so disappointed in the venture that he destroyed the manuscript.[12]

However, Melville was still interested in the story of desertion. Sometime after September 1853 he no doubt read a piece, printed in the *Albany Evening Journal,* titled "A Female Robinson Crusoe," that told of a woman who had been abandoned on the South Pacific island of Santa Barbara. Melville became reengrossed in the story of an abandoned woman and, finally, in 1854, in "The Encantadas" (which has its own curious history, by the way), Agatha Hatch/the female Crusoe appears as Hunilla, the Chola Widow, in "Sketch Eighth: Norfolk Isle and the Chola Widow."[13]

12. See Hershel Parker, "Herman Melville's *The Isle of the Cross:* A Survey and Chronology," *American Literature* 62 (1990): 1–16.

13. See Robert Sattelmeyer and James Barbour, "The Sources and Genesis of Melville's 'Norfolk Isle and the Chola Widow,'" *American Literature* 50 (1978): 398–417.

Thus we have an intertextual chain letter: An unknown magazine or newspaper article connects to "Wakefield" connects to Melville's Agatha letters connects to the unpublished and apparently destroyed novel *The Isle of the Cross* connects to the newspaper story of a female Crusoe connects to the story of the Chola Widow. Nothing is to be causally (or vertically) regarded here, but we nevertheless do have a sequence of events (textual linkages, if you will) that constitutes a very small and very complicated piece of literary history.

These linkages present an intricate combination of textual and biographical problems. Not only do they shed some light on the perplexing and always fascinating relationship of Hawthorne and Melville, but also they provide a lens through which we may view and come to interpret any of these several texts in relation to the others. Of course, selecting a focal text from this chain letter is not dictated by the sequence itself, and the "privileging" of one text over another has more to do with the critic's or interpreter's temperament and interest than it does with hierarchy or cultural hegemony. The possible combinations of these several texts seem limitless.

If one's focal text is the Chola Widow sketch, then all of the others may be seen as tributary sources and influences, though not as "causes" as such. If the focal text is on the opposite end of the spectrum—that is, Hawthorne's "Wakefield"—then the Agatha letters may be seen as an intertext to that tale. The story of Agatha Hatch was obviously not a source for "Wakefield," but we may read the tale through the association of the two in Melville's mind and thereby gain access to how Melville "read" Hawthorne, as well as to how his own creative imagination functioned. Indeed, we might even attempt to infer the nature of the absent text, *The Isle of the Cross*, from the several texts that bracket it. In whatever fashion we choose to relate these several texts, what is, in one formulation, a source or an influence may be, in another, an effect. But any of the several possibilities for textual linkage will never be completely random or "free." They will of necessity be conditioned by temporal sequence and therefore subject to the economies of scholarly inquiry and a responsibility to rules of evidence. And they will be further restricted by an appeal to notions of the author, or at least the author function. In fact, the poststructuralist's desire to do away with the author makes the sort of combinations I have just described improbable, if not impossible.

The Great-Books/Little-Occasions
Source-Influence Symptom

I have often wondered whether or not it snowed in Pittsfield, Massachu-setts, on January 1, 1856. If it did, then the Melvilles might well have stayed home from church that Sunday, but they also would likely have done the scriptural readings as outlined in the Book of Common Prayer, and among those readings would have been this passage from 1 Corinthians 12: "And God hath set some in the church, first apostles, secondarily prophets, third-ly teachers, after that miracles, then gifts of healings, helps, governments, diversities of tongues." This passage, as I have argued elsewhere, supplied the masquerade for Melville's title character in *The Confidence-Man: His Masquerade* (1857), and in turn a structural principle for the novel he had begun probably in September 1855.[14]

There is no causal connection here, in the sense that the source might "explain" Melville's text, because the adaptation of this biblical passage to his narrative is clearly multilayered and ironic and because Melville's reli-gious attitudes are so complex. In fact, it is the very complexity of Melville's mind that makes source-influence study of his fiction so challenging and stimulating. In Herman Melville we have an author who often relied upon sources in developing his narratives, but we also have a man with a near-photographic memory of what he had read combined with what he once called an "ungovernable thing" within him that made his imagination near-ly always unpredictable and original. The way that Melville used the Bible in this instance might be described, to borrow a phrase from Kenneth Burke, as the "dancing of an attitude." Besides, Melville was so familiar with the Bible that he would not have necessarily needed the Book of Common Prayer to call the scriptural passage to mind. However, to offer a conjectural ac-count of when Melville might have contemplated this scriptural text and appropriated it to the purposes of his then unfinished novel might likewise provide a way to link (systematically, and hence thriftily) the several other intertexts operating in *The Confidence-Man*, from the familiar *Don Quixote, Hamlet,* and *Paradise Lost,* to the virtually unknown *Sketches of History, Life, and Manners in the West* (1835) by James Hall, each of which was in

---

14. See my "Saint Paul's Types of the Faithful and Melville's Confidence Man," *Nineteenth-Century Fiction* 28 (1974): 472–77.

some fashion "federated" in the fancy of the "author function" that goes by the name of Herman Melville.

The passage from 1 Corinthians may be established as a source or influence for Melville's text on the basis of verbal echoes and representational parallels. But the identifications of that same source may, in turn, serve as the impetus to speculation about biographical circumstance and the genesis of a text. The conventional source hunter has never shared the New Critical assumption that literary texts are discrete, atemporal verbal artifacts. On the contrary, source hunters have typically assumed that texts are products of the imagination and that such formal integrity as texts may possess was acquired by degrees and over a period of time. It is at least possible that the so-called "instability" of literary texts may as easily be explained by the vacillations of an author's thoughts and feelings and shifting aesthetic purposes as by the free play of linguistic signification.

The "Them Are My Squirrels!"
Source-Influence Symptom

I take my cues from Boon Hogganbeck here. At the end of William Faulkner's *The Bear*, Isaac McCaslin has agreed to go hunting with Boon and is walking through the woods to meet him. He hears a furious sound coming from the direction of a large gum tree, and as he comes through the briers, Ike sees Boon sitting at the base of the tree frantically hammering on the breech of his dismantled gun. The tree is alive with squirrels. Without looking up, Boon says, "Get out of here! Don't touch them! Don't touch a one of them! They're mine!" The point is hoarding—the author's futile wish to claim dominion over his or her texts.

Often, the author's own corpus provides the most provocative intertexts for the text under consideration (consider, for example, Walt Whitman's anonymous reviews of the first edition of *Leaves of Grass* or the preface to the 1855 edition itself). Indeed, in a sense, the totality of the writing (poems, fictions, journals, letters, etc.) of any author provides multiple intertexts for a particular text that is lifted from the block of a lifetime's work. And, for their part, individual writers sometimes find the means to scatter and at the same time control their meanings from text to text; textual boundaries are effaced and the author's proprietary relation to his or her significations are extended and enlarged.

Wallace Stevens had at one time contemplated following Whitman's lead and had thought of calling *Harmonium,* his first book of verse, "THE GRAND POEM: PRELIMINARY MINUTIAE." For several years Ezra Pound scholars had their pencils sharpened waiting for the day when the hundredth canto should be published and his major work rounded off symmetrically and finally, but Pound defeated their nice expectations and sense of closure by running his cantos well beyond one hundred. Whatever else might be said about the agglutinizing activity (of Whitman or Pound), it tends to keep the critics at bay for a time.

Another strategy is observable in texts as remote from one another as *Uncle Tom's Cabin* and *The Waste Land.* Harriet Beecher Stowe's massive mustering of "intertexts" or sources in *A Key to Uncle Tom's Cabin* as a way of validating her portrayal of the conditions of slavery in the novel surely finds its analogue in T. S. Eliot's collateral clarifications (or evasions) in his notes to *The Waste Land*—both authors would preserve authority over the range of meanings to be constructed around their texts. The same is true of Henry James's remarkable prefaces to the New York Edition, and, indeed, of his meticulous revisions of the New York Edition itself.

An author's creation of a comprehensive scene provides yet another example, for it points almost allegorically away from any particular text to other texts enacted upon the "same" stage. The invention, say, of Edgar Lee Masters's Spoon River, Stephen Crane's Whilomville, E. A. Robinson's Tilbury Town, James Branch Cabell's mythical country of Poictesme, Sherwood Anderson's Winesburg, Faulkner's Yoknapatawpha County, even A. A. Milne's Hundred Acre Wood in the Winnie the Pooh stories (which, by the way, Faulkner once said he wished he had written) serves to extend meanings and possibilities beyond the boundaries of a single text. The ruptures and relocations of meanings may remain, by virtue of an indefinite potentiality for texts still to be created, quietly under an author's control, and, in fact, may help shape his or her career.

The One-More-Time-with-Feeling
Source-Influence Symptom

A familiar example of a literary source is the text that acts as fulfillment, clarification, or alteration of meanings set forth in an earlier work. The "complementarity" of such texts is too obvious to require argument. Willa

Cather published a short story titled "The Professor's Commencement" in 1902. It was written when Cather herself was teaching high school in Pittsburgh and deals with a man who has discovered, too late, that, in promoting the interests of youth, he has squandered his own vitality and energy. The creative work that the man wished to do has not been, will never be, accomplished. There was a strong identification in 1902 between the author and her professor, for she realized that her own ambitions would be forfeited should she continue to encourage her pupils at the expense of her own interests. (Not long after the publication of this story, Cather quit teaching and moved to New York.) In this sense, the story serves as a spiritual prophecy for Cather as artist. Over twenty years later, she published *The Professor's House* (1925). Her second professor's career has so many parallels with her own that James Woodress has described the novel as Cather's "spiritual autobiography."[15] The first story is a cautionary tale, written when her future still seemed to spread out before her. The second was written in the full confidence of achievement and public acclaim, but is no less—in fact is far more—disturbing. In both, there was a profound identification with her title character. And I must confess that I don't know how to teach or even describe the meanings and emotional register of either tale without reference to the other.

The It's-in-the-Text Source-Influence Symptom

We know that *The Sound and the Fury* had its origins in a short story called "Twilight," which was never published and, it had long been supposed, was not extant. But Leon Howard has demonstrated that the short story is embedded in the Benjy section of the novel itself; in fact, he reconstructed the story for publication. This ur-story was neither discarded nor modified. Instead, Faulkner's apparent stream-of-consciousness method of disclosing the thoughts of an idiot was in fact far more calculated, and perhaps more daring.

Howard's method was simple enough. He explained, "In an attempt to investigate Faulkner's own creative process in this combination of order and chaos [that characterizes *The Sound and the Fury*], I attacked the Benjy

15. James Woodress, *Willa Cather: Her Life and Art* (Lincoln: University of Nebraska Press, 1970), 207.

section directly: I simply cut it up into the fragments of what were obviously its constituent parts and pasted them together again in order to recreate the separate parts and arrange them in a normal time sequence."[16] The result was a chronological text in which a discernible story, "Twilight," emerged without so much as a single word missing. Here, within the text of the novel (literally absorbed into the disjointed narrative) was a conventional chronological narrative that, through the resources of scissors and paste, not to mention an explosive creative surge in the author, becomes an "inner text" or perhaps an "infratext" that points both without and within, one whose traces are scattered throughout the Benjy section, but which can be reconstituted (again by means of scissors and paste) by a reader patient and systematic enough to do so. Needless to say, Random House, which granted permission to publish the reconstructed tale, did so with some hesitation and perplexity. Did the publisher, in fact, have the rights to this story? It had, in effect, already published the work in the novel itself. Was "Twilight" an unpublished story, or, instead, a massive and selective quotation employed to demonstrate a scholarly point about the genesis of the novel?

I could multiply instances, but I hope my essential point—that source and influence study is not so narrow as is sometimes supposed—is suggested by this rough-and-ready taxonomy. By now it should be apparent that I find the several charges leveled against source and influence study specious or mistaken. However, I will not be so rash as to predict the demise of intertextuality. Nor do I even wish it. Intertextuality, in all its manifold forms, may confidently contribute to our understanding of literary texts, and I would be the last to say that the several configurations intertextualists offer us as readers of imaginative literature are "banal," or "narrow," or even "tedious."

But, perhaps, it is important to note that life, too, has something to do with the construction of meanings, far more to do with it than "textuality." As William James observed in *The Principles of Psychology*, "You can no more make a new thought out of 'ideas' that have once served than you can make a new bubble out of old triangles."[17] The same might be said for

16. See Leon Howard, "The Composition of *The Sound and the Fury*," *Missouri Review 5*, no. 2 (1981–1982): 111–28. (The "reconstituted" text of "Twilight" is published in the same issue, 128–38.)

17. William James, *The Principles of Psychology*, 2 vols. (New York: Henry Holt, 1890), 1:279.

textuality and signification generally. I will risk one final illustration that may help to clarify the relation between source-influence study and intertextuality, and note an important difference between them.

Most sources imported into an author's text are not so neatly disguised as "Twilight" in *The Sound and the Fury*. But sources, as distinct from allusions, typically have passed through the alembic of the author's imagination and have been transformed to suit a personal literary purpose, and they serve as sources only when the author's imagination is ready to receive them. This was surely the case when Richard Wright, who was about halfway through a first draft of *Native Son*, learned of the arrest in Chicago of Robert Nixon and Earl Hicks for the murder of a white woman. Wright wrote to Margaret Walker, asking her to send everything she could about the case, and he spread out the newspaper clippings on the floor and read and studied them again and again. As Keneth Kinnamon points out in his essay on the composition of *Native Son*, Wright's meticulous research into the Nixon case was appropriated to his own thematic purposes, but the patently racist newspaper accounts recorded in the novel are interlarded with unexaggerated echoes of actual pieces from the *Chicago Tribune*.[18] The point is worth making because Wright was deliberately grotesque in his rendering of Bigger Thomas's life and often attempted the melodrama of a Dreiser or the gothicism of a Poe,[19] and it is not always easy to distinguish in the novel between his romantic effects and his realistic ones.

Richard Wright insisted that Bigger Thomas's consciousness was to a large degree inscribed upon him by a white racist society and that he had known many Biggers in both the North and the South. In his essay, "How Bigger Was Born," Wright further acknowledged the impact certain un-

---

18. Keneth Kinnamon, "How *Native Son* Was Born," in *Writing the American Classics*, ed. James Barbour and Tom Quirk (Chapel Hill: University of North Carolina Press, 1990), 209–34.

19. Wright's concluding remark in his "How Bigger Was Born," in *Native Son* (restored text, New York: HarperCollins, 1993, 505–40)—"If Poe were alive, he would not have to invent horror; horror would invent him"—suggests some indebtedness to Poe, as well as to the newspaper accounts of the Nixon/Hicks murder case. More particularly, a newspaper account had compared Nixon to Poe's "giant ape" in "Murders in the Rue Morgue." Interestingly, as Richard Kopley has shown in *Edgar Allan Poe and "The Philadelphia Saturday News"* (Baltimore: Enoch Pratt Free Library, Edgar Allan Poe Society, and Library of the University of Baltimore, 1991), Poe's first detective tale had its own sources in newspaper accounts (also racist) of a black man named Coleman who had killed his wife, and these were fused with reports in the same periodical of an escaped ape or baboon. These cross-connections suggest yet another kind of textual linkage.

named white writers and their novels had had upon him and how he had adapted and had "bent" their literary strategies "until they became *my* ways of apprehending the locked-in life of the Black Belt areas."[20]

To study the bending and twisting of those sources and those influences is to discover the individual genius of Richard Wright; to understand that the Nixon/Hicks murder case, as source, is anchored in a historical reality is to comprehend more fully the urgency of the political ideology of the novel, as well as its artistic achievement. If we dismiss the role of the author in interpretation (and along with it the role the study of influences and sources plays in our more precisely understanding the unique qualities of the individual imagination and historical occasion), we may also risk trivializing the values we want most to sustain. As Frederick Crews has so trenchantly remarked, "Once writers have been discounted as the primary shapers of their works, critics are free to 'liberate signifiers from the signified'—that is, to make a text mean anything or nothing according to whim. From Roland Barthes through Jacques Derrida to Foucault himself, poststructuralism has conflated such quasi-libidinal play with political liberty, as if a carnival of unconstrained textuality could somehow serve as a proxy for the actual release of oppressed social groups from neglect and exploitation."[21]

Derrida's dictum that there is nothing outside the text notwithstanding, everyone, including poststructuralists, knows that there is an extratextual world to which memorable literature makes its powerful appeal. It is a world stuffed with extratextual pleasures and riddled with unspeakable pain and suffering. That mute and hungry world has its claims upon us, not as a text to be deciphered, but as a palpable condition. In any event, it simply will not do to sit plumply on one's political and moral prepossessions and at the same time practice a theory that essentially says, "Let them eat discourse."

Sources and influences can attain to the status of a "cause" only through the auspices of the creative imagination, and the imagination is located in a largely unknowable but reasonably inferable concept of the author. Without the author, sources and influences are indistinguishable from any other sort of intertext, except perhaps for the fact that they are frequently more

---

20. Wright, "How Bigger Was Born," 517.
21. Frederick Crews, *The Critics Bear It Away: American Fiction and the Academy* (New York: Random House, 1992), xix.

arcane than those texts commonly attributed to a reader's literary repertoire. So considered, they are no more than textual shards, parts of some
linguistic mosaic, and they become everything the intertextualists say they
are: infinitely detachable and perpetually implicated in an unchecked "sig-
nifying chain" that, in its turn, cascades into some huge and general interpretive drift.

Literature is a symbolic action that we may approach by means of criticism and interpretation. But between the text and the source or influence
stands the author (or author function), and what we continually do by turning our attention from a focal text to the sort of intertext we designate as
source or influence is to construct on an empirical and systematic basis a
more precise notion of the author as the creative cause of a literary artifact.
The match between text and intertext, between author and work, is never
exact, however, and we must continually adjust private conviction to an
ever-shifting body of demonstrable fact and a fuller comprehension of historical occasion.

Interpretation (including the sorts of interpretation that source and influence invite, but do not in themselves demonstrate) may, if it does nothing more, help to prevent the irresponsible squandering of intellectual perceptions and to check the cancerous proliferation of meanings. If it is to do
so effectively, however, perhaps it is wise, and surely it is economical, to
preserve some working notion of the author as an originating and shaping
intelligence. To adapt the language of Emerson in his essay "Experience,"
amidst the "vertigo of shows and politics" one may yet settle for a firm
creed: "That we not postpone and refer and wish, but do broad justice
where we are."[22] Let us treat our authors (and our texts as well), Emerson
might have said, as if they were real. Perhaps they are.

---

22. Emerson, *Oxford Authors*, 223.

III

Authors, Intentions, and Texts

One of my favorite remarks about the nature of literary criticism comes from Allen Tate. Literary criticism, he wrote, "is like a mule: it cannot reproduce itself, though, like a mule, it is capable of trying."[1] Surely Tate meant to apply the observation to formalist criticism, of which he was an uneven representative, as well as to other forms of critical inquiry. At any rate, when it became clear that the whole business and future of formalist analysis was to explicate texts ad infinitum, formalism as a lively and fertile enterprise was dead, though other theoretical schools would, without invitation to do so, pronounce the postmortem on altogether different grounds. But what is true for formalism is equally true for deconstruction, semiotics, and so forth. In other words, the popularity of any critical method is its undoing, and one has to admit that the farmer with a bunch of amorous mules on his hands ought to apply for a federal subsidy.

Literary criticism must always seek new ways to assert itself and to define its interests, not so much for the sake of interpretation as for its own survival. One of the most interesting and provocative possibilities for criticism these days lies, I believe, in the responsible combination of the methods of critical theory and the practice of textual scholarship. I wish to make a few observations about the nature of authors, intentions, and texts as they relate to the state of criticism at this interesting period in literary study and, wherever possible, to apply some examples to make my point. And let me begin with the basic stuff of literary criticism: the author—the author as creative cause, as authenticating presence, as biographical subject, as explanatory principle, and as damned nuisance.

We know that many critics and theorists would just as soon dispense with the author altogether. There are all sorts of ways to kill off the "au-

---

1. Allen Tate, "Is Literary Criticism Possible?" in *Essays of Four Decades* (Chicago: Swallow Press, 1968), 40.

thor," of course, and not merely by pronouncing him or her, as Roland Barthes did, dead on arrival—dead on the arrival of the reader, that is. W. K. Wimsatt and Monroe Beardsley had killed him off much earlier and quite cleverly by suggesting (partly on psychoanalytic grounds) that the author's intentions may be so obscure to the creating intelligence as to be virtually useless to the critic. Then (on grounds other than psychoanalytic), they had determined the text to be a verbal icon, insulated from the pesky claims of the creator. But an author may be killed with kindness as well, and before the intentional fallacy was articulated, romantic and impressionist critics exalted the author to the point of irrelevance by insisting that the imagination is merely a conduit for the divine afflatus; and E. D. Hirsch's emphasis in *Validity in Interpretation* on "pure" intentions may be not much more than a tough-minded survival of this impulse.

In what amounts to the same thing, in the long run, an author may be killed with condescension by maintaining that he or she was socially constructed and inscribed upon by the dominant culture. One problem with this maneuver is that it denies the motive one might have for imaginative writing in the first place. No one whose consciousness is congruent with its culture has much use for the imagination at all. Still, while the means and opportunity for authoricide may vary from critic to critic, the motive is pretty much the same: authors (their intentions, circumstances, and prepossessions) make things messy for interpretation. But critics and theorists have never been very successful in authorial assassination. Authors seem more like Fearless Fosdick or (for those whose memories do not reach back so far) like Freddy Kruger; they have remarkable powers of rejuvenation.

But equal and opposite sins exist as well, and critics sometimes cunningly invoke the author for altogether specious reasons. One may smuggle into critical discourse all sorts of untested generalizations under the name of the author, for example. One of my favorite specimens of this sleight of hand resides in the statement I once read in an essay on Nathaniel Hawthorne's psychological themes: "Hawthorne anticipated Freud by eighty years." Whatever the critic might have meant by this fanciful claim, he was not thinking of Hawthorne as biographical subject, creative intelligence, or anything that has much at all to do with Hawthorne. For most of us, however, our interest in Hawthorne, or any other author, is less in his or her anticipations than in a person who had and tried to realize certain literary intentions. Authorial intention, however, is as vexing an issue as the notion of an author is.

Even to begin a discussion of intention as it relates to the business of literary study, one must clear away some of the brush that has tended to obscure the question rather than to have, in fact, legitimately problematized the issue. I shall avoid the term *intentionality* altogether for the simple reason that it invites, and is misleading on just this score, comparisons to Edmund Husserl. For Husserl, intentionality is a law of consciousness. We "intend" objects; that is, through the operations of consciousness, we carve out of undifferentiated Being objects of contemplation or activity. Martin Heidegger gave to this metaphysical postulate both its existential and its linguistic character (in a way that is analogous to John Dewey's *instrumentalism*). Heidegger's reformulation of the Husserlian phenomenological method ultimately provided two rather divergent hermeneutical possibilities. One direction is the way of Hans-Georg Gadamer, which, rather than bringing us closer to resolutions about the issue of authorial intention, implicates us in the displacement of Spirit with Language and the Subject with the Linguistic. The other is the way of Roland Barthes, who would have us as readers intend the unintended; we would hand over to the consciousness of the reader (in an eternalized Present, one must suppose) the meaning-making process without recourse to the author or authorial intention. Intentionality, in the Husserlian sense, however, merely makes "things" possible; it has little if anything to do with notions of literary intention as it is customarily understood or with the general aims of literary interpretation.[2]

Another, and far more frequent, obfuscation is the naive assumption that the assumptions of intentionalists are naive. That is, there is the prevailing

2. Insofar as they apply notions of intentionality, structuralists and poststructuralists alike are more interested in the reader's rather than the author's side of things. Thus, Paul de Man in *Blindness and Insight: Essays in the Rhetoric of Contemporary Criticism* (New Haven: Yale University Press, 1971) speaks of intentionality as "neither physical nor psychological in its nature, but structural, involving the activity of a subject regardless of its empirical concerns, except as far as they relate to the intentionality of the structure. The structural intentionality determines the relationship between the components of the resulting object in all its parts, but the relationship of the particular state of mind of the person engaged in the act of structurization to the structured object is altogether contingent" (25). Clearly, in the case of the author this description of intentional acts cannot apply because the creative act is concerned with other objects than the poetic object, which has not yet come into being, and, moreover, the only way one can come by the consciousness of the author is by way of identification of empirical concerns and states of mind. In this sense, the structured object is altogether contingent, not the other way round.

idea that intentionalism is a survival of a "positivistic" *post hoc, ergo propter hoc*ism. Few intentionalists do now, or have ever believed that the antecedent conditions that may have motivated a particular creative act somehow "explain" the text either as a creative work or as a textual system. The study of sources and influences, for example, often gives us access to the operations of the creative intelligence and occasionally supplies such textual linkages as would be unavailable, indeed unthinkable, without the normal resources of scholarly investigation and corroboration, governed by certain more or less agreed upon rules of evidence. A source or influence may help us determine the occasion for the creative act, but neither determines the act itself. The same may be said for other ingredients in literary intention—announced artistic ambition, biographical (which is to say, personal, economic, or social) circumstance, authorial revision, amendment, and all other forms of second or third thoughts.

While it is true that we may speak of an "author" as the creative cause of a work, it is only through a study of the literary "effects" of any given text that one derives a concept of "author" at all, apart from the rather pedestrian ones having to do with copyright or with literature as a social commodity. As logicians are quick to point out, an effect is logically prior to its cause. Though it is habitual to think of a cause as explaining an effect, in fact, the process is all the other way around—an effect is the cause of a cause, so to speak. Thus, Harriet Beecher Stowe becomes an "author" by virtue of the publication of *Uncle Tom's Cabin,* but the novel does not become what it is because she is an author. Viewed in this sense, the author (as concept) is the conclusion, not the foundation, of literary investigation and interpretation. While that same conclusion may appear to emanate outward—to stamp a style or vision as Kafkaesque or Dickensian, for example—that application is merely a name for certain distinctive features that have been observed and experienced over a period of time in such a way that the name, by the process of conventional definition, absorbs these several features into it.

The procedures and rules of textual editing both clarify and complicate matters of literary intention. The Center for Scholarly Editions, whose CSE imprimatur designates "An Approved Edition" and thus would guarantee the authenticity and authority of a given text, takes it as a matter of due course that a scholarly edition reflects as fully as possible an author's "intentions." But the CSE does not insist that the copy text chosen for such purposes be the earliest possible form of a given text; those choices may

vary with the circumstances and compositional habits of individual authors. Indeed, we are told that the CSE seal indicates "An" not "The" approved edition, and the Center concedes that "it is not unlikely that two
careful scholars may disagree about certain readings in a critical text; and
it is certainly possible that *two different texts of the same work could meet
CSE standards and qualify for the emblem.*"[3]

It is sometimes an easy matter to determine what Whitman wrote as opposed to what his printer published, but it is not necessarily so easy to prefer one text over the other. The typesetter's "improvement" may actually
be one from an aesthetic point of view; the copy editor's fiddling with an
author's prose may clarify "meanings" and at the same time violate an
author's "intentions." The author's original impulses may have fashioned
such and such a phrase, and later ones may have motivated a dramatic revision of it. I substitute the word *impulse* for *intention* here because the issue has less to do with whether one prefers original or final intentions in
the establishment of a given text than it does with whether the intention itself is discoverable either in literary texts or outside of them, in the author's
psyche, say, or in his or her social circumstance.

Then there are equal and opposite problems, epitomized on the one hand
by Robert Browning's famous remark when asked about his meaning in a
certain passage in *Sordello*: "At one time only God and I knew what that
line meant. Now, only God knows." On the other hand there is what might
be called the Pee-Wee Herman Principle. In one of his movies Pee-Wee Herman is showing off on his bicycle. He falls in the shrubs, and his friends
laugh. He dusts himself off and indignantly declares, "I meant to do that."
For example, in the *Typee* manuscript Herman Melville spoke of "bloody
cannibals." The English edition changed the phrase to "bloody-minded
cannibals"; the American edition printed it as "booby-minded"; and in
the American Revised edition Melville himself changed it back to "bloody-
minded," presumably preferring that phrase to his own original "bloody."[4]
Yet still another problem arises when, as in the case of certain early poems
of Robert Frost, all the evidence points to Frost as their creator, but the author not only denies intention in the poems but even authorship itself.[5]

3. "Center for Scholarly Editions: An Introductory Statement," *PMLA* 92:4 (1977):
586; italics mine.
4. See John Bryant, "Melville's L-Word: First Intentions and Final Readings in
Typee," *NEQ* vol. 63, no. 2 (1990): 120–31.
5. In "The Case of the Orphaned Poems" (in *Mysteries and Manuscripts,* privately

What is at stake for editors and critics alike is not intention at all, whatever one may mean by the word, but coherence, or, better, comprehensibility. Some people temperamentally find psychoanalytic explanations more compelling than economic ones, in fact find economic explanations altogether mysterious; matters of gender may be for some of greater interest than matters of race or class; "facts" may consist in eyewitness accounts, corroborating testimony, the a priori requirements of language or consciousness, the forces of the marketplace, or metaphysical postulates. These are differences about what constitutes evidence, nothing more and nothing less, and while one may stand outside of texts and interpret them and their authors' intentions according to a variety of evidentiary procedures and assumptions, one may not stand outside what one takes to be evidence itself.[6] One may prefer the notion that the divine spirit circulates through the creative soul only in moments of inspiration and enlist cognitive psychology and speech act theory to assist in the articulation of one's preferences for "original intentions." Another may find that the shaping hand operates steadfastly and minutely in the direction of an aesthetic ideal and believe that symmetrical second thoughts subdue confused and discordant passions. Romantic or classical, these preferences enlist our interest and assist in our detection of evidence, but they really don't have much to do with intentions as such.

---

published, 1976, 38–44), Leon Howard, with reference to Frost poems in the Huntington Library, asked the interesting question, "What is the status of a literary manuscript which is denied by its purported author but which has a provenance that makes impossible its attribution to anyone else?" (38). His essay concludes with a related question: Does a writer who denies authorship of unpublished manuscripts thereby place the work in the public domain? This is a copyright question that awaits a legal decision.

6. Walter Benn Michaels and Steven Knapp, in "Against Theory," in *Against Theory: Literary Studies and the New Pragmatism,* ed. W. J. T. Mitchell (Chicago: University of Chicago Press, 1985), 11–30, make a similar but by no means identical point. Intention and meaning, knowledge and belief, are inseparable terms, they contend; theorists separate these terms and thereby arrive all unknowingly at a form of question begging that in itself argues against theory as a useful or even possible activity. For them, intention and meaning are the same thing and therefore cannot be isolated from one another. Only within the precinct of certain theoretical assumptions does this antitheoretical claim make any sense, however. An Olympic diver, for example, chooses a certain dive that carries with it a degree of difficulty, and the actual dive is measured against this intention. Not for a moment does the diver suppose that his intention is synonymous with his performance. Nor for that matter do writers themselves make the sort of assumption Knapp and Benn Michaels postulate—Faulkner described *The Sound and the Fury* as a "magnificent failure"; Melville knew that his achievements, considerable though they were, fell short of his ambitions for *Moby-Dick.*

What distinguishes the occupation of textual editing is an open allegiance to a provisional attitude toward its subject. Precisely to the degree that one is committed to being speculative, the less one can afford to be provisional. The obverse is also true. If, to return to the example of *Typee,* the editors of the Northwestern/Newberry edition of the novel take into account all extant evidence and establish a text in a way that allows it to be acknowledged as an "approved text," and then some years later a fragment of the manuscript of the novel is discovered in a trunk, their conclusions must be altered or amended in ways that take this new evidence into account. A different trunk containing a different manuscript (that is, the first half of *Adventures of Huckleberry Finn*) will undoubtedly modify if not finally discredit Walter Blair's *Mark Twain and Huck Finn* (1960), the Iowa/California CSE edition of the novel (1989), and Victor Doyno's *Huckleberry Finn: The Evolution of a Novel* (1991).[7] Scholars would not need to be so provisional and tentative, of course, if only history would keep its place in the past, but that is an impossibility.

In any event, textual editors are sometimes dismissed as antiquarian, fastidious, or timid, when in fact they are merely resisting the easy urge to have their faith exceed their facts. This latter attitude, I hope it is unnecessary to point out, is not "positivistic" but scholarly. Of late, textual editors have had theory thrust upon them, and the resulting debate both within and without the precincts of textual editing has been provocative and enriching. In the heyday of New Criticism, there was a kind of détente between scholars and critics, a strict separation of duties and disciplines, but postmodern critiques have effaced these nice boundaries. In part, this turn of events derives from the inadvertent intersection of two distinct uses of the term *text.* For the textual editor, the text is the *terminus a quem;* for the poststructuralist, or most any other critic, it is the *terminus a quo.*

This last point may be clarified by briefly comparing an unlikely pair: Ronald Crane and Hershel Parker. Apart from the fact that both have said some provocative things on matters of intention, the two men have little in common—except the assumption that texts are suffused with meaning only by and through the artistic or creative process. Crane and Parker agree,

---

7. Advocates of hypertext solutions to editorial uncertainties will no doubt watch with interest the reception and sales of the new Random House "comprehensive" edition of *Huckleberry Finn,* for the publishers have paid hard coin for the rights to put into the novel what Twain took out.

more or less, that knowledge of authorial intention may be arrived at inductively while at the same time insisting on what Crane called a "strict relativism" in critical discourse, but their methods and understanding of this process are quite different.

For Crane, as he expressed it in *The Languages of Criticism and the Structure of Poetry* (1953), a book too commonly ignored these days and surely still worthy of our attention, the whole method of poetics consists in "reasoning back from the inductively known nature of any such [poetic] whole to the necessary and sufficient internal conditions in the [poetic] structure to be fashioned by the poet of a maximum achievement of the specific form of beauty of which it is capable." Crane is not concerned with poetic creation, however, but with "poetic reasoning," that is, with the artistic ends to be achieved in terms of the necessary or desirable poetic means to achieve them. I might add that Crane, though he does not say so explicitly, arrives simultaneously through this backward motion at intention and the author, or perhaps it is more precise to say that for Crane intention and author are one and the same force or entity. Crane obviously takes his cues from Aristotle; Parker prefers John Dewey. For Parker, citing Dewey, "meaning is infused into the text at the moment each part is written. The 'artist is controlled in the process of his work by his grasp of the connection between what he has already done and what he is to do next.' He must 'at each point retain and sum up what has gone before as a whole and with reference to a whole to come'; if this does not happen, there will be 'no consistency and no security in his successive acts.'"[8]

I must confess that I do not know, precisely, what the expressions "poetic reasoning" and the "security" of successive creative acts may mean. Certainly plot figures centrally for both Parker and Crane and is one of those artistic means that sometimes seems to inhere in narrative or, in the case of Parker, may be quickly enough detected when it does not. Thus Parker will sometimes identify nonsense statements in what he calls "flawed texts," as for example Huckleberry Finn's statement in one paragraph that he is going ashore to find out how far Cairo is and, in the next, that there was nothing left for him to do but to "look out sharp" for the town from

---

8. Ronald Crane, *The Languages of Criticism and the Structure of Poetry* (Toronto: University of Toronto Press, 1953), 81, 46; Hershel Parker, *Flawed Texts and Verbal Icons: Literary Authority in American Fiction* (Evanston: Northwestern University Press, 1984), 73.

their raft.[9] Is this an aesthetic shortcoming and artistic blunder, or is it rather a rupture in the text caused by the circumstantially imposed interruption of the successive acts of creation?

The answer, of course, or one answer, is that there are at least two notions of text to which this question may be addressed. The non sequitur in Twain's poetic reasoning may be accounted for, extratextually, by the fact that Twain deleted the raftsmen's episode from *Huckleberry Finn* and neglected to repair the remark in conformity with the altered text before it went to press. The question of aesthetic wholeness is thus referred to two very different occasions—to a literary text whose formal integrity has been violated or to a text that may be "established" by textual editors in order to rectify the error and thus dramatize the "intentions" of the author. However, I do not wish simply to make the established point that good criticism requires good texts, but rather to identify two distinct operant notions of intention.

The distinction between Crane and Parker on matters of intention may be accounted for by identifying the differing points of view of those from whom they take their cues: Aristotle and Dewey. As W. V. Quine points out, "The Aristotelian notion of essence was the forerunner, no doubt, of the modern notion of intension or meaning." Thus may Crane speak of the discoverable *dynamis* supplying a text both with a concrete wholeness and an aesthetic beauty, which is at the same time its meaning. For Dewey, by contrast, meaning is "primarily a property of behavior"; hence, "primarily meaning is intent." Thus may Parker say in *Flawed Texts and Verbal Icons* that a work is infused with authorial intention "during the process of composition, not before and not afterwards."[10]

For Crane poems are forms of discourse that act on behalf of an aesthetic idea and, for the critic, demand in turn a method, a language, and a framework, in sum a poetics, appropriate to them. For Parker, so far as I can tell, poems, or any other texts we deem literary, are the residue of a form of essentially prelinguistic compositional behavior, which I take to mean that poems are acts in the process of self-discovery rather than artic-

9. See Hershel Parker, "Lost Authority: Non-sense, Skewed Meanings, and Intentionless Meanings," in *Against Theory: Literary Studies and the New Pragmatism*, 72–79.

10. W. V. Quine, *From a Logical Point of View: Nine Logico-philosophical Essays* (Cambridge: Harvard University Press, 1980), 22; John Dewey, *Experience and Nature* (New York: Dover, 1958, 179–80; Parker, *Flawed Texts and Verbal Icons,* 23.

ulations of an idealized form of beauty. Likewise, the textual editor's object (regardless of whether one prefers original or final intentions) remains provisional to the extent that circumstances, including new and ever-accumulating evidence, alter cases, and cases determine texts.

The point here, once again, is that intention is not the beginning point but the ending point, perhaps never to be achieved, of critical and scholarly deliberation. The critical interpretation of a text (whether or not one takes into account authorial intention) is the establishment of a text. The opposite is also true: The establishment of a text is perforce an interpretation and a critical statement.

Rodolphe Gasché names three usual concepts of a text: 1) "The sensibly palpable, empirically encounterable transcription of an oral discourse"; 2) "an intelligible object"; and 3) "the dialectical sublation, either as 'form' or 'content,' of both its sensible and ideal determinations." And he offers an account of Derrida's "general text" as a superior formulation of, "phenomenologically speaking, an intentionality without an intentum." Hershel Parker would have us deal with 1 and 2; Crane with 1 and 3. Both, I suspect, would reject the Derridean general text as "intentionality without an intentum" and, I am sure, would reject as too neo-Platonic the proffering of Derridean "textuality" as, in Gasché's words, "an essence or substance, that is, a more authentic and more fundamental mode of being than that of the texts which in their empirical variety, depend on it as to their last reason."[11]

I have said elsewhere and in another connection that imaginative literature is no more made of words than the economy is made of money, and I would further propose that the stuff out of which literature is made is feelings, not words. Or to put it more bluntly, Marshall MacLuhan notwithstanding, the medium is still the medium, not the message. I do not wish to pause to argue this rather unfashionable notion, but if one assents to the proposition, then one comes round, rather oddly I suppose, to the conclusions that 1) literature is antirepresentational, in the sense that it does not mean to depict reality (real or imagined); and 2) that literature is realistic,

---

11. Rodolphe Gasché, *The Tain of the Mirror: Derrida and the Philosophy of Reflection* (Cambridge: Harvard University Press, 1986), 279, 281, 283. Since, at least in the Husserlian construction of phenomenology, all consciousness is consciousness-of, this Derridean formulation, despite its linguistic character, appears more to resemble Spinoza's notion of the *conatus* as tendency or drive independent of its objects.

in the sense that literature is to be measured not against the "real" (whatever that may be) but against experience, what in Henry James's words one "cannot not know one way or another" by virtue of having been alive and observant. The intentions of an author are the attempts to render, somewhat totemically, equivalents of a quite fluid state of being that may or may not communicate to readers some portion of that state but are surely meant to be compelling renderings nonetheless. So understood, one can't take authorial intention as the ground for interpretation; nor can one ever decide absolutely, except in such concrete matters as what word or words he or she at first or at last settled on, what the intention of an author was, since the text or texts (simultaneously in all their possible versions) are the intended.[12]

Literary intentions may be forever inscrutable, but that does not require one to give up the term or the search. however. If one were to abandon every question to which there could never be a satisfactory answer, there would be few questions to ask and the answers would likely be so mundane as to be entirely unremarkable anyway. What one really means, or ought to mean, by the term *authorial intention* is this: The literary expression (that is, a passage, a poem, a text) is adequate (at least for the moment) to the whole physiological and emotional condition that impelled it. The poem, as Wallace Stevens observed, is the "cry of its occasion." That cry is in some sense satisfactory (in Stevens's idiom, we may say that it "suffices") despite the fact that it may later undergo innumerable revisions and alterations; and each successive cry is also satisfactory, though the original occasion has been supplemented by other occasions (the desire, say, to make oneself understood, or to get published in such and such a journal whose audience is typically of such and such a character, or, perhaps, simply to make money).

The difficulty is not so much identifying intention as such, since the writing is itself the intended, but how to characterize what motives or impulses have been satisfied. Any given piece of writing may temporarily satisfy a

---

12. Even when all the pertinent evidence is available, as John Bryant has shown in regard to Melville, the determination of the word an author intended is sometimes no easy matter. Bryant notes that in the recently discovered fragment of *Typee* what he calls Melville's "L-word" is indecipherable. The word may be "literally" or "liberally," and the meaning of the passage as well as how we are to take the narrator's attitude toward his subject vary considerably according to which construction we choose. None of the three editions over which the author had some say, nor the manuscript itself, can resolve this question.

rational or an irrational impulse, a conscious or an unconscious design, an ideological position or a perverse curiosity. And original impulses may change in the course of composition; this is particularly true of extended works such as novels. It would seem to go without saying that the author of a novel intended first and foremost to write a novel, but Ernest Hemingway's *The Sun Also Rises* grew out of multiple desires that were first figured forth as the impulse to write a short story, then a series of connected stories, and finally a multilayered novel.[13] Richard Wright appears to have wished to dramatize a Communist ideological perspective in *Native Son,* but by the end he was more interested in presenting the existential dilemma of his black hero in a way that undercut or at least modified his political agenda.

And even if an author's intentions were "pure"—synthetically unitary, poetically rational, and above all knowable—the recalcitrance of the world at large would serve to deflect, erode, disperse, or otherwise separate intention from meaning and leave us with a host of significances determined by, say, popular whim (as in a sudden contemporary interest in Vienna over Paris); political perspective (for example, Upton Sinclair's socialism as it was expressed in *The Jungle* was obscured by a vague social nausea that ultimately resulted in the establishment of the FDA); happy or unhappy coincidence (as, for example, in the nearly concurrent release of the film *The China Syndrome* and the accident at Three Mile Island); nonliterary inventions or discoveries (such as Alfred Lord Tennyson's reference in "Locksley Hall" to "airy navies" or Edgar Allan Poe's proposal in *Eureka* of what amounts to a "big bang" theory of the origin of the universe);[14] not to mention those more gradual and comprehensible alterations in critical focus, reception, and perspective.

Of course authors *feel* that they have intentions invested in their works, but their own status in terms of any given text, particularly when it has entered the public domain, is as an interpreter, not as one who authorizes its

13. For an account of the composition of this novel, see William Balassi, "Hemingway's Greatest Iceberg: The Composition of *The Sun Also Rises,*" in *Writing the American Classics,* ed. James Barbour and Tom Quirk (Chapel Hill: University of North Carolina Press, 1990), 125–55.

14. Jim O'Connor, in Tennessee Williams's *The Glass Menagerie* (1945), was surely meant to be seen as a well-meaning but oafish character. However, the fact that he is going to night school and intends to cast his lot with the newfangled television industry makes him appear to a contemporary reader more like a visionary (a budding Walter Cronkite, say) than a pathetic dreamer.

meaning. They are privileged interpreters, to be sure, since their connection to the genesis of a work is an intimate one and forms a part of their own experience and to a greater or lesser degree their projection of a public identity into the community. They are privileged, too, in that they may at times exert, sometimes legally, more than readerly influence over the production or nonproduction, revision, suppression, or interpretation of their work. But that same authority does not insure that as interpreters they enjoy incontestable intelligence about or power over the text.

Anyone who has ever taught composition knows the familiar student complaint about a paper that received a low grade: "But you know what I meant to say!" And indeed we frequently do. But we know it by virtue of some extratextual, often extraverbal information—the nature of the assignment, the readings in the course, class discussion, the temper of the times, the personality and temperament of the student, and of course a broader or at least teacherly knowledge of conventional usage. Recently, for example, a student of mine wrote of the relative complacency of third- and fourth-generation Puritans and their delay in receiving adult baptism. These Puritans, she wrote, failed to "pass the mustard."

Once the paper is handed in, the letter mailed, the novel published, the text is socialized and fends for itself, though it often gathers allies in the form of critics, reviewers, and, of course, scholarly textual editors, along the way. Nevertheless, the disposition of editors and publishers, the prepossessions of readers (both contemporary and future), even the revisionary and conciliatory consciousness of the author when he or she has the opportunity to alter a text, all these and other factors enter into the meaning-making process. Thus one may speak significantly of textual and publishing history, the history of popular and critical reception, and the like. And to do so is to soon discover that there is no "text," but instead a record (often consisting of several conflicting and contradictory "texts") of private expression and public response and the subsequent and ongoing negotiating of meanings into the world.

Truth, said William James, is what *"happens"* to an idea.[15] Meaning, likewise, is what happens and continues to happen to texts. And it is just this "what happens" that might profitably concern the critic. But one ought not err in the opposite direction, as it seems to me Jerome McGann comes

15. William James, *Pragmatism, and Four Essays from "The Meaning of Truth"* (New York: Meridian Books, 1955), 133.

awfully close to doing.[16] Some urns are better wrought than others, and good texts, arrived at by scholarly consensus, focus our attention and coordinate our energies. In any event, recent attempts to drain texts of their formal and unique integrity by connecting them to processes of production, literary protocols, and ideological formations, or by ignoring or denying human agency in the creation of memorable literature is sheer vanity. To "contextualize" texts is a worthy activity, but contextualizing that dissolves the object in the articulation of its political or historical surround calls its own methods into question. I recur once again to William James: "Let the *q* be fragrance, let it be toothache, or let it be a more complex kind of feeling, like that of the full-moon swimming in her blue abyss, it must first come in that simple shape, and be held fast in that first intention, before any knowledge *about* it can be attained. The knowledge *about* it is *it* with a context added. Undo *it,* and what is added cannot be *context.*"[17]

No doubt to accept the proposals that 1) there are no "texts" as such, but merely the ever shifting record of appearances and amendments of texts; 2) that there is no "author" as a separable entity responsible for a given text, but instead the author concept, again shifting, whose name indicates not merely a historical personage, but a composite of beliefs and attitudes we adopt about the creative cause of a work; and 3) that "intention" (first, middle, or final) means the assumed adequacy of the expression for the emotional condition that impelled it—no doubt these proposals, and the several implications that flow from them, will distress those who hanker after some absolute ground for meaning, belief, and, ultimately, culture itself. On the other hand, the fact that meanings and the determination of meanings are negotiated into existence does not imply that interpretation is exclusively a political matter, that one must engage in some sort

16. In the chapter entitled "The Problem of Literary Authority," in *A Critique of Modern Textual Criticism* (Charlottesville: University Press of Virginia, 1983), for example, Jerome McGann asserts that "Authoritative texts are arrived at by an exhaustive reconstruction not of an author and his intentions so much as of an author and his context of work." It may well be and almost certainly is the case that "the location of authority necessarily becomes dispersed beyond the author" (84), but if, in the process, the author evaporates as a focal point of that authority, the conditions of production can no longer be defined as "context." In this sense, the concept of the author is absolutely necessary in order to determine what sorts of social and contractual arrangements have any bearing upon the production of any given text. It seems to me to be at least a mild contradiction that a working concept, the "author," is still required in order to argue that the author is socially constructed.

17. James, *Pragmatism,* 211.

of pork-barrel lobbying effort in order to make texts serve a special and preconcerted purpose. There are in place, after all, parliamentary procedures, which we may designate broadly as the scholarly method, that both promote and organize critical discourse but do not thereby predict its conclusions.

What is more important, there is also the almost perverse human desire to know more than we know already and to wish to act on behalf of rather than through this thing we call literature, to bring into being a completer picture, a more compelling account, a fuller and more viable record not only of texts, authors, and intentions, but of the processes of the creative imagination itself. Curiosity, too, is a value, and it well may be that our desire to solve problems outstrips our desire to problematize issues.

In any event, I offer in the next few pages a case study that I hope will reveal the complications inherent in discerning the nature of authors, texts, and intentions. The case is the curious history of Mark Twain's play *Colonel Sellers*.[18] Twain's play is virtually unknown, even to many Twain scholars. If nothing more, the unfamiliarity of the play provides an adequate substitute for critical detachment.

If one is concerned with matters of authorship and the "authority" a writer does or does not have over a text, it is necessary to sift through the intricate and sometimes tedious evidence of the author's actual role in the production of a text. Let us take the circumstances surrounding the play *Colonel Sellers*.

These are the facts of the case:

In May 1873, Twain sailed to England to negotiate copyright for the novel *The Gilded Age,* which he had coauthored with Charles Dudley Warner. At that time he wrote Warner that a man named Boucicault was interested in dramatizing the book: "I know it ought to dramatize well," he wrote, and Twain was determined that Boucicault should not get more than one-third profits for dramatizing it (1:57). On May 19, Twain filed for joint copyright for himself and Warner for any dramatic production of the novel, and he began to "map out" a dramatization of the novel but was diverted from the project (1:57).

---

18. The information concerning the composition and circumstances of production of this play is drawn from Jerry Thomason's "*Colonel Sellers:* The Story of His Play" (2 vols., Ph.D. diss. University of Missouri–Columbia, 1991). References to this dissertation are hereafter cited parenthetically in the text.

By February 1874, Twain reported that he had written a "queer play"; perhaps this was a play based on *The Gilded Age* (1:58). Whatever Twain's dramatic aspirations may have been at the time, on April 17 the *Alta Daily Californian* announced that John T. Raymond was preparing a production of *The Gilded Age*, dramatized by G. B. Densmore. On April 22, the play opened before a small but receptive audience. By the end of April news of the production had reached the east coast and Warner wrote Twain, needlessly reminding him of their copyright on any dramatic production of the novel. Twain responded, saying that he knew Densmore well enough and that "he shan't run any play on MY brains" (1:66).

At this point the issue of authorship begins to get sticky. Twain had thought of enjoining the production of the Densmore play, but he learned from reviews that the San Francisco production was restricted to portions of the novel that he, and not Warner, had written and that its principal attraction was the character of Sellers. Twain's main concern at this point suddenly turned to renegotiating the terms of his and Warner's copyright and dissolving their agreement in order that he might develop on his own a play based only on that portion of the novel he had written. In point of fact, however, the play he was to write, contrary to their agreement, did draw upon portions of the novel that Warner had written.

What one can see thus far is an intricate history of the "authority" of a text: A coauthored novel and the joint intention to protect with copyright their combined intention to at some future time carry *The Gilded Age* material from one genre to another conflicts with an independent piracy of the subject matter by a third party. But the terms of that conflict shift as soon as Twain recognizes that "his" part of the novel has been well received on the stage. By May Twain had enjoined the Densmore play against future performances and proceeded to write his own. He wrote *Colonel Sellers* at Quarry Farm in about a month and finished it by July 15, 1874, presumably having John Raymond in mind to play the title role.

Twain bought the Densmore script for two hundred dollars, promising to pay another two hundred if his own play proved successful. (By Thomason's reckoning, the *Colonel Sellers* play eventually earned Twain about $180,000 dollars.) On July 20, Twain submitted an amanuensis copy of his play for copyright, and he wrote Robert Mackenzie that he was well enough satisfied with his rendering of Sellers: "I meant him to be at all times & under all circumstances a *gentleman* & so he is, now, as Raymond plays him. . . . I am very glad you like the old speculator (he still lives, & is drawn

from life, not imagination—I ate a turnip dinner with him years ago)"
(1:72).

Let us turn for a moment to the authorship of the play. Densmore's script
does not survive, and there is insufficient evidence to corroborate rumors
that were at the time circulating that Twain had plagiarized from Densmore's play. In a letter he wrote to the *Hartford Post,* but never mailed,
Twain insisted that he had rewritten Densmore's script three separate times.
"I had expected to use little of his language & but little of his plot. I do not
think that there are now twenty sentences of Mr. Densmore's in the play,
but I used so much of his plot that I wrote him & told him that I should
pay him about as much more as I had already paid him, in case the play
proved a success. I shall keep my word. . . . I furnished all the characters in
this play, & put in their mouths almost every individual word they utter"
(1:93). (One notes that, in terms of his own claims to authorship and artistic intention, Twain divides for separate consideration individual words
from plot. A narratologist might have a field day with this distinction.)

But whatever Twain's artistic ambition, it vied with another intention—
that the play should make money. Twain assisted in rehearsals for the New
York City production, and he wrote his brother Orion Clemens that "I
wanted the play played *my* way unless my way was radically wrong"
(1:86). His way, remember, was that Sellers should remain a gentleman
throughout. But the basis of the popularity of *Colonel Sellers* was its comedy, not its pathos. "I threw all my strength into the character of Colonel
Sellers," Twain recalled, "hoping to make it a very strong tragedy part, and
pathetic. . . . [Raymond] *tries* hard to play it right and make it majestic and
pathetic; but his *face* is against him. . . . Oh! I can see that he tries hard to
make it solemn and awful and heroic, but really sometimes he almost makes
me laugh" (1:90).

Twain's reservations notwithstanding, the money was rolling in. He
grumbled, but apparently he never even considered sacrificing profits at the
altar of his muse. Twain attempted to advise Raymond on how to portray
the Colonel, but Twain's intentions and Raymond's dramatic renderings
never fully merged. Twain remembered in his *Autobiography* years later
that "The real Colonel Sellers was never on the stage. Only half of him was
there. Raymond could not play the other half of him; it was above his level." But theatergoers and critics responded to Raymond's half, commending the production for (in the words of reviewers) its "grotesque humor"
and its continual "merriment" (1:91).

What we have in this episode is the record of converging and diverging intentions; copyrights arranged, dissolved, renewed; capitalistic ambitions conflicting with democratic loyalties to the man Twain one time ate turnips with; multiple authorship, and the neat separation of plot from language; enthusiastic public reception and frustrated private artistic purpose; stated intentions and thwarted artistic aspirations. And what is true of authors is equally true of texts. In the case of the Colonel Sellers play, there are three scripts extant, but the basis of choosing one over another goes beyond the conventional dispute over first or final intentions, since Twain's intentions are known and his authority over the text was absolute, but the two could not be satisfactorily fused. Sociolinguistics, narrative theory, psychoanalysis, Marxist critique, reception theory, all manner of theoretical positions might shed some light on the production of this text, but one thing is sure, the case does not need to be problematized; it is too complicated already.

What I am suggesting finally is that the consideration of the complete record of authorship, a record disclosed by conscientious scholarly investigation and clarified by responsible contemplation and reasonable inference, is a rewarding enterprise. The fusion of theory and scholarship will likely yield ambiguous but instructive results, and some concessions are required on both sides—but the relation is mutually beneficial. Virginia Woolf put it best, perhaps: "From the collision of many converging ideas a theory forms. It may be helpful. For if we allow sensations to accumulate unchecked they lose their sharpness; to test them by reason strengthens and enriches. But fascinating as theories are . . . they too must be controlled or they will form a crust which blocks the way for further experience. Theories must always be brought into touch with facts. The collision may prove fatal to these delicate and intricate constructions. It does not matter. The risk must be run."[19] At all events, it does not seem very profitable for me stubbornly to keep my mules penned up against the incursions of yours. Especially when letting down the barriers that separate us might yield such unpredictable and feisty hybrids.

19. Virginia Woolf, *Roger Fry: A Biography* (New York: Harcourt, Brace, 1940), 227–28.

The Pudding

IV

What If Poe's Humorous Tales Were Funny?

Poe's "X-ing a Paragrab" and Twain's "Journalism in Tennessee"

"What If Poe's Humorous Tales Were Funny?" There are imbedded in this gimmicky title a couple of presuppositions and a couple of questions: First, there is the presupposition that Poe's humorous tales are not funny, entirely an impression on my part, though one largely borne out by general neglect of Poe's humor. Second, there is the suggestion that some alteration in manner or conception might actually render them funny. The corollaries of these assumptions may be phrased as questions: What would it take to make Poe's humorous tales funny? and Why aren't they funny?

Any discussion of Poe as comedian requires a brief examination of his qualifications as a humorist. For my purposes, his familiar letter of justification of "Berenice" is a sufficient instance. In writing to the owner of *The Southern Literacy Messenger*, Thomas W. White, on April 30, 1835, Poe defends the grotesque tale as a thoroughly magazinish piece, in keeping with articles to be found in the *London New Monthly* or *Blackwood's*. One observes in such pieces, he writes, "the ludicrous heightened into the grotesque; the fearful coloured into the horrible; the witty exaggerated into the burlesque; the singular wrought out into the strange and mystical. You may say this is bad taste. I have my doubts about it. Nobody is more aware than I am that simplicity is the cant of the day—but take my word for it no one cares anything about simplicity in their hearts."[1]

Poe was a shrewd editor and a canny judge of popular taste, of course, and his assessment of what the public is apt to respond to must be taken seriously. And it should also be noted how much importance he places on

---

1. Quoted in Thomas Dwight and David K. Jackson, comps., *The Poe Log: A Documentary Life* (Boston: G. K. Hall, 1987), 150.

literary treatment to carry his intended effects home. As with Twain, in "How to Tell a Humorous Story," Poe emphasizes manner over and above subject matter, though Poe relied more upon a certain stylistic elegance than on the pause or the sound of the human voice. However, here, as elsewhere, he claims the authority to speak of what he several times called in the "Philosophy of Composition," a "universality" of effect or sentiment; and one is rather more reluctant to credit Poe's acuity when it comes to democratic impulse and what the masses care for most deeply in their hearts.

But what of the dramatic situation of "Berenice" itself? Has it, in fact, been heightened into the grotesque? This tale told by an infirm monomaniac betrothed to his cousin, who has suddenly lost her health and vitality, surely has something ludicrous about it. As Berenice withers away, the narrator's love of the ethereal and immutable finds its obsessive object in that which neither molds nor rusts—her teeth. Through a bit of transference neurosis, the narrator fixes upon her teeth as the emblem of the ideal: "For these [teeth] I longed with a frenzied desire. All other matters and all different interests became absorbed in their single contemplation. They—they alone were present to the mental eye, and they, in their sole individuality, became the essence of my mental life. . . . I pondered upon their conformation. I mused upon the alteration in their nature. I shuddered as I assigned to them, in imagination, a sensitive and sentient power, and even when *unassisted by the lips*, a *capability of moral expression*."[2] It is grotesque, not to say bizarre, to contemplate how this feat of imagination, this figuration of the Cheshire cat–like grin of Berenice, might be translated, even in the mind of a madman, into a moral maxim.

How, precisely, Poe has escaped the ludicrous here quite baffles me, though I have no reason to doubt the sincerity of his claim to White. Nevertheless, when, at the end, the reader discovers that the narrator, bespattered with mud and gore, had recently violated Berenice's tomb in order to forcibly extract "thirty two" "ivory substances" and that Berenice herself is still alive, we may concede Poe's observation, made in the same letter, that, indeed, the tale "approaches the very verge of bad taste." If there is, in fact, a moral to this tale, Ralph Waldo Emerson, coincidentally, expressed it more succinctly, and without a detectable trace of humor or of a sense of the grotesque. In a journal entry for January 1841 he wrote: "A

---

2. Poe, "Berenice," in *Complete Tales and Poems of Edgar Allan Poe* (New York: Vintage, 1975), 146–47; italics mine. Hereafter cited parenthetically in the text.

tooth is excellent in the <mouth> jaws but would not be pleasing in the hand."[3]

At any rate, had Poe a keener sense of the ridiculous, or at least a blunter sense of the sublime, he might have better succeeded as a humorist. If, in "Berenice," he had followed out the logic of his tale and had converted downward instead of upward, Poe might have returned the grotesque to the ludicrous, and perhaps to some darkly comic effect. For we know that the narrator, fastidious and studious as he is, is to be married to his cousin Berenice in a matter of weeks. To imagine a forlorn and toothless Berenice gumming "I do" at the altar, and beside her a disconsolate groom with a pocketful of grinders, is to imagine that the teeth might indeed have had the "capability of moral expression."

In this imagined extension of the tale we have our demented narrator paying the social price for his obsession. If, as Poe insisted, the death of a beautiful woman is the most poetic of all subjects, what, one wonders, according to this logic, is the revivification of an ugly one? What else but an at least mildly amusing social comedy? But Poe's narrators hardly ever face social consequences; they are too busy paying psychological blood money to the imp of the perverse. Such a narrative alteration is not unthinkable, after all. Poe had himself done something in this vein in his tale "The Man That Was Used Up," in which the darling of society and the object of amorous attention is shown to be made up of several detachable parts. Nathaniel Hawthorne, too, had created in "Mrs. Bullfrog" an analogous comedy; in that tale, a carriage accident reveals to the newlywed narrator that his wife is a bald and toothless shrew, though, as it agreeably turns out, a rich one.

But, to bring these speculations round to my announced topic, I offer a comparison of Poe's "X-ing a Paragrab" to Twain's "Journalism in Tennessee." My justification for putting these two stories together in order to tell them apart is flimsy enough: They both deal with the furious and comic rivalry of country newspaper editors. I do not know whether this subject matter was sufficiently widespread and frequent for me to speak of it in generic terms. Burlesque relies upon a general familiarity with the object of humorous exaggeration to achieve the intended comic effect, and both Poe and Twain assume in their readers some acquaintance with the dramatic

---

3. *The Journals and Miscellaneous Notebooks of Ralph Waldo Emerson*, ed. A. W. Plumstead and Harrison Hayford (Cambridge: Harvard University Press, 1969), 7:413.

situation of the contest between newspaper rivals. We can be certain, at any rate, that such rivalries, real or imagined, were common enough.

Witness the actual exchange conducted during the winter of 1874–1875 between the editor of the Yuma paper, the *Arizona Sentinel,* and the Prescott paper, the *Weekly Arizona Miner.* The first editor, Judge William J. Berry, refers to his rival as a "dirty nincompoop" and a "blackguard" and responds to an earlier charge of being a drunkard:

> In regard to our being a "judge of whiskey," we will simply say that no man ever saw Wm. J. Berry laid out under its influence; while we had the extreme mortification of seeing the editor of the *Miner,* . . . laid out in the refreshment room, dead drunk, with candles placed at his head and his feet, and a regular "wake" held over him. It was then for the first time that we discovered Darwin's connecting link . . . [here] was a connecting link between the catfish and the jackass.

Not to be outdone, John Marion, the editor of the *Miner,* replies to the man he variously calls a "mammoth ape" and a "natural and artificial liar." Surely, he continues, the editor of the *Sentinel* cannot have forgotten

> his visit to Lynx Creek, in 1864, when he rolled over a pine log dead drunk, and served a useful purpose for a j[o]cose man. Yes, Judge, we own up to that little drunk of ours; but unlike you, we were not pointed out and derided as a regular whiskey bloat; nor did any person ever attempt to use us for a water-closet, as you were used that day on Lynx Creek.[4]

Needless to say, this is frontier humor in a form too raw to appeal to Poe's sensibility. What is perhaps not so apparent is that even in this vituperative exchange there is the concern for social respectability. In point of fact, Berry and Marion were longtime friends, and their published exchange of insults is something of a journalistic version of doing the dozens. More to the point, their editorials are comic to the extent that they disclose behavior measured against accepted social ritual and communal feeling—that is, holding a wake for a man dead drunk or bragging that no one ever used me as a water closet—and imply a trust in civilized life as, if nothing more, the protection against catfish and jackasses.

4. Reprinted in Tony Hillerman, ed., *The Best of the West: An Anthology of Classic Writing from the American West* (New York: Harper Collins, 1991), 470–73.

The social requirements for comedy are nicely summarized in a few stray remarks by Henri Bergson in his familiar essay, *Le Rire* (Laughter): "You would hardly appreciate the comic if you felt yourself isolated from others. Laughter appears to stand in need of an echo." "Our laughter is always the laughter of a group." "To understand laughter, we must put it back into its natural environment, which is society, and above all must we determine the utility of its function, which is a social one. . . . Laughter must answer to certain requirements of life in common. It must have social signification."[5] And in light of these observations I will here predict my conclusion about Poe's humor: It is not funny because it is fundamentally antisocial. Or, to put it another way, if Poe really wanted to be funny, he should have had a mother to advise him to "Get out more! Meet people! Join in! Have Fun! Laugh a little!" But we know that Poe had no such mother and that, whatever else was bothering him, he suffered from the feeling of being a socially displaced person. One senses in Poe's humorous tales that the author is having a great deal of fun, but one also senses that he is laughing up his sleeve, immunized against the social contagion of general good humor and fellow feeling.

That said, we might consider the salient differences between "X-ing a Paragrab" and "Journalism in Tennessee." Both Poe and Twain were sometime journalists who meant to transcend (in public estimation if not always in actual achievement) the narrow limitations of that vocation, and both had motive to regard the journalistic enterprise with a certain condescension. For rather different reasons, Poe and Twain considered themselves outside the house of the dominant literary culture—by half, they both desired entrance into this culture, and by half, they wished to burn the house to the ground. All the anxious extenuations and self-accusing recriminations that Twain expressed in the aftermath of the famous "Whittier Birthday Speech" are not nearly so affecting, or so pathetic, however, as the fact that the Virginian Poe published his first volume, *Tamerlane and Other Poems* (1827), as "by a Bostonian."

The use of a literary persona is central to both men, of course, but the important difference is that Clemens soon settled on a mask ("Mark Twain") that acquired a life of its own and in whom Clemens had both a practical and sympathetic interest. Poe, by contrast, was a literary chameleon and randomly adopted personae that typically had no other function than that

5. Henri Bergson, *Le Rire* (Laughter), reprinted in *Comedy*, ed. Wylie Sypher (Garden City, N.Y.: Doubleday, 1956), 64–65.

of a literary device or offered a certain protective coloring for an overly sensitive personality.[6] "Mark Twain" was a fully developed sensibility, capable of absorbing as well as delivering his comedy. Poe's literary personae, on the other hand, came out of a remarkable literary sophistication that never acquired the firmness or confidence that might deploy humor in any other fashion than through self-justification, grotesque exaggeration, or nervous derision. Clemens's humor was grounded in a more stable and, often, more morally indignant perspective, which seldom stooped to the effects of mere wit or cleverness.

Still, both were gifted writers, and they were ever alert to the techniques and appeal of popular literature and expert in the technical and rhetorical journalistic process. These two tales are strikingly parallel in any number of incidental ways, but their interest for us here is how, precisely, they disclose differences in humorous technique. In short, "Journalism in Tennessee," even though it is not one of Twain's better burlesques, is funny, while Poe's isn't. And it is worth our attention to inquire into the difference.

Both writers exploit the conventions of burlesque with a seemingly casual indifference to public perception of them as professional writers. The plots of the stories are similar—a rivalry between country editors is dramatized from the point of view of a witness to events, though Twain's narrator more than once literally gets caught in the cross fire. In Twain's tale, the narrator travels south to Tennessee for his health and takes a berth on the paper, the *Morning Glory and Johnson County War-Whoop.* The chief editor of the paper conducts an ongoing battle, both verbal and physical, against rival editors for such papers as the *Moral Volcano,* the Higginsville *Thunderbolt and Battle Cry of Freedom,* the Mud Springs *Morning Howl,* and the Blathersville *Daily Hurrah.*

Twain is given the task of condensing the news of the week in a column entitled "Spirit of the Tennessee Press," which he does in bland and courteous tones. The chief editor is not pleased and revises this piece into a "peppery" prose not unlike the editorials from the Arizona *Miner* and *Sen-*

6. Poe had a natural aptitude for literary emulation, and among the several writers from whom he drew inspiration are Byron, Keats, Milton, Thomas Campbell, and Coleridge. For an insightful treatment of this dimension of Poe's creative imagination, see Leon Howard, "Artificial Sensitivity and Artful Rationality," in *Poe Studies* 20:1 (June 1987): 18–33.

tinel. Thus, for example, the narrator decorously observes: "We are pained to learn that Col. Bascom, chief-editor of the *Dying Shriek for Liberty*, fell in the street a few evenings since and broke his leg. He has lately been suffering with debility, caused by overwork and anxiety on account of sickness in his family." The chief editor translates this "mush and milk journalism" into something a bit more vigorous: "That degraded ruffian Bascom, of the *Dying Shriek for Liberty*, fell down and broke his leg yesterday—pity it wasn't his neck. He says it was 'debility caused by overwork and anxiety'! It was debility caused by trying to lug six gallons of forty-rod whisky around town when his hide is only gauged for four, and anxiety about where he was going to bum another six."[7]

Meantime, the multitudes that the chief editor has offended pay their several visits to exact their revenge, and by the end, the narrator has received the assaults meant for his boss and has lost two teeth and a finger, chipped a knuckle, suffered a cowhiding, and taken bullets in the arm and thigh. By the end, Twain decides that he will leave Tennessee for the same reason he came, for his health. This is common tall-tale humor, but, however exaggerated this sketch is, Twain's narrator is himself vulnerable to the fictive events and implicated in the comedy itself; he is literally a casualty of the ongoing war between the chief editor and, it seems, most of the citizens in the state.

By contrast, Poe's tale is only casually a first-person narrative, and the narrator stands as an uninvolved, bemused recounter of incident. The setting of Poe's tale is vaguely western (external evidence indicates that he had the utopian Fourierite community of Alphadelphia, Michigan, in mind). An eastern editor, "Mr. Touch-and-go Bullet-head" travels from "Frogpondia" (Poe's name for Boston) to the city of "Alexander-the-Great-o-nopolis" and establishes the paper the *Nopolis Tea-Pot*. For Poe, the battle between rival editors consists solely of vituperative complaints about literary style, and the missiles they fire are entirely textual.

John Smith, the editor of the *Alexander-the-Great-o-nopolis Gazette* and himself from Concord, thus cementing the transcendentalist qualities Poe means to satirize, complains of Bullet-head's excessive use of the letter O in his inaugural issue. Bullet-head is incensed and, after rejecting the idea

7. Mark Twain, *Collected Tales, Sketches, Speeches, and Essays, 1852–1890*, ed. Louis J. Budd (New York: Library of America, 1992), 310–11; hereafter cited parenthetically in the text.

of writing an editorial free of the dreaded letter, decides to outdo himself in his rejoinder. His composition begins: "So, ho, John! how now? Told you so, you know. Don't crow, another time, before you're out of the woods! Does your mother know you're out? Oh, no, no!—so go home at once, now, John, to your odious old woods of Concord! Go home to your woods, old owl,—go! You won't? Oh, poh, poh, John, don't do so!" (363).

Meantime, however, Smith has sent one of the printer's devils to the *Tea-Pot* offices to steal the Os from the print box. Thus, it so happens that Bullet-head's typesetter is forced to "x" the paragraph—that is to substitute the letter X for the missing Os. The printed version of the passage quoted above now reads: "Sx hx, Jxhn! hxw nxw! Txld yxu sx, yxu knxw. Dxn't crxw, anxther time, befxre yxu're xut xf the wxxds . . ." (365). The next morning the town feels there is some "diabolical treason" involved in this mysterious paragraph and vows to lynch the new editor. But Bullet-head has skipped town, and the citizens, by means of a series of sorry visual puns, are left to speculate on the man and the deed. One says that it was an "X-ellent" joke, another the result of the "Xu-berance of fancy," and yet another that he was merely "X-centric." The opinion of Bob, the typesetter who had x-ed the paragraph, is that Bullet-head had indulged himself too much in "XXXale," which "made him X (cross) in the X-treme" (366).

In any event, one senses in the tale that the author was enjoying himself enormously in writing this burlesque. For my part, however, I get the punch line, but I fail to see the humor in the joke itself. There is wit here aplenty, but has it really been exaggerated into the burlesque? The jokes are too exclusively private. Poe's satire of the transcendentalists is at best a bank shot from Alphadelphia, Michigan, to Concord, Massachusetts. Perhaps, in his emphasis on the O as the symbol of eternity and perfection, Poe had the self-described "circular philosopher," Emerson, in mind, and more particularly the essay "Circles," as the object of his satire, but if so, the wit is too obscurely delivered while the self-satisfaction is too annoyingly evident. Perhaps, too, there is some personal delight in transforming before the readers' very eyes the Frogpondian's orphic pronouncements into a cryptogram of the sort that Poe took a special pride in solving in the pages of *Graham's* magazine. In fact he invites this sort of comparison in the tale when he notes that the "town mathematician" could not solve the problem; for "X, everybody knew, was an unknown quantity; but in this case (as he properly observed), there was an unknown quantity of X" (365). Perhaps, too, he had in mind Immanuel Kant (whom he sometimes referred to

as "cant") as satirical object; for it was this metaphysician who had announced in *The Critique of Pure Reason* that the transcendental object
equals X.

All these are possibilities, I suppose, and I leave their unraveling to some
eager decoder of discourse. Perhaps they bear witness to Poe's semiotic
cleverness; I do not know. But I do know that the letter X is not funny. L
is funny. And I know this in the same way that Steve Allen, in the company of other comedians, decided that the word "spoon" is funny, but not
"knife" or "fork." "Hat" is funny, but "cap" isn't. And the way that they
made these discoveries, Allen recalled, was by saying these, and several other words besides, out loud. However, Poe most often writes for the "mental eye," not the "laughing" ear; or to phrase it in Bergsonian terms, there
is no echo in his humor, but the muffled snicker of self-satisfaction.

So what would it have taken to make Poe's humor funny? The answer,
I suspect, lies in a parable I draw from the *Mary Tyler Moore Show.* When
the newscaster Ted Baxter asks Lou Grant "What's wrong with me, Lou?"
Grant replies, "Ted, you know the way you are? Well, don't be that way."
Or, to rephrase the advice in the language of Bullet-head, "So, ho, Poe how
now! Oh, poh, poh, Poe, don't do so!" But Edgar Allan Poe was too help-
lessly himself to risk the revision of his life. At least Poe himself implied as
much when, in answer to James Russell Lowell's request for an estimate of
his life, he replied: "I am not ambitious—unless negatively. I, now and then,
feel stirred up to excel a fool, merely because I hate to let a fool imagine
that he may excel me. Beyond this I feel nothing of ambition."[8] With few
exceptions, Poe's humor does not risk self-exposure and does, indeed, seem
to emanate from an entirely negative ambition. "How to Write a Blackwood Article" and the accompanying tale "A Predicament" are two such
exceptions because, not only do they parody the literary manner of the typical *Blackwood's* tale, but they also disclose and ridicule, however oblique-
ly, Poe's own indebtedness in serious horror tales to the formulaic tale he
undertakes to burlesque. In other words, Poe is actually capable of humor
when he is willing to expose a certain personal vulnerability; more often,
however, his passivity and a settled pride obstruct any genuine move toward the social basis of laughter and comedy.

What strikes me as finally more mysterious and fascinating than Poe's

---

8. In Dwight and Jackson, *Poe Log,* 466.

ineptness at humor, however, is his motive to write comedy at all. Kenneth Burke, before he founded so much of his social and political philosophy on what he came to call "comic correctives," wrote a novel called *Towards a Better Life* (1929).[9] In it, the hero, John Neal, through a series of "epistles and declamations" addressed to his friend Anthony, arrives unassisted at the knowledge that Lou Grant would impose on Ted Baxter. Neal knows the way he is. He knows that he should make a move towards a better life, but he is paralyzed and infatuated by his own gift for clever self-justification. Of his created character, Burke once remarked, "if my hero lacks humor, he does not lack grotesqueness—and the grotesque is but the humorous without its proper adjunct of laughter."[10] In the final chapter ("Testamentum Meum"), John Neal characterizes his lamentable existence through a series of aphorisms, cast in the protective second or third person, but which refer to himself.

To me, Neal's self-inflicted aperçus shed interesting cross lights on the enigma of Edgar Allan Poe's humor, and I cite a few specimens here: "speech being a mode of conduct," Neal writes, "he converted his faulty living into eloquence. Then should any like his diction, they would indirectly have sanctioned his habits" (211). Elsewhere he observes, "had he found the matter ludicrous, he could have spared himself much indignation" (214). And finally, "though you, in learning, brought trouble upon yourself, let no man discredit your discoveries by pointing to your troubles. Nor must you turn against your bitterness. The sword of discovery goes before the couch of laughter. One sneers by the modifying of a snarl; one smiles by the modifying of a sneer. You should have lived twice, and smiled the second time" (217–18).

---

9. Burke most fully defines his notions of "comic correctives" and "comic frames of reference" in chapter 6 of *Attitudes toward History*. To my knowledge, the student of the social uses of humor has not yet fully made use of Burke's important claims about the relation between the comic and political awareness, and these notions are worth noting because they have a special appropriateness to the distinctions I am making between Twain and Poe as humorists. The comic frame of reference, Burke argues, "opens up a whole new field for social criticism" (167). In recent years, social critics have often been absorbed with the notion of "constructing the subject," but Burke's proposal treats human beings as agents in the world, whose acts and determinations are still in the process of completion: "The comic frame should enable the people *to be observers of themselves, while acting*. Its ultimate would not be *massiveness,* but *maximum consciousness*. One would 'transcend' himself by noting his foibles" (171; italics in original).

10. Kenneth Burke, *Towards a Better Life* (Berkeley and Los Angeles: University of California Press, 1966), xvii; hereafter cited parenthetically in the text.

Perhaps no American writer had a greater personal stake in eloquence than Poe, and innumerable American high school students, as well as the French in general, have been inclined to sanction his habits merely out of love of his diction. Without the resources of that eloquence, I suspect all Poe's tales would appear quite ludicrous, though I doubt that his imagined dramatic situations spared him much indignation, so used was he to snarling and sneering at New York literati or Frogpondian philosophy. What, finally, would it have taken to make Poe's humor funny? Perhaps he should have lived twice, and smiled the second time.

V

Hawthorne's Last Tales and "The Custom-House"

After the publication of *Mosses from an Old Manse* (1846), Nathaniel Hawthorne wrote (in addition to his "chapter from an abortive romance," "Ethan Brand") four other stories, which represented his final contribution to the art he had been practicing for nearly two decades: "Main-street," "Feathertop," "The Snow-Image," and "The Great Stone Face."[1] It has often been noted that "The Artist of the Beautiful" and "Drowne's Wooden Image," which appeared in *Mosses from an Old Manse,* deal with theories of artistic (and by implication, literary) composition. But relatively little attention has been given to the fact that the four later stories reveal a similar preoccupation with that subject and address specific problems of artistic creation even more directly and in sharper focus than do those earlier tales. "Main-street" dramatizes the writer's concern with narrative, "Feathertop" and "The Snow-Image" with the creation of believable characters, and "The Great Stone Face" with aesthetic response. This last is the most interesting and significant because it was apparently written only shortly before *The Scarlet Letter* and is clearly paralleled by "The Custom-House," which reiterates the same aesthetic ideas after the completion of Hawthorne's greatest romance. "The Great Stone Face" and "The Custom-House" may be considered companion pieces, expressing the author's most mature and firmly held aesthetic principles, and the latter gives Hawthorne's critical estimate of his own place in the hierarchy of ethical and aesthetic sensibility that he portrayed in "The Great Stone Face."

These four stories and "The Custom-House" sketch are products of a

---

1. "Main-street" was published in *Aesthetic Papers* in May 1849; "The Snow-Image" in the *International Miscellany,* November 1850; "The Great Stone Face" in the *National Era,* January 1850; and "Feathertop" in the *International Monthly Magazine,* February and March 1852. The first three of these were collected in *The Snow-Image and Other Twice-Told Tales* (1851), and "Feathertop" was included in the second edition of *Mosses from an Old Manse* (1854).

crucial period in Hawthorne's literary development: an interim period in which he might at once reflect upon his long career as a writer of tales and sketches and, to some extent, anticipate his vocation as a novelist. Terence Martin is no doubt right in asserting that *The Scarlet Letter* represents Hawthorne's "final accomplishment in the tale even as it signals the beginning of his achievement in the romance." But the description is true only of the formal properties of the novel itself. Certain artistic decisions, emotional commitments, and narrative adjustments were prior and enabling acts that, just as clearly, pressed the author forward in that accomplishment. Those decisions and adjustments, when they came, came in a flurry. It was during the last two years before the publication of *The Scarlet Letter* that Hawthorne reached what Leon Howard describes as the "crossroads" of his development as a writer.[2] He might either continue as a writer of moral parables and allegories, or he might attempt a romance, but the talents he had cultivated for the first would carry him only so far in a legitimate achievement in the second, and indeed might prove a liability. In his last tales he contemplated and dramatized, with customary intellection and imaginative insight, the practical difficulties he foresaw. And the solutions he worked out in those tales he reaffirmed in "The Custom-House."

Careful attention to these texts reveals that they are statements about the specific artistic concerns of a writer who had often seen in his materials the "foundation" for a romance but who, as he had announced in his prefatory remarks to "The May-Pole of Merry Mount," had attempted only a "sketch." It further demonstrates that, while Harry Hayden Clark may be right in suggesting that Hawthorne has "little to say, relatively, about technical matters," he said more, however covertly, than is sometimes supposed. These tales reveal that Hawthorne had a great deal to say about the technical matters of his craft during a period when he was moving toward the recognition that his works, when viewed with "a cold or critical eye," "do not make their appeal to the popular mind."[3] To trace

2. Terence Martin, "The Method of Hawthorne's Tales," in *Nathaniel Hawthorne: A Collection of Criticism*, ed. J. Donald Crowley (New York: McGraw-Hill, 1975), 1, 23; Leon Howard, *Literature and the American Tradition* (Garden City, N.Y.: Doubleday, 1960), 113.

3. *The Works of Nathaniel Hawthorne*, Centenary Edition (Columbus: Ohio State University Press, 1962–1980), 9:54; hereafter cited by volume and page number parenthetically. Harry Hayden Clark, "Hawthorne's Literary and Aesthetic Doctrines as Embodied in His Tales," *Transactions of the Wisconsin Academy of Sciences, Arts, and Let-*

the development of Hawthorne's aesthetic argument as it appears in these tales and that eventuated in certain firmly held artistic principles is to see Hawthorne self-consciously grappling with problems of craft and invention in new and practical ways. And the conclusions he reached are of special interest because they reveal Hawthorne's final thoughts about how he or any author ought to be read.

The tales of "The Artist of the Beautiful" and "Drowne's Wooden Image" most perfectly illustrate what Roy R. Male termed the "organic-mechanistic antithesis"[4]—two opposing modes of artistic creation. The first tale is the most familiar and has received the most critical attention. In it Owen Warland attempts to vivify his conception of the beautiful in the form of a toy butterfly invested with the mechanical precision necessary to give it life. Warland is an artist of the will, a creator rather than a discoverer of imaginative forms, whose impulse is to "give external reality to ideas as irresistibly as any of the poets or painters, who have arrayed the world in a dimmer and fainter beauty, imperfectly copied from the richness of their visions."[5] Only gradually does he come to learn, however, that "the reward of all high performance must be sought within itself or sought in vain" (10:473). By contrast, Drowne escapes the mechanical mode of creation and becomes a servant to his art; he says of the wooden maiden taking shape under his hand, "the figure lies within that block of oak, and it is my business to find it" (10:311).

Because these two tales were probably composed within a few weeks of each other, in the spring of 1844, they quite naturally invite comparison.

---

ters 50 (1961): 274; Hawthorne to James T. Fields, 1860, as quoted in Arlin Turner, "Hawthorne as Self-Critic," *South Atlantic Quarterly* 37 (1938): 138. Turner termed the comment one of Hawthorne's "most penetrating and unbiased critical self-estimates."

4. Roy R. Male, *Hawthorne's Tragic Vision* (Austin: University of Texas Press, 1957), 20–37, passim.

5. 10:458. Critical opinion of this tale divides about Hawthorne's attitude toward the artist figure. Richard Harter Fogle, *Hawthorne's Fiction: The Light and the Dark,* rev. ed. (Norman: University of Oklahoma Press, 1964), 78, expressed the once dominant opinion that the tale is a "Romantic affirmation of the value of art and of the spiritual preeminence of the artistic imagination." Other critics have questioned this view. See Millicent Bell, *Hawthorne's View of the Artist* (New York: State University of New York, 1962), 94–111; Nina Baym, *The Shape of Hawthorne's Career* (Ithaca: Cornell University Press, 1976), 110–11; and Kenneth Dauber, *Rediscovering Hawthorne* (Princeton: Princeton University Press, 1977), 81–86. Baym, in fact, believes that "the narrator and the narrative flatly contradict each other" (111), that the story itself calls for another sort of artistry than the one it dramatizes.

By the time he came to write them, Hawthorne was beginning to favor the organic over the mechanical method of creation because it makes the artwork less dependent upon a receptive audience. Warland's butterfly pales and droops under the gaze of a practical man; and though the innocent eye of a baby temporarily revives the contraption, the same child, putting on his "grandsire's sharp and shrewd expression," crushes it in his hand. Drowne's wooden maiden, on the other hand, may indeed possess a life of its own.

For Hawthorne, artistic creation and aesthetic response had always been integrally related, and during his career as a writer of tales, he had sought the narrative means to join reader and writer in a collaborative effort of the imagination. But he seems to have come late to the recognition that the least artificial, most natural act of creation produces an artwork that touches rather than requires a responsive chord in the audience. In "Drowne's Wooden Image," Hawthorne dramatized his conviction that the organic mode of creation was the more authentic and, finally, the more useful attitude to adopt toward one's material; as Nina Baym has remarked, "more than any other work of the Manse period, this story looks ahead to the long romances."[6] Nevertheless, even in 1844, Hawthorne's speculations and conclusions about artistic creation and audience response in these two tales were, at best, general and tentative. It was not until his last stories that these considerations received fuller attention and more specific treatment.

In the first of these later tales, "Main-street," Hawthorne returned to a consideration of a mechanical artwork of the sort represented in "The Artist of the Beautiful," but this time the mechanics bore a closer relation to the artistic problems of a writer, the problems of narrative. It is an obvious point, but one worth making nonetheless, that the artistic "problems" Hawthorne contemplates in this and other tales exist quite apart from his artistic achievement in them. If in "The Artist of the Beautiful," Hawthorne dramatized the moral and emotional costs of an inferior artistic mode of creation, it does not follow that the tale itself is an inferior work of art. Yet as astute a critic as F. O. Matthiessen, who recognized "The Artist of the Beautiful" as altogether superior to "Drowne's Wooden Image," as indeed it is, apparently confused his moral sympathies with his critical acumen in discussing these two tales, for he describes Owen Warland

---

6. Baym, *Shape of Hawthorne's Career,* 111.

rather than Drowne as a "sensitive" and "suffering" "carver." A similar discrimination must be made concerning "Main-street." As Leland Schubert long ago pointed out, the "rhetoric of meaning" and the "rhetoric of feeling" may exist quite separately in Hawthorne's work; more recently, critics such as Edgar Dryden, Kenneth Dauber, and John Carlos Rowe have refined our understanding of these distinctions in provocative ways.[7] My purpose in this essay is more conventional—to examine the ways in which these late tales betray Hawthorne's interest in the practical difficulties of the writer's craft.

In "Main-street," the location of this interest may be found in Hawthorne's exploration of the relation between a historical sketch and the mechanical means that sustain it and upon which the showman too exclusively depends. Here he again recognized the need of the artist to enlist the interest and sympathies of the observer, but he rejected artistic contrivance as sufficient in itself, beautiful in its own right. In this story an unnamed gentleman has invented a machine, presumably a diorama, which he claims will "call up the multiform and many-colored Past before the spectator." The machine revolves by means of a crank and presents a "shifting panorama" of historical events. In complete confidence, the showman announces to his audience that "the little wheels and springs of my machinery have been well oiled; a multitude of puppets are dressed in character, . . . the lamps are trimmed and shall brighten into noontide sunshine, or fade away, in moonlight, or muffle their brilliancy in a November cloud, as the nature of the scene may require" (11:49).

Before its demonstration has advanced very far, however, a spectator complains about the unreal quality of the forest scene: "The trees look more like weeds in a garden, than a primitive forest." And the narrator of the history courteously replies: "Human art has its limits, and we must now and then ask a little aid from the spectator's imagination." The critic asserts that the showman will receive no aid from *his* imagination, for he

---

7. F. O. Matthiessen, *American Renaissance: Art and Expression in the Age of Emerson and Whitman* (New York: Oxford University Press, 1941), 223–24; Schubert, *Hawthorne, the Artist: Fine-Art Devices in Fiction* (Chapel Hill: University of North Carolina Press, 1944), 3–13, passim; see Edgar Dryden, *Nathaniel Hawthorne: The Poetics of Enchantment* (Ithaca: Cornell University Press, 1977); Dauber, *Rediscovering Hawthorne;* and John Carlos Rowe, *Through the Custom-House: Nineteenth-Century American Fiction and Modern Theory* (Baltimore: Johns Hopkins University Press, 1982).

makes it a point to "see things precisely as they are" (11:52). Undiscouraged, the inventor continues to crank out his historical sketch, but when certain Puritan characters appear upon the scene the critic once more interrupts: "Here is a pasteboard figure, such as a child would cut out of a card, with a pair of very dull scissors" (11:56). The showman subdues the irate customer and persuades him to move back one row for a more ideal point of view, from which the proper combination of light and shadow may transform the scenes into a very different experience.[8] Pacified for only a time, the critic again complains that a "sermon" is not part of the bill when the showman starts editorializing.

Despite similar intermittent exchanges, the show runs fairly smoothly until it arrives at the "Great Snow of 1717," which all but buried the New England countryside. The showman recognizes that this scene has a "dreary monotony" about it; however, he assures the audience that "that vast icicle, glittering so cheerlessly in the sunshine, must be the spire of the meeting house, incrusted with frozen sleet. Those great heaps, too, which we mistook for drifts, are houses, buried up to their eaves, and with their peaked roofs rounded by the depth of snow upon them. There, now, comes a gush of smoke from what I judge to be the chimney of the Ship Tavern; and another—another—and another—from the chimneys of other dwellings, where fireside comfort, domestic peace, the sports of children, and quietude of age, are living yet, in spite of the frozen crust above them" (11:80–81). In short, the creator of this entertainment tries to transform this snowy waste into a vivid experience by breathing life into the scene. The chimney does emit a few puffs of smoke, but as the showman turns the crank, a wire breaks within the machine and the landscape is left to fill up with snow. The machinery that tells the tale is simply inadequate for its purpose, and no amount of narrative choreography can disguise the fact. Needless to say, the critic is not unjustified in demanding his money back.

In this story Hawthorne was making a more sophisticated statement

8. Interestingly, Hawthorne pleads for the same sort of indulgence in his readers on cultural rather than aesthetic grounds in the preface to *The Blithedale Romance.* American readers, unlike European readers, tend to measure the romancer's work against nature, thus denying the fiction a "suitable remoteness," an "atmosphere of enchantment." "This atmosphere," he continues, "is what the American romancer needs. In its absence, the beings of imagination are compelled to show themselves in the same category as actually living mortals; a necessity that generally renders the paint and pasteboard of their composition but too painfully discernible"; 3:2.

about art than he had in "The Artist of the Beautiful." Although the complaining spectator is disgruntled, he is, as Nina Baym has observed, not
"unliterary." He is a critic, and his criticisms are particular and valid.
Through this character Hawthorne makes it clear that he is dealing not
simply with misguided but with incompetent artistic invention of the sort
which, in popular fiction, produces unbelievable scenes, "pasteboard" characters, and didactic interruptions, or "sermons." Although the artist may
require the aid of the spectator's imagination, the viewer cannot be expected to collaborate in a basically inferior project. Nor can the creator rely
upon the introduction of popular subject matter, such as "fireside comfort"
or "domestic peace," to revive his story. Nor, for that matter, may the teller
of the tale always rely upon his ability to coax his reader into the ideal point
of view. Yet the essential inferiority of the Main-street entertainment is the
result of its mechanical makeup. The machinery of the diorama, even more
than the machinery of Warland's butterfly, is inadequate, and though the
showman tries to breathe life into his creation through the artistic contrivance of narrative intervention, his special pleading and the machine itself break down. Such a contraption has no life of its own; it is, rather, the
product of the willful imposition of the creator's idea upon the material
world. And Hawthorne, unlike Ralph Waldo Emerson (as Richard J. Jacobson has pointed out), refused to believe the creative process "an act of
will."[9]

Hawthorne may have originally planned "Main-street" as a short book;
certainly he was contemplating or attempting longer pieces of fiction in
1848–1849. In this regard, the tale is especially illuminating about Hawthorne's interest in the means of narrative presentation sufficient to sustain
a longer work, for that was a subject much on his mind and had been at
least since 1846, when he had expressed in "The Old Manse" his desire to
"achieve a novel" (10:5). And he may have been speaking through his
character when he had his showman apologize for failing to bring his
story to its fit conclusion, that his ambitions, "like most other human purposes, lie unaccomplished" (11:82). "Main-street" is telling too in the now
obsequious, now insistent attempts of the showman to "manage" his audience, for this was a proven talent for Hawthorne. To borrow James Cox's
phrasing, Hawthorne might place himself as writer rather than as artist be-

---

9. Baym, *Shape of Hawthorne's Career*, 119; Richard J. Jacobson, *Hawthorne's Conception of the Creative Process* (Cambridge: Harvard University Press, 1965), 16.

fore his fictions, and to indulge in this sort of narrative manipulation is to acknowledge tacitly the absence of "an inner action of a character which the style pictures, pursues, analyzes, and judges. Substituted for such an action is the activity of the author seeking for, perceiving, and sketching his subject."[10] If he were to forfeit this known quantity of his craft, he necessarily must fall back upon a created character whose inner workings were neither artificially manufactured nor reliant upon their creator's spontaneous capacity to generate interest in them.

Hawthorne contemplated such inauthentic character creation in "Feathertop,"[11] a story that supplements "Main-street" as a commentary on character creation rather than scene and story. For in this "moralized legend," Hawthorne deepens his criticism of the art of contrivance and gives his aesthetics more definite focus by considering the type of character who, made of straw, passes for flesh—a pasteboard prop created merely to satisfy superficial and conventional expectations.

Like the diorama of "Main-street" or the toy butterfly of "The Artist of the Beautiful," Feathertop is yet another mechanical contrivance, though he is put together with a competence that deceives the most hardheaded of his fellow townspeople. He is, as the narrator describes him, a "well-digested conventionalism" (10:242) pieced together from knickknacks and clichés. He has a pumpkin for a head, a London coat, a pair of French breeches, and a pair of silk stockings that hang loosely upon his legs. Mother Rigby, his creator, also makes Feathertop a man of property, with a gold mine in El Dorado, a vineyard at the North Pole, a castle in the air, and a thousand shares in a broken bubble. More successfully than the showman of "Main-street," she attempts to breathe life into her creation—the occasional gush of smoke from the chimney in "Main-street" is a faint mist compared to the billowing clouds of smoke that issue from the limping scarecrow's pipe. As a created character, Feathertop is a fraud; Hawthorne describes him as "merely a spectral illusion, and a cunning effect of light and shade, so colored and contrived as to delude the eyes of most men" (10:228–29).

10. James Cox, "*The Scarlet Letter*: Through the Old Manse and the Custom House," *Virginia Quarterly Review* 51 (summer 1975): 434.
11. In *The American Notebooks,* Claude M. Simpson suggests that the tale was not written until November 1851 (8:627). Nevertheless, it was conceived much earlier. The "germ" of the story was recorded in 1840, and an entry in the *Notebooks* (8:286) anticipates the story almost in its present form.

In this tale Hawthorne shifts his attention from inadequate artistic creation to indiscriminate public reception. A notebook entry indicates that the character of Feathertop, early in its conception, had been intended as "a symbol of a large class" (8:286)—presumably the sort of character that appealed to the undiscerning readers of the "popular mind" for whom Hawthorne refused to write. In any event, despite his awkward construction, Feathertop proves attractive enough to win the admiration of the public at large and the affection of Polly Gookin, the prettiest girl in town. Equally witless and more vain than Feathertop, she is tempted to match her own beauty with that of her newfound beau by standing side by side before a mirror. The mirror, however, is so highly polished that it is "incapable of flattery," and the illusion is broken. Feathertop and Polly at last perceive what a truly awkward character the scarecrow is, and, heartbroken, Feathertop limps home only to destroy himself by throwing his pipe (which provides in this story the gush of smoke required to keep him alive) into the fire.

The only unaided human eye that sees Feathertop aright is that of an innocent baby, like Annie's child in "The Artist of the Beautiful" who appreciated the contrivance though he treated it as a toy. Here, the innocent eye, as well as the realistic reflection, recognizes and rejects fraud, and Hawthorne makes it clear that he too rejects the artificialities of popular fiction: "Shall I confess the truth? At its present point of vivification, the scarecrow reminds me of some of the lukewarm and abortive characters, composed of heterogeneous materials used for the thousandth time and never worth using, with which romance-writers (and myself, no doubt, among the rest) have so overpeopled the world of fiction" (10:230). If Hawthorne were in earnest in his parenthetical self-condemnation, he surely undervalued his genuine achievement in the creation of characters such as Goodman Brown, Robin Molineux, and even Owen Warland himself; but in the grotesque figure of Feathertop he purposely fashioned a fit emblem to represent his distaste for the contrived characters of popular fiction.

In these three stories Hawthorne dealt with artistic contrivance and its relation to the response of the audience or viewer. In "The Snow-Image" he considered the more fruitful organic method of creation in the same relation. Here, as in the earlier "Snow-flakes" (1838), Hawthorne used snow as a symbol for the artist's medium. "The Snow-Image," in fact, is almost an allegorical lesson in artistic creation and appreciation, neither so "carelessly conceived" as Nina Baym believes, I think, nor so shrewdly ironic as Dennis Berthold has maintained.[12] The children in the tale, Violet and Peony, represent the two requirements of poetic creation: fancy or imagination and obedient labor. But, unlike artists of contrivance, in constructing their snow image Violet and Peony do not try to make the snow conform to their idea of what a snow figure should look like. Rather, like Drowne, they discover it in the act of creation, for the snow girl seems "not so much to be made by the children, as to grow up under their hands" (11:10). The children *find* rather than design their "snow-sister" who, when complete, seems to have grown up with them, to have been waiting for the children to recover her from the icy waste outside. Both children have full confidence in their undertaking; and, as the narrator states, "if miracles are ever to be wrought, it will be by putting our hands to the work, in precisely such a simple and undoubting frame of mind" (11:9).

The children are unhampered by egoistic impulses; their very simplicity and willingness to labor in a "natural state" account for the living quality of the snow figure. Their mother, from whom the children had inherited a "strain of poetry," represents the perceptive and sympathetic audience in this tale. She has perfect confidence in the goodness and ingenuity of her offspring; her heart is "as pure and clear as crystal; and, looking at all matters through this transparent medium, she sometimes saw truths so profound, that other people laughed at them as nonsense and absurdity" (11:20). Her husband, a man of common sense, is, on the other hand, the type who considers children's productions just such works of nonsense. Despite his good intentions, Mr. Lindsey destroys the figures of imagination with his philosophy of "stubborn materialism." His demand that the snow image come inside to get warm results in her destruction.

Here Hawthorne wrestles once more with the problem of audience response and how an author ought to be read. The practical demands of stubborn materialists can easily destroy the work of imagination because art does not answer the claims of practicality. The imagination of the audience instead must collaborate with the artist's to bring a work of art to life, though there are limits to the assistance an artist may require of his audience. The complaints of the critic in "Main-street" are legitimate, and the mirror in "Feathertop" is realistic; artist and audience must meet on some

---

12. Baym, *Shape of Hawthorne's Career,* 118; and Dennis Berthold, "Anti-Idealism in Hawthorne's 'The Snow-Image,'" *Arizona Quarterly* 38 (1982): 119–32.

true ground between the poles of reality and imagination, where those "profound truths" available to a poetic sensibility, such as Mrs. Lindsey's, reside. Thus "The Snow-Image" reasserts Hawthorne's preference for the organic mode of creation exemplified in "Drowne's Wooden Image."

Hawthorne's preoccupations with an authentic mode of creation, the legitimate approach to narrative, convincing characterization, and audience response were by no means new. They go back as far as the early 1830s, and they prefigure such pronouncements as he would make in the prefaces to all the later romances. But the aesthetic statements these last tales embody are notable for the specificity with which they address particular problems of the writer's craft and apparently resolve to the author's satisfaction, on an intellectual level, problems of art. They are notable, too, because they express such a clear preference for a creative method that, if it does not preclude it, suggests that Hawthorne's customary impulse to hang a narrative veil between his story and his reader would have to be judiciously restrained. That is, if he were to write a sustained piece of fiction, then Hawthorne, like Drowne, must submit to his subject completely; he could neither rely upon his proven talent to sustain interest by means of authorial intrusion and commentary nor shape his figures into an allegory by means of calculation, contrivance, or diverting speculation. The story of "Wakefield" is at once the most impressive example of Hawthorne's capacities in this regard and the most revealing of the problem of character creation that would sustain a longer work. As J. Donald Crowley has observed, Hawthorne seems to create this story out of its donnée before our very eyes;[13] yet the artistic question the story implies is, simply put, how to shape a figure whose actions simultaneously supply a moral and imply a motive. The manner of telling rather than the tale told is the true subject of "Wakefield"; and if we glimpse Hawthorne's potentiality as a novelist in the inquisitive attitude he adopts toward Wakefield, we get it all from the wrong side of the cloth. Hawthorne's ability to sustain interest in a tale independent of, almost in spite of, the interest the tale itself might possess is as familiar as it is remarkable; yet, as Kenneth Burke observed, assets sometimes convert themselves into liabilities,[14] and certainly Hawthorne was

---

13. J. Donald Crowley, "The Unity of Hawthorne's Twice-Told Tales," *Studies in American Fiction* 1 (1973): 35–62.

14. This idea pervades Burke's writings; for a succinct plotting of this sort of transformation, see "Compensatory Gains" and "Margin of Persuasion," nos. 35 and 36 in

suspicious of the writer (perhaps himself included) who might at will breathe life into his characters only to fool an all too easily deluded multitude. For this reason, "The Great Stone Face" occupies an especially important position in Hawthorne's aesthetic dialectic during these years.

"The Great Stone Face" is sometimes taken as a peculiar instance of transcendentalism in Hawthorne's writings; in fact, it is an expression of his aesthetics. In the very idea of a monumental natural profile set upon a distant mountainside, Hawthorne found an adequate metaphor to convey his thoughts on the relation of art to reality. As John Carlos Rowe has observed, "Hawthorne struggles endlessly to define the nature of the imagination and to determine its function in relation to consciousness, the emotions, and the objective world."[15] In "The Great Stone Face" he found an apt and enabling symbol that might promote his struggle toward useful artistic ends. Moreover, because the great stone face is the creation of Nature rather than art, Hawthorne could deal with aesthetic perception so as to avoid such complications as the artist's values, competence, and honesty, complications that were dramatized in "Main-street" and "Feathertop." Instead of the playful creation of a human being, the great stone face is "a work of Nature in her mood of majestic playfulness," the happy combination of enormous rocks upon a mountainside. Of course, the cliff is not the exact representation of a face, but when viewed from the proper distance "it seemed as if an enormous giant, or a Titan, had sculptured his own likeness on the precipice." Like the panorama in "Main-street," the lifelike effect of the stone face requires the proper aesthetic distance, lest the human features dissolve into "a heap of ponderous and gigantic rocks piled in chaotic ruin one upon another" (11:27).

In addition, Hawthorne combines the symbolic device of a natural art

---

his "Lexicon Rhetoricae" included in *Counter-Statement* (Berkeley and Los Angeles: University of California Press, 1968), 175–78.

15. Rowe, *Through the Custom-House*, 54. Rowe's phenomenological treatment of *The Blithedale Romance* is insightful and, if only by implication, assists in disputing the notion that "The Great Stone Face" is an odd instance of transcendentalism in Hawthorne. Clearly, Hawthorne is not at all interested in the noumenal world in this story, as is evident from his *Notebooks*. He had recorded its "germ" in January 1839 (8:184), but, more to the point, he had also recorded in the same month his thoughts about the relativity of point of view as they related to written language: "Letters in the shape of figures of men, &c. At a distance the words composed by the letters are alone distinguishable, close at hand, the figures alone are seen, and not distinguishable as letters. Thus things may have a positive, a relative, and a composite meaning, according to the point of view" (8:183).

work with a local legend that someone from the neighboring valley whose features would replicate those of the great stone face would one day become the greatest and noblest person of his age. By means of this prophecy Hawthorne symbolized a hierarchy of ethical and aesthetic sensibility and represented in the character of Ernest the noblest expression of human capability.

As a young boy, Ernest was told the legend and forever after believed the prophecy would one day prove true. During his lifetime, three of the valley's inhabitants earn a certain reputation, each in turn leading the community to believe that the prophecy has been fulfilled. But Ernest, the profoundest and most sensitive and sympathetic student of the stone countenance, rejects each candidate in turn: "Mr. Gathergold," a man with the Midas touch, lacks the generous features of the stone face; in "Old Blood-and-Thunder," a great soldier, Ernest can not detect the same tenderness which the natural profile seems to possess; and though a noble and wise statesman, "Old Stony Phiz" seems "vague and empty," with a face that "no high purpose had endowed . . . with reality" (11:41).

Above and apart from these men of affairs, however, stands the poet. Of the poet's gift the narrator remarks that "the Creator had bestowed him as the last best touch to his own handiwork. Creation was not finished till the poet came to interpret and so complete it." By interpreting the works of Nature, the poet reveals the common bond of humanity and shows "the golden links of the great chain that intertwined them with an angelic kindred" (11:43). Needless to say, the poet who visits the aging Ernest bears little resemblance to the egoistical artist of the beautiful. However sympathetic Hawthorne may have been toward artists such as Owen Warland in 1844, he finds little to recommend them in this later tale: "Some, indeed, there were, who thought to show the soundness of their judgment by affirming that all the beauty and dignity of the natural world existed only in the poet's fancy. Let such men speak for themselves, who undoubtedly appear to have been spawned forth by Nature with a contemptuous bitterness; she having plastered them up out of her refuse stuff, after all the swine were made. As respects all things else, the poet's ideal was the truest truth" (11:44). The artist, in other words, must attempt to reveal the inherent truth of his subject matter; he must at once possess a creative and a perceptive or critical imagination. The poet who visits Ernest is neither vain nor proud and for a time seems to be the fulfillment of the prophecy. But as he frankly confesses, he is unworthy of this honor because his life has not entirely corresponded to his high thoughts, and Ernest reluctantly agrees.

The person who fulfills the prophecy is Ernest himself. This loyal student of the natural artistry of the stone countenance read the face of Nature, gathered in its wisdom, and lived accordingly. Ernest developed a kind of noble faith and action that the poet lacks; and, over the years, his face became a living replica of the stone profile. In contemplating the visage, he was unhampered by a "stubborn materialism." Instead, his imagination actively engaged the horizon and elevated the face above the "chaotic ruin" a practical man might find there, and in this perceptive state he glimpsed certain truths forbidden those of a more practical nature and reflected them in his own life.

Ernest's imagination is creative as well as receptive. Much like Drowne or the children in "The Snow-Image," he discovers the design and form of the natural statue. He does not impose his fanciful expectations upon the landscape as do his neighbors, whose conventional notions of greatness lead them to impute a likeness of certain supposedly worthy persons to the natural landscape. Rather, he allows the natural play of light and shadow to reveal the great stone face in its many moods, and it sometimes seemed that the stone figure smiled approvingly upon Ernest, for he was creating within himself the fulfillment of the prophecy and subtly developing the external qualities that allowed others to recognize the fact.

Ernest symbolizes Hawthorne's conception of the ideal artist, but he is also, in a sense, an ideal reader—an unprofessional version of that "all sympathizing critic" for whom Hawthorne was to claim in the preface to *The Marble Faun* (1860) he had always written. Ernest's generous and trusting attitude toward the natural artwork brings it to life. Yet while Ernest's sympathies are pure and honest, his imagination is discerning; he possesses "poetic insight" that, as Hawthorne would define it in *The House of the Seven Gables,* is the "gift of discerning, in this sphere of strangely mingled elements, the beauty and the majesty which are compelled to assume a garb so sordid" (2:41). It is Ernest who first rejects the possibility that "Gathergold," or "Old Blood-and-Thunder," or "Old Stony Phiz" might fulfill the prophecy, though the indiscriminate public finds in the features of each successive candidate a perfect resemblance to the stone face. Ernest's sensibility is of such a refined character that it easily discerns the false from the true, much as the innocent baby perceived the grotesque nature of Feathertop.

What Hawthorne suggests in this tale is that the ideal reader and the ideal artist are much the same. In contrast to those readers too coldly critical and stubbornly materialistic and those too foolishly gullible, Ernest serves as one to whom the "truth of the human heart" may be effectively communicated. In contrast to those egoistical, impulsive artists who attempt to impose their personal fancy upon the natural world, he is an ideal artist who translates the beauty and truth of the natural world into his life and reflects it to others. And the meeting ground of the ideal reader and ideal artist is that realm where poetic perception and critical discrimination combine to reveal profound natural truths.

In "The Great Stone Face," then, Hawthorne most explicitly articulated his ideal solutions to the artistic problems of audience response, aesthetic distance, authentic creativity, and the relation of art to reality. The author must write for that sympathetic reader who willingly assumes the proper distance from his subject matter, a distance that allows light and shadow to vivify the creation, and whose imagination gladly collaborates with the artist's in the imaginative experience. The mature and competent artist does not resort to contrivance or deceit but rescues the profound truths of nature and translates them into vivid forms. He interprets and therefore completes the artistry of nature, and Ernest himself embodies "the last best touch" of the Creator's handiwork.

Significantly, in these tales about art, Hawthorne resolved certain aesthetic problems that troubled him prior to the composition of *The Scarlet Letter*. The preface to that work, "The Custom-House," manifests extraordinary parallels with "The Great Stone Face" and echoes some of the other tales in ways that suggest that Hawthorne wished to reaffirm these principles after the completion of his masterpiece. "The Custom-House" has the same sort of hierarchy of sensibility that exists in "The Great Stone Face." The patriarch of the custom house, like "Mr. Gathergold," is representative of pure appetite, a man who had "no soul, no heart, no mind; nothing as I have already said, but instincts" (1:18). A second official, "Old Ticonderoga," a military hero, recalls "Old Blood-and-Thunder" of the earlier tale. Finally, Hawthorne describes the administrator of the institution, who, like "Old Stony Phiz," was honest and a perfect man of affairs with "a law of nature . . . rather than a choice or a principle; nor can it be otherwise than the main condition of an intellect so remarkably clear and accurate as his" (1:24–25). But however admirable these qualities might be, clarity of intellect, Hawthorne implies, interferes with imaginative response.

The place of the poet in this hierarchy Hawthorne modestly chooses for himself, even specifying a kinship with Chaucer and Robert Burns in his custom-house position. Like the poet in "The Great Stone Face," he can glorify "the man or woman, sordid with the common dust of life, who crossed his daily path" (11:43). But clearly the poet is a lesser figure than Ernest. He can write "thoughts divine" but lacks the "faith in the grandeur, the beauty, the goodness, which my own works are said to have made more evident in nature and in human life" (11:46). And he recognizes Ernest's superiority. Similarly, the narrator of "The Custom-House" is of a lower order than is Mr. Surveyor Jonathan Pue, who had "borne his Majesty's commission" and was therefore "illuminated by a ray of the splendor that shone so dazzlingly about the throne" (1:33); the narrator is mere "editor, or very little more" (1:4) of the "several foolscap sheets" (1:32) containing Pue's account of Hester Prynne.

"The Custom-House" also reaffirms aesthetic principles Hawthorne sketched out in the earlier tales. For imaginative creation, he advocates, in a famous passage, "moonlight, in a familiar room, . . . making every object so minutely visible, yet so unlike a morning or noontide visibility," an "unusual light" in which particulars "seem to lose their actual substance, and become things of intellect" (1:35). A warmer light from a dim coal fire "mingles itself with the cold spirituality of moonbeams, and communicates, as it were, a heart and sensibilities of human tenderness to the forms which fancy summons up. It converts them from *snow-images* into men and women." Moreover, Hawthorne reasserts his belief that there exists a proper aesthetic distance, a distance that at once would satisfy the critic of "Main-street" yet not bow to the pressure of a "stubborn materialism." The firelit chamber is an ideal place for his imagination to function in complete faith and freedom; it is "a neutral territory, somewhere between the real world and fairy-land, where the Actual and the Imaginary may meet, and each imbue itself with the nature of the other" (1:36; italics mine). As Ernest does, for the great stone face is neither real nor unreal, Hawthorne contemplates the scarlet letter in its aspects of reality and imagination and seeks to interpret and therefore complete the significance of this relic of an age gone by.

If we take "The Custom-House" sketch as a work of fiction rather than as an autobiographical recollection, and if we take that fiction as an aesthetic statement as well as a sardonic comment upon his disenfranchisement from his post, it becomes clear that Hawthorne intended the sketch to be more than a simple preface. It is, as Cox has observed, the "foreground" to *The Scarlet Letter* in which Hawthorne places himself as artist between the romance and the reader and reaffirms the artistic beliefs that he had adopted only after gradual and painstaking speculation upon the nature of his craft and that were to remain with him for the rest of his career.[16] In the prefaces to his later works, he would remind his readers— readers not of the popular mind, with conventional expectations, but those ideal readers whose imaginations might conspire with his in vivifying his work—that the realm of imaginative literature exists somewhere between brute fact and pure fancy: He claims that *The House of the Seven Gables* has a "great deal more to do with the clouds overhead, than with any portion of the actual soil of the County of Essex" (2:3); that *The Blithedale Romance* (1852) offers "an atmosphere of strange enchantment," a "Faery Land," and though the Blithedale story invites comparison to Brook Farm, the romance itself merely offers a "foothold between fiction and reality" (3:2); and, finally, in the preface to *The Marble Faun* (1860), that "Italy, as the site of his Romance, was chiefly valuable to him as affording a sort of poetic or fairy precinct, where actualities would not be so terribly insisted upon" (4:3). These remarks were addressed not to the multitude but to those ideal readers who might be enjoined in the collaborative art of fiction.

It has been frequently observed that the aesthetic theories expressed in "The Custom-House" govern, to some extent, the shape and content of *The Scarlet Letter,* as indeed they do. But because the sketch was probably written after the romance it introduces, it also serves as a reassertion, in the full confidence of achievement, of the aesthetic conclusion he had tentatively reached in "The Great Stone Face." And Hawthorne may even have been contemplating his next novel when he wrote, "Soon . . . my old native town will loom upon me through the haze of memory, a mist brooding over and around it; as if it were no portion of the real earth, but an overgrown village in cloud-land, with only imaginary inhabitants to people its wooden houses, and walk its homely lanes, and the unpicturesque prolixity of its main street" (1:44).

16. Cox, *"The Scarlet Letter,"* 447.

VI

The Judge Dragged to the Bar

Melville, Shaw, and the Webster Murder Trial

In November 1849, Herman Melville was in London negotiating the terms for the English publication of his latest novel, *White-Jacket,* and on the thirteenth of that month he walked across town to witness, along with some thirty thousand other curious spectators, the public hanging of George Frederick and Marie de Roux Manning. The couple had been convicted of murdering a friend of Mrs. Manning's named O'Connor and burying the body underneath the kitchen flagstones. Each had claimed the other guilty of the murder and had written pious letters printed in the *Times* and elsewhere calling for the other to acknowledge full guilt for the killing for the good of his or her soul. Herman sent to his father-in-law, Judge Lemuel Shaw, a broadside depicting the execution and containing letters written by both husband and wife.[1] Shaw had presided over many murder cases and had heard diverse protestations of innocence; no doubt Melville thought the circumstance and notoriety of this one would perhaps amuse the judge. Barely a week after the Mannings were executed, however, another murder was committed, this time in Shaw's native Boston. The sensational interest this Boston murder case and trial aroused eclipsed the public attention paid to the Manning case, but it is unlikely that Shaw found it altogether amusing, for he became the subject of damning accusations and was himself dragged to the bar of public judgment.

The story of the murder of Dr. George Parkman by Professor John White

---

1. Jay Leyda, comp., *The Melville Log: A Documentary Life of Herman Melville* (2 vols., New York: Gordian Press, 1969), 1:331. The story of the O'Connor murder case is told by Albert Borowitz in *The Woman Who Murdered Black Satin: The Bermondsey Horror* (Columbus: Ohio State University Press, 1981).

Webster is a familiar one.[2] However, few have discussed the trial and the public reaction to it with particular reference to the Chief Justice of Massachusetts or to the Shaw family. Fewer still have speculated upon the influence these events might have had upon Melville himself, who at the time was about to begin *Moby-Dick,* and who had displayed an interest in and some knowledge of legal matters and at the end of his life would contemplate in *Billy Budd* many of the same issues raised by this famous trial.[3]

The Crime

Dr. Parkman, one of the wealthiest and most respected of Boston Brahmins, was by turns altruistic and tightfisted. Only a few years before his death, he had donated land for the new medical college at Harvard and had endowed the Parkman Chair of Anatomy (occupied at the time of his murder by Dr. Oliver Wendell Holmes). But he was known to keep an intrepid eye on his money as well. He had loaned Professor John Webster some $400 in 1842, and in 1847, along with a few others, had loaned Webster $2,000. Professor Webster held the Erving Chair of Chemistry and Mineralogy at Harvard, but perhaps not so surprisingly he had trouble making ends meet on his professor's salary and was continually in debt. He had not repaid the most recent loan when he approached Robert Gould Shaw to sell for $1,200 (the full equivalent of his annual teaching salary) a cabinet of valuable minerals he had collected over the years. There were two problems

2. See Stewart Holbrook, "Murder at Harvard," *American Scholar* 14 (autumn 1945): 425–34; Cleveland Amory, *The Proper Bostonians* (New Yolk: E. P. Dutton, 1947), 207–27; and Richard B. Morris, *Fair Trial: Fourteen Who Stood Accused from Anne Hutchinson to Alger Hiss* (New York: Alfred A. Knopf, 1952), 156–203. These essays, along with George Bemis, ed., *Report of the Case of John W. Webster* (Boston: Charles C. Little and James Brown, 1850), which published the complete proceedings of the case from notes taken at the trial, provide the factual basis for the subsequent discussion of the murder and the trial.
    3. See Brook Thomas, *Cross-Examinations of Law and Literature: Cooper, Hawthorne, Stowe, and Melville* (Cambridge: Cambridge University Press, 1987), 202–6, 211–14, for an interesting discussion of the relation between the Webster case and *Billy Budd.* Jonathan Cook has also detected Judge Shaw in Melville's fiction; he argues that Shaw is the model for the man with gold sleeve buttons in *The Confidence-Man;* see "Melville's Man in Gold Sleeve Buttons: Chief Justice Lemuel Shaw," *ESQ* 34 (1988): 257–81.

with this business venture: First, the minerals, along with his other personal property, had already been offered as security for the earlier loan; and, second, Robert Shaw was Parkman's brother-in-law.

Parkman, of course, discovered the double-dealing through Robert Shaw, and on Friday, November 23, he visited Professor Webster in his laboratory. Parkman had badgered Webster several times before for repayment of the loan, but what precisely happened that particular day in Webster's laboratory would not be known until the investigation and trial had run their course. And the guilt of Webster, even after his conviction for the murder of Parkman, would not be completely believed until he confessed to the crime the following July. In that confession, Webster acknowledged that he had invited Dr. Parkman to his laboratory on that Friday, and Parkman, supposing Webster had at last collected the money due him, began their conversation with, "Are you ready for me, sir? Have you got the money?" Webster began to make his appeal to the sympathies of his creditor, but Parkman was in no mood; he heaped on the man "the most bitter taunts and opprobrious epithets" and threatened to have him removed from his post.[4] In a fury, Webster grabbed a piece of stovewood and hit him. Parkman fell instantly dead upon the floor. Desperate but methodical, Webster dismembered the body, disposing of it in various locations in the building.

On Saturday, November 24, Robert Shaw offered a $3,000 reward for information concerning Dr. Parkman's whereabouts. Webster himself provided the first positive information about Parkman's disappearance when he visited Rev. Francis Parkman, the doctor's brother, on Sunday and announced that he had been visited by Dr. Parkman at 1:30, Friday afternoon, and that he had paid his creditor $483. That Parkman should now be thought to have been carrying so much money on him supplied a motive for foul play, and by Wednesday, Shaw and the Parkman family suspected the worst. Robert Shaw once again issued an announcement, this time offering $1,000 reward for the location of his brother-in-law's body.

By coming forward as he did, Webster might well have been satisfied that he had thrown the detectives off the trail. And since the police had been receiving letters (some mysteriously signed "Civis") instructing them that Dr. Parkman had been seen after 1:30, or that the body was buried in East

---

4. Quoted in Morris, *Fair Trial*, 197.

Cambridge, or that it had been cut up and thrown in the Charles River, Webster's laboratory seemed an unpromising place to begin their investigation. Nevertheless, the police did search the medical college and found nothing. But the janitor of the building, Ephraim Littlefield, was not so easily satisfied. Littlefield had several reasons to be suspicious. He had overheard parts of a heated conversation between Webster and Parkman, and he had noticed that Professor Webster had behaved oddly of late. But the most suspicious act of all was that the typically penurious Webster had given Littlefield money for a Thanksgiving turkey.

Indeed, it was on Thanksgiving day that Littlefield satisfied his suspicions about the contents of the vault by breaking into it from below. It was heavy work; the stone wall separating the cellar from the privy was a thick one. But Littlefield knew no one would be around on this holiday, and he interrupted his work to dine with his wife on the turkey he had purchased thanks to Webster. When he eventually broke through, he found within a pelvis and two leg fragments, and in the furnace in Webster's laboratory were several other bones and a blackened set of china dentures. This was enough for the police. When Webster was informed that he was charged with the murder of Dr. Parkman, he attempted suicide by swallowing a strychnine tablet.

By the time Melville arrived in New York from his trip abroad on February 1, the whole country had become engrossed in the Parkman murder case. The degree and persistence of public interest here and abroad may be suggested by the fact that in 1862 Atremus Ward bragged that his road show included "wax figgers of G. Washington Gen. Taylor John Bunyan Capt. Kidd and Dr. Webster in the act of killing Dr. Parkman."[5] And in 1869 Charles Dickens, while in Boston, was particularly anxious to see the room in which Dr. Parkman was murdered. More immediately, a writer for the *Boston Transcript* would characterize the public reaction at the time: "Incredulity, then amazement, and then blank, unspeakable horror have been the emotions, which have agitated the public mind as the rumor has gone on. Never in the annals of crime in Massachusetts has such a sensation been produced."[6] And he would call upon Hamlet to give adequate words for the scandal—"O, horrible! O, horrible! most horrible."

---

5. Walter Blair, *Native American Humor* (Chicago: Chandler Publishing, 1937), 400.
6. Quoted in Amory, *Proper Bostonians*, 220.

The Case

The public feasted on each new disclosure published in the press, and by the time the trial began on March 19, 1850, interest had reached a fevered pitch. Barricades were put up and gallery tickets permitting ten-minute viewings were issued. The trial lasted only eleven days, but, in all, some sixty thousand people were permitted their brief glimpse of the proceedings.

Everything about the trial was sensational. One of the wealthiest and most respected citizens of Boston had been murdered. A distinguished Harvard professor was accused of the crime. The most eminent jurist in the country, himself a Boston Brahmin, would preside over the case. Character witnesses for the defense included Harvard President Jared Sparks, Congressman and former editor of the *North American Review* John Gorham Palfrey, and Dr. Oliver Wendell Holmes. A largely blue-collar jury would hear the prosecution claim that Webster had dissected Dr. Parkman's body with a hunting knife, and that if this were so, it was accomplished, according to Dr. Holmes, with considerable skill. They would find that Webster erred in trying to burn human flesh and bone in his furnace when his iron stove would have been far more effective. They would hear Dr. Parkman's dentist claim with certainty that the china dentures found in the furnace were those he had made for Parkman only four years earlier, and they would hear from another dentist that the same set could belong to any number of his own patients. They would learn that a skeleton had been assembled from the bones found at the medical school. And though the resulting figure was a half inch taller than that of the living Dr. Parkman, no one in the press seriously doubted that this was indeed the *corpus delecti* or that Webster was the murderer. And they would hear a handwriting expert testify that the so-called "Civis" letters were in fact written by Webster himself.

Throughout the proceedings, Shaw ruled with customary decision and authority, and he hastened matters along probably because he did not wish to prolong a trial that every moment threatened to become an unruly public spectacle. Though some might have questioned his refusal to disqualify a juror who was opposed to capital punishment and therefore wished to be released from duty, or his decision to allow the jury to inspect the alleged scene of the crime, Shaw's reputation and lucidity on legal precedent held him above reproach. However, when the trial was concluded and Judge Shaw gave what seemed to be interminable instructions to the jury, public attention shifted from the accused to the judge.

The defense had maintained that without positive proof that the gathered remains were those of Dr. Parkman no charges of murder could be brought against the defendant. But Judge Shaw explained to the jury that this was not in itself sufficient to acquit the accused, for circumstantial evidence may often provide the basis for conviction: "It has sometimes been said by judges that a jury never ought to convict in a capital case unless the dead body is found. That, as a general proposition, is true. It sometimes happens, however, that it cannot be found, where the proof of death is clear. Sometimes, in a case of murder at sea, the body is thrown overboard on a stormy night. Because the body is not found, can anybody deny that the author of that crime is a murderer?"[7] He went on to say that if the jury was convinced that the set of china teeth were those of Parkman, this fact, along with the other less certain evidence of the bone fragments, would provide compelling evidence that indeed the *corpus delecti* had been found. Shaw further informed the jury that character witnesses (of which the defense had summoned several) may in fact prove instructive about the general character of the defendant, but in a case where the crime is extraordinary and the circumstances of the murder so atrocious as the one before them, the evidence of good character ought to play a far inferior role in their judgment than it might in lesser crimes. But the most disturbing aspect of Shaw's statements had to do with the question of malice.

The defense had also argued that in murder cases the prosecution was required to show malice. If in fact Webster had killed Parkman, so the defense claimed, it was done in a fit of unthinking passion. Shaw's instructions to the jury on this point proved to be nearly as much an object of public attention and outrage as the murder itself. Judge Shaw observed that in the absence of other evidence that might excuse or extenuate the criminal act, *the act of murder itself implied malice.* Seen in this light, malice was a matter of legal interpretation not a determination of motive subject to the judgment of the jury. The implication of this ruling, so it was popularly held, was that Shaw had shifted the burden of proof from the prosecution to the defense. This judgment along with the other salient characteristics of his three-hour-long instructions to the jury, according to Richard B. Morris, constituted a "hanging charge if ever there was one."[8]

Actually, this ruling was neither new nor so deadly to democratic legal

---

7. Morris, *Fair Trial,* 192.
8. Ibid., 194.

protection processes as it might be supposed. Shaw had in fact made the same point in an earlier case, *Commonwealth v. York,* in 1845. However, that case involved a drunken Irish laborer who solicited a black woman in the Negro section of Boston, and his murder presumably did not stir the public imagination because it involved the lower orders of society. But Richard Henry Dana Jr., who served as defense counsel for the York case, asked for a new trial on the grounds that the jury had been misdirected and was granted the motion, even though there was no higher court to which he might appeal. He was in effect asking the Supreme Court to reverse itself. The appeal was heard in "full bench," and the ruling was upheld.

In law, as legal historian Leonard W. Levy explains, *malice* does not mean ill will but instead has to do with *mens rea,* the particular state of mind accompanying the intention to do an unlawful act. Because the exact state of mind of a murderer cannot ever accurately be known, malice can only be implied from the proved facts of the case. Malice aforethought does not have to do with premeditation or deliberation but with the willful act of a person who intends to do harm to another. Thus considered, malice aforethought may occur at the very moment of the criminal attack. The legal question hinges only on whether the murderous act was voluntary and done with the intention to do harm; unintentional acts were to be governed by other rules of law. Moreover, as he remarked in the Webster ruling, "It is a settled rule of law that no provocation by words only, however opprobrious, will mitigate an intentional homicide, so as to reduce it to manslaughter."[9]

"The true rule of the Webster case," writes Levy, "was this: in a case where it has been proved to the jury beyond reasonable doubt that the accused committed the homicide intentionally, and where no evidence is adduced showing extenuating circumstances, the law will imply malice. In such a case, that is, the Court will instruct the jury that malice has been established as a matter of law, whereas it is normally left to the jury to determine the existence of malice from all the evidence." And as Levy goes on to explain, the defense is only required to establish a preponderance of belief that the act was not one of malice, whereas the prosecution is required to prove "beyond reasonable doubt" the fact of malice. If intentional homicide is established, malice can only be disproved by showing ex-

9. Leonard W. Levy, *The Law of the Commonwealth and Chief Justice Shaw* (Cambridge: Harvard University Press, 1957), 223, 224.

tenuating circumstances that prove the murder was somehow excusable. In such a case, however, it would be for the jury not the court to determine malice on the basis of all the evidence presented in the case. This was not the case in the Webster trial, for the defense made no attempt to extenuate an act for which the defendant consistently claimed perfect innocence.[10] And Shaw was simply interpreting the law rather than subverting due process by shifting the burden of proof to the defendant.

This was not how the ruling was understood in the popular mind, or even in the minds of several members of the bar. After Judge Shaw charged the jury, the jurors met for a little over two hours—they gave most of that time to prayer and spent only a few minutes in deciding that Webster was guilty. John Webster was sentenced to be hanged, but the sensationalism of the Webster case was far from over. It was now Lemuel Shaw's turn to be judged.

The Aftermath

Almost immediately, the popular press redirected the focus of its attack to what seemed to be the implication of Shaw's ruling, and the public transferred its sympathies from Parkman to the accused. The interest generated throughout the country made the aftermath of the trial as newsworthy as the crime itself: Bostonian respectability had been severely compromised by the disclosures of the philanthropic Dr. Parkman's niggardliness and a Harvard professor's violence. Moreover, the severity of Judge Shaw's ruling reminded some of the imperious judgments of the earlier "witchburners of Salem." The *New York Daily Globe* predicted that Shaw will "be the last of American Judges associated in position and character with the band of cruel and corrupt English Judges, of whom Jeffries is the first."[11] On April

---

10. Ibid., 221. In point of fact, Webster had wanted the skillful lawyer, Rufus Choate, to defend him, but Choate would only accept the case if Webster would admit the homicide and allow him to defend him on the grounds that the killing was no more than manslaughter. Webster refused this condition. The court appointed Pliny Merrick and Edward D. Sohier as Webster's defense attorneys. See Frederic Hathaway Chase, *Lemuel Shaw: Chief Justice of the Supreme Judicial Court of Massachusetts, 1830–1860* (Boston: Houghton Mifflin Company, 1918), 194–95.

11. "Judicial Murder in Boston," *Philadelphia Daily Sun* (April 3, 1850), 1; the *New York Daily Globe* clipping is among the Shaw papers; it is without a date.

5, the *Boston Transcript* reprinted comments from the *Philadelphia North American* and The *Richmond Whig* to the effect that Webster had not received a fair trial and that the prosecution had not proved its case. And the *Transcript* also mentioned the next day that there was a petition circulating in New York on Webster's behalf. In an April 6 letter to the *Philadelphia North American,* an unnamed writer described the Webster case as a "judicial mockery," observing that the "repeated violations of the simplest and safest rules of law, have excited the most profound astonishment from observers of Bench and Bar" and condemned the "laxity in applying proper tests of evidence." The *Transcript* reprinted this letter on Tuesday, April 9, but dissented from these "assumptions and conclusions." Presumably, the Boston paper felt local respectability was on trial and wished at once to capitalize on interest in the case but at the same time to uphold a certain sense of civic self-righteousness.

With the notable exception of Harvard law professor Joel Parker's essay criticizing Judge Shaw's ruling in the Webster case,[12] most of the judge's accusers preferred to remain anonymous. Besides, Parker's thoughtful critique did not appear until the following January. The immediate response was to damn Shaw under the protection of anonymity. Thus, an open letter in the *Transcript* on April 18 arguing that requiring the defendant to prove his innocence was a "relic of barbarism" and tantamount to "judicial murder" was signed "One of the Suffolk Bar." Similarly, a 36-page pamphlet entitled *A Statement of the Reasons Showing the Illegality of That Verdict upon Which Sentence of Death Has Been Pronounced against John W. Webster* was written by someone who identified himself only as a "Member of the Legal Profession." Judge Shaw, incidentally, received a copy of this pamphlet with the inscription written on the front cover— "From the Author."[13]

The fact that Judge Shaw, or someone in his household, saved several of these newspaper clippings suggests a certain bemusement toward the public reaction, however unflattering it may have been toward the Chief Justice. Among the Shaw papers is also a quite long and purely descriptive

12. Joel Parker, "The Law of Homicide," *North American Review* (January 1851): 178–204.

13. This pamphlet, published in New York in 1850, is among the Lemuel Shaw Papers at the Massachusetts Historical Society. I inspected the Shaw Papers on microfilm at the Law Library of the Library of Congress.

piece from the *Pittsburgh Weekly Dispatch and Temperance Banner* dated May 15, 1854. The Webster trial was sufficiently newsworthy to justify such a lengthy piece four years later, and this too likely amused Shaw to the extent that he would save the Pittsburgh clipping along with other reminders of his supposed infamy. But there were reasons to be distressed as well. The man who in 1850 had served as Chief Justice of Massachusetts for twenty years and would serve ten more before he was through and who was to write over 2,200 opinions may have felt in the spring of 1850 that he would be remembered only as a hanging judge, as the man who sentenced Professor Webster to death.

Criticisms were not confined to the press; various threats, accusations, and importunings were delivered to his door. One anonymous letter accused Shaw of performing the "double duty of judge and juror" and thereby of having consigned his name to "everlasting infamy" and becoming a "disgrace to mankind." Another anonymous correspondent remarked "Your coat of arms will be and now is a gallows sable, with a chemical professor pendant."[14] An unsigned letter dated April 4, 1850, was sent to Shaw directly: "You disgraced the Bench," it reads, "with the villainous charge you made against a persecuted & oppressed man like Webster[;] if you have a Soul within you the least bordering on Humanity it must gnaw you when you look back on your charge to that Jury; for this Sin you have committed there is an all Seeing Providence that will when the Day arrives for you to appear before Him give you a Trial which will be juster than the one you have awarded to an unfortunate man." Two other letters made their appeals to Shaw's authority as judge in the case, though ironically the authors made their incredible disclosures after the trial was concluded. One dated April 1, 1850, and signed "A friend to justice," announces "I am not the murderer." But the author goes on to say that he was an accomplice in the crime and therefore knows that Webster is an "innocent sufferer." And another dated April 4 also asserts Webster's innocence. The charges brought against him were a scheme designed to "ruin an innocent man." The letter is signed simply "Truth."[15]

14. Chase, *Lemuel Shaw*, 208. Mrs. Shaw was sufficiently alarmed by threats made against her husband should he sentence Webster to die that she insisted that their two sons accompany him to and from the courthouse.

15. These materials are in the microfilm collection of the Shaw Papers at the Library of Congress on reel 15, folder 4.

One can only speculate about Shaw's reaction to these letters or about the public vilification he received after the trial. We do know that he helped George Bemis, who had served as the assistant to the prosecuting attorney in the Webster case, prepare his *Report of the Case of John W. Webster,* which included verbatim the long and complicated and now controversial instructions he gave to the jury. And he may have wished to cooperate in the publication of a complete record of the trial because, as he said, many of the published reports were grossly inaccurate and therefore contributed to the criticism he had received.[16] Nor do we know very much about the Shaw family's reaction to the publicity. For that matter, there is no concrete evidence that Melville concerned himself much about the case, either as a writer who was intensely interested in the sorts of issues the case raised— the nature of innocence and guilt; the determination of malice and malicious intent; the fate of murderers; or the incompatibility of divine judgments, absolute and incontrovertible, and human judgment, flawed and contingent. Less still is known about his reaction as Shaw's son-in-law to what must have seemed something of a family crisis. While the temperament of the judge makes it likely that he regarded, or at least would have others believe that he regarded the whole affair with a cool matter-of-factness or barbed sardonicism, his wife and children, including Herman's wife Elizabeth, probably felt quite differently. It is impossible that Herman was not acquainted with the case, however, and when he began writing *Moby-Dick* that spring, some of the same questions the trial raised entered into the new book, and at times there seem to be references to the case itself.

Melville may have had his father-in-law in mind when, in chapter 132, "The Symphony," he put in Ahab's mouth the painful and intense words of his troubled hero's self-interrogation: "Look! see yon Albicore! who put it into him to chase and fang that flying-fish? Where do murderers go, man! Who's to doom, when the judge himself is dragged to the bar?"[17] The passage, of course, has immediate reference to Ahab's self-doubts, and he asks himself what "hidden lord" drives him on and whether he or God lifts his arm against the natural urgings of his heart. But the language is oddly gratuitous. Not even crazy Ahab would truly think the albicore a murderer, though he does seem to think his own desires for revenge somewhat murderous. And who has dragged the divine judge to the bar but Ahab himself

16. Chase, *Lemuel Shaw,* 206.
17. NN *Moby-Dick,* 545; additional references are cited parenthetically in the text.

when he asks what mysterious power so crowds him and pushes him on? There is, then, at least a residual suggestiveness here that is reminiscent of the circumstance of his father-in-law, who by virtue of his own commentary on the implied malice of a murderous act, had himself been dragged to the bar of public judgment.

And Ishmael's comment in chapter 16, "The Ship," has at least passing reference to the means whereby Judge Shaw argued for the determination of malice as logically implicated in any act of willful violence. When Ishmael learns from Peleg how Ahab has lost his leg, his response echoes and perhaps affirms Shaw's judgment: "What you say is no doubt true enough, sir, but how could I know there was any peculiar ferocity in that particular whale, though indeed I might have inferred as much from the simple fact of the accident" (72). Again, the language is strangely, and comically, gratuitous. Peleg is hardly interested in Ishmael's ability to draw logical or legal inferences from the facts of the case and finds the response peculiar and suspicious—does Ishmael not "talk shark a bit?" he asks.

Not too much ought be made of these stray passages, I suppose, but, in a way, much of *Moby-Dick* is the extenuation of acts of malice. Starbuck's contemplation of and reasoning on Ahab's tyrannical and irresponsible stewardship of the *Pequod* is identical to Ahab's attempted self-absolution in "The Symphony" chapter. Starbuck says Ahab would "fain kill all his crew" by driving relentlessly and incautiously into a gale: "But shall this crazed old man be tamely suffered to drag a whole ship's company down to doom with him?—Yes, it would make him the willful murderer of thirty men and more, if this ship come to any deadly harm." And then, to save Ahab from his crime, Starbuck himself, because two oceans and a continent stand between him and the law, contemplates murdering Ahab to save the crew from murder: "Is heaven a murderer when its lightning strikes a would-be murderer in his bed, tindering sheets and skin together?—And would I be a murderer, then, if—" (514–15). But the question dissolves in the benign promptings of Starbuck's natural heart.

The Afterthought

All this is to say that Melville was intrinsically interested in the sorts of difficult questions raised by the Parkman/Webster case. Toward the end of his life, Melville's mind may have drifted back to the notorious judgment of

Judge Shaw in this murder trial, as it undoubtedly drifted back to the *Somers* mutiny case in which his cousin had played an important role. And Brook Thomas has detected many parallels between the drumhead court that judges Billy Budd and the Webster/Parkman case, as well as between the temperaments of Judge Shaw and Captain Vere themselves.[18] In any event, *Billy Budd* dramatically frames the same sorts of legal and moral issues raised by the Webster trial nearly forty years earlier and, because Billy's trial is conducted before a drumhead court in time of war, gives them sharp accent.

The "honest scholar, my senior," long since dead, whom the narrator refers to in chapter 11, may be, as Harrison Hayford and Merton Sealts observe, no more than an invented spokesman created to dramatize a certain point of view.[19] The point of view and certain details concerning this invention bring Judge Shaw to mind nevertheless. Like Shaw, Melville's "senior scholar" was "so unimpeachably respectable that against him nothing was ever openly said though among the few something was whispered" (74). The public damnations of Shaw in the newspapers were hardly whispers, but it should be pointed out that the accusations were typically anonymous. More important, Judge Shaw was likely to believe, like this invented spokesman, that knowledge of the world and knowledge of human nature are two "distinct branches of knowledge, which while they may coexist in the same heart, yet either may exist with little or nothing of the other" (75). As Leonard Levy remarks, Lemuel Shaw believed that the law "was a symmetrical and scientific system of principles, based on 'reason, natural justice, and enlightened public policy,' from which a rule could be deduced and adapted for every case."[20] The hard matter-of-factness of Lemuel Shaw might well have perplexed or irritated a younger and more earnest Melville. And whether or not his latter-day unnamed spokesman bears even so slight a resemblance to his deceased father-in-law, the narrator's admission of the gentleman's wisdom in leaving the knowledge of the

---

18. See Thomas, *Cross-Examinations*, 202–6, 211–14. My own conclusions about the relation between the Webster case and *Billy Budd* do not so much differ from Thomas's in substance as in emphasis. I choose to view the notion of malice and judgment as of primary interest to Melville and central to Vere's arguments.

19. See Harrison Hayford and Merton M. Sealts Jr., ed., *"Billy Budd, Sailor: (An Inside Narrative)* (Chicago: University of Chicago Press, 1962), 74; Hayford and Sealts's note appears on p. 161.

20. Levy, *Law of the Commonwealth*, 4.

world to Coke and Blackstone and the knowledge of human nature to the Hebrew prophets is revealing of Melville's state of mind in the late 1880s: "At the time, my inexperience was such that I did not quite see the drift of all this. It may be that I see it now."[21]

Melville as much as admits that when he was a younger man he was too ready to regard life's "ambiguities" with a certain moral urgency. But by the time he came to write *Billy Budd,* if the degree of sympathy he evokes for Captain Vere is any measure, Melville may have concluded that the jurisdiction of law and the jurisdiction of virtue must sometimes be regarded as quite distinct. Like Captain Vere, Judge Shaw was apt to regard the "mystery of iniquity" as "a matter for psychologic theologians to discuss" (108). By virtue of the way he forces the court to contemplate the matter before them, Vere (as Shaw supposedly had done) delivers a "hanging charge" to his drumhead court. When he steps out of his role as witness to the crime and undertakes to become the "coadjutor" in the case, Vere insists that military duty must be distinguished from moral scruple—"scruple vitalized by compassion" (110).

Melville, by contemplating murder, malice, and judgment under the rule of naval law, reduces the terms of this opposition to their barest and severest construction. Though Vere believes Billy when he says that he never bore any "malice" toward Claggart, he also declares motive and occasion extraneous to the case they are now considering: "Quite aside from any conceivable motive actuating the master-at-arms, and irrespective of the provocation to the blow, a martial court must needs in the present case confine its attention to the blow's consequence, which consequence justly is to be deemed not otherwise than as the striker's deed" (107).

It is the brute fact of the deed alone, the criminal act, that must concern the court. Vere himself gives voice to the court's hesitancy. Do not your

---

21. *Billy Budd,* 75; further citations included parenthetically in text. In another passage, Melville also seems to be admitting to a similar misjudgment on his part: "Says a writer whom few know, 'Forty years after a battle it is easy for a noncombatant to reason about how it ought to have been fought. It is another thing personally and under fire to have to direct the fighting while involved in the obscuring smoke of it. Much so with respect to other emergencies involving considerations both practical and moral, and what it is imperative promptly to act'" (114). The passage follows a reference to the *Somers* case, but that occurred in 1842, more than forty-five years before Melville began in late 1888 to develop that part of the novel that deals with Captain Vere's judgment. The date of the Webster trial comes closer to the forty-year estimate.

scruples import something like this, he asks: "If, mindless of palliating circumstances, we are bound to regard the death of the master-at-arms as the
prisoner's deed, then does that deed constitute a capital crime whereof the
penalty is a mortal one. But in natural justice is nothing but the prisoner's
overt act to be considered? How can we adjudge to summary and shame-
ful death a fellow creature innocent before God, and whom we feel to be
so?" (110). But he also answers the perceived complaint; they are but agents
of military law: "That however pitilessly that law may operate in any instances, we nevertheless adhere to it and administer it." And to the officer
of marines's objection that Billy "purposed neither mutiny nor homicide,"
Vere explains: "Surely not, my good man. And before a court less arbitrary
and more merciful than a martial one, that plea would largely extenuate.
At the Last Assizes it shall acquit" (111). "Budd's intent or non-intent," he
concludes, "is nothing to the purpose" (112). Vere's strict adherence to
duty, we know, is difficult for him. And his dying words ("Billy Budd, Billy Budd."), whether or not they were uttered in the "accents of remorse"
(129), indicate that the problem, formerly legal and military in its nature,
has withdrawn from the precinct of experience of the world to that of human nature, a precinct more fit for the consideration of Hebrew prophets
than bench and bar.

    Billy Budd, as Leon Howard observed, in part derived its creative im-
petus from Melville's contemplation of the *Somers* mutiny case and the
family's conviction that his cousin Guert Gansevoort's actions were in the
last analysis *"approved* of God."[22] Certainly this "inside narrative" drew
upon the interior history of the author and to a degree upon his reflection
on family associations. But the author had another analogue, again within
his family history, that might have clarified his own thinking about the
problematic position of his created character, Captain Vere.[23] We know at
any rate, and must assume that Melville likewise knew, that pronouncing

    22. Leon Howard, *Herman Melville: A Biography* (Berkeley: University of Califor-
nia Press, 1951), 325.
    23. Had Melville desired to, he could have read a complete account of the Webster
trial, including the passage quoted above, in Bemis's *Report of the Case of John W. Webster;* which was published in November 1850. Shaw himself probably owned a copy, and
much closer to Melville's Pittsfield residence, Oliver Wendell Holmes had one as well.
Holmes's copy, presented to him by G. C. Shattuck and dated "Dec. 6th 1850," is in the
rare book room of the Library of Congress.

the death sentence of John Webster was no easy task for Judge Shaw—he found it, he said, an "unspeakably painful" duty.[24] His statement to the prisoner was, as George Bemis observed, sometimes interrupted by an emotional quiet and hesitancy, but he, like Vere, remained true to the command of duty. Webster was sentenced in late March; he was hanged the following August.

24. Chase, *Lemuel Shaw,* 210.

VII

Mark Twain in His Short Works

When Samuel L. Clemens published "Letter from Carson City" in 1863, he signed the sketch "Mark Twain." Clemens had adopted pen names before—"W. Epaminondas Adrastus Perkins," "Thomas Jefferson Snodgrass," "Josh"—but this was the first time he used the name that would eventually become a registered trademark and a universally recognized literary identity. It was a fateful gesture. Much of the experience that Clemens would use in his later fiction was already behind him, but his career as a professional "literary person" (as he one time described his almost accidental occupation as a writer) largely lay before him. Sam Clemens had been places and seen things; by his own admission, his early adult life consisted of a string of apprenticeships and misdirected ambitions. "Mark Twain" took the boy in tow. He offered a young journalist's perceptions a point and his wit a barb; he gave a mature man's memories of childhood a literary shape and solidity; he transformed a personal delight in the joke, the hoax, and general mischief-making into a moral point of view; he offered an old man the bitter solace of philosophy. For the persona that was "Mark Twain" was something more than a mere literary device; it became a means of being in the world and of speaking to that world in ways that Clemens might not venture in his own person.

In part, Samuel Clemens had fame, or at least celebrity, thrust upon him. He sent his jumping frog story east to Artemus Ward in 1865 to be included in a collection Ward was assembling, but the tale he had heard (along with so many others) in a California mining camp and had cast in the familiar mode of the frame tale arrived too late for inclusion. It was published instead in the *Saturday Press* the same year. The story was an instant success and was widely reprinted, and its creator thereafter became a figure of some interest. Inevitably, the "Mark Twain" available to us now is a diminished presence, however much we instinctively feel ourselves to be his familiar acquaintance.

In his own day, Twain was primarily known as a public personality who also happened to be a writer. The public knew him equally through his lectures and readings, through the more than three hundred interviews he granted to intrepid reporters, and through the frequent accounts of his doings and sayings in newspapers and magazines. A whole generation grew up with Mark Twain as a living voice and a responsive and frequently outrageous and outraged critic of the times. Though he spent much of his adult life abroad, as George Ade rightly observed, Americans typically thought of him not as an expatriate but as their trustworthy emissary to the world at large. When he died in 1910, much of the country mourned the loss of a genial companion.

Since that time readers and critics have tried to define Twain's significance to American literary culture, to analyze his multiform and largely elusive personality, to somehow recapture the distinctive flavor of his humorous idiom, and to describe the mechanics of his wit. Unlike, say, Herman Melville, whose deep-diving imagination is so aptly linked to the sea, there is nothing especially deep about Twain. Like the Mississippi River itself, he is intricate, shifty, and sometimes treacherous, driven by some strong current of earnestness or indignation; he is complicated, but he is not profound. In an essay written for *Harper's* and titled simply "William Dean Howells," Twain identified the qualities he envied in his friend, and many of them he could claim as his own. But Howells's easy prose, "unconfused by crosscurrents, eddies, undertows," was not his. It is true that Twain made it his business to have a point and to get to it as unmistakably and forthrightly as possible, but even so, there is nearly always a sly wrinkle or unanticipated snag likely to catch us by surprise. Witness this letter written in 1907 to the editor of the *New York Times:*

> To the Editor
>
> Sir to you, I would like to know what kind of a goddam govment this is that discriminates between two common carriers and makes a goddam railroad charge everybody equal & lets a goddam man charge any goddam price he wants to for his goddam opera box.
>
> W. D. Howells
Tuxedo Park Oct 4
>
> Howells it is an outrage the way the govment is acting so I sent this complaint to N. Y. Times with your name signed because it would have more weight.
>
> Mark

Even a cursory survey of Mark Twain's short fiction and prose disclose not merely the variety of his imaginative invention and diverse talents but the range of his emotional condition as well. As if by instinct, he seems to have been naturally adept in virtually every prose genre—the fable, the sketch, the tale, the anecdote, the maxim, the philosophical dialogue, the essay, the speech—and to have understood generic requirements sufficiently to burlesque and satirize them as well. (His "An Awful—Terrible Medieval Romance" was in the tradition of such burlesques that parodied the popular romance in only 500 to 2,500 words; and he indulged in the well-known burlesques of popular poetry and the Shakespearean soliloquy in *Huckleberry Finn*.) At the same time, his imagination seemed always to outrun literary conventions and accepted forms, as though formal discipline were inimical to thought and expression and unequal to the many moods that motivated him to write. He mastered the frame tale—a form featuring a story within a story—of the Southwestern humorists easily, but this same form that played upon the comic contrasts between genteel refinement and vernacular coarseness acquired a sudden seriousness when he adapted it to the poignant and accusing story of the former slave Aunt Rachel in "A True Story."

It is tempting to describe Clemens's career as an arc, a slow ascent to a perfect mastery of his craft and then a falling off. By this view he is to be seen as a rough, untutored, slightly reckless humorist who by degrees acquired the literary sophistication and confidence to produce one exquisite novel, *Huckleberry Finn* (1884), and, likewise by degrees, who gradually turned bitter, polemical, and churlish and permitted his fiction to suffer the depletions he felt as a man until he was unable to produce anything more interesting than quasi-philosophical dialogues or false starts toward extended narratives that were ill-conceived to begin with. There is more than a grain of truth in this depiction; it is far more appealing, however, to those who assume that the mark of a writer of distinction resides chiefly in the capacity to produce the novel, not the tale, the essay, or the sketch. But Mark Twain's imagination was constitutionally unruly and eruptive. For that reason, he often worked most coherently if not most memorably in short compass.

In his "Reply to the Editor of 'The Art of Authorship,'" Twain compared his own unconscious and associative creative process to bricklaying. Though the remark refers to the making of individual sentences and the all but unconscious acquisition of a literary "style," the figure applies as well to those discrete compositional blocks that make up so many of his extended narratives. Twain often casually interpolated self-sufficient episodes, tales, and sketches into his books, sometimes without supplying even a flimsy excuse for doing so, and some of these were detachable enough to move from one book to another. Whatever formal integrity critics have been able to discern in Twain's novels and travel books, they remain nevertheless highly episodic narratives, a series of adventures or journeys more often held together by narrative sensibility or a travel itinerary than by sure and comprehensive artistic purpose. Little wonder that he preferred Cervantes to Jane Austen.

It is certain, at any rate, that Twain's short fiction and prose better exhibit his volatile temperament and erratic genius than do the novels, even if they complicate a familiar portrait of the writer. "The Man That Corrupted Hadleyburg," perhaps the most formally perfect of his tales, follows relentlessly its own cynical logic, to the enormous and practically debilitating discredit of the American village and the moral and democratic values it so sanctimoniously symbolizes. The story was published in 1899 and epitomizes the dark brooding of the late Twain, though he was destined to have darker moments still. A few years later, however, he published "Early Days" (a "chapter" from his ongoing autobiography), with its litany of recollected pleasures experienced in his native Missouri. However penetrating his analysis of the false virtues of Hadleyburg, to turn to that tale after reading his description of dinnertime at his uncle's farm is to experience a certain sensory deprivation:

> In the summer the table was set in the middle of that shady and breezy
> floor, and the sumptuous meals—well, it makes me cry to think of them.
> Fried chicken, roast pig, wild and tame turkeys, ducks and geese; veni-
> son just killed; squirrels, rabbits, pheasants, partridges, prairie-chickens;
> biscuits, hot batter cakes, hot buckwheat cakes, hot "wheat bread," hot
> rolls, hot corn pone; fresh corn boiled on the ear, succotash, butter beans,
> string-beans, tomatoes, pease, Irish potatoes, sweet-potatoes; butter-
> milk, sweet milk, "clabber"; watermelons, muskmelons, cantaloups—
> all fresh from the garden—apple pie, peach pie, pumpkin pie, apple
> dumplings, peach cobbler—I can't remember the rest.

Have butter beans ever appeared in better company? And can there be any doubt that Twain's ability to summon from the resources of his memory the rich advantages and pleasures of youth was a form of personal indulgence and the ecstatic privilege of his creative imagination?

W. D. Howells once observed the apparent lack of design in Mark Twain's method of composing. He drew from the "divine ragbag" of his mind whatever it offered and left it to the reader to discern the relevancies and sequences. "It is imaginable that he pursues [this creative method] from no wish but to have pleasure of his work, and not to fatigue either himself or his reader; and his method may be the secret of his vast popularity." Twain more than once represented himself as the "amanuensis" of his creative imagination, and he confessed in an 1883 letter how personally satisfying the work was when the writing was going well: "I used to restrict myself to 4 & 5 hours a day & 5 days in the week; but this time I've wrought from breakfast till 5:15 p.m. six days in the week; & once or twice I smouched a Sunday when the boss wasn't looking. Nothing is half so good as literature hooked on Sunday on the sly." The "literature" he was hooking was not what he was reading but the fiction that was taking shape under his hand.

It is that same happy submission to the spontaneous and immanent terms of the tale to be told, the remembered scene to be summoned and described, the emotion to be recast under the friendly auspices of nostalgia—all with the audacious flair of inconsequence—that is so often imparted to his readers, as though we were copartners in creation. These are the vital qualities so vividly conveyed in the opening chapters of "Old Times on the Mississippi," but they are features of his humor as well. It was the confidently spontaneous quality in Twain that Howells (still his most cordial and astute critic) characterized as his "fine, forecasting humor," a willingness to stand so far back from comic effect that "one, knowing some joke must becoming, feels that nothing less than a prophetic instinct can sustain the humorist in its development." Again, the observation is corroborated by Twain himself. In "How to Tell a Story," he insists that the truly American humorous story relies upon the manner of the telling, not the matter of the tale told: "The humorous story may be spun out to great length, and may wander around as much as it pleases, and arrive nowhere in particular; but the comic and witty stories must be brief and end with a point. The humorous story bubbles gently along, the others burst."

The comic percolations of "Jim Smiley and His Jumping Frog," "Jim Blaine and His Grandfather's Old Ram," "Buck Fanshawe's Funeral," or "Jim Baker's Blue Jay Yarn" exhibit in print the rich vein of humor Twain had mined in storytelling communities on the river or the Pacific slope, but they retain, as well, the felt quality of the human voice speaking at its pleasure. Jim Blaine, in a state of "serene" and "symmetrical" drunkenness, begins his story of the old ram with,

> "I don't reckon them times will ever come again. There never was a more bullier old ram than what he was. Grandfather fetched him from Illinois—got him off a man by the name of Yates—Bill Yates—maybe you might have heard of him; his father was a deacon—Baptist—and he was a rustler, too; a man had to get up ruther early to get the start of old Thankful Yates."

Of course those times do come again with each rereading of the yarn. We will never find out about the old ram or know why, precisely, Bill Yates is thankful. The stiff and formal narrator who introduces the tale may feel he has been "sold," but readers are more likely to feel that they have been tricked into an awfully good time.

This ambulatory style that winds down as the author's own interest wanes is only one of Twain's many signatures, however. He could speak succinctly and pointedly when he chose:

> Truth is the most valuable thing we have. Let us economize it.

> Pity is for the living, envy is for the dead.

> Adam and Eve had many advantages, but the principal one was that they escaped teething.

> There are two times in a man's life when he should not speculate: when he can't afford it and when he can.

In some ways Twain's comic genius appears at its best advantage in the aphorism and the maxim. Even when Twain chooses to be epigrammatic or merely witty (forms of humor, he once remarked, that made one "want to renounce joking and lead a better life"), there remains something lavish and unexpected in him. Who else could have formulated such a maxim as this?: "She was not quite what you would call refined. She was not quite what you would call unrefined. She was the kind of person that keeps a parrot."

But Twain was known as well as a commentator on the national scene; his remarks upon all sorts of injustices and cruelties had the force of conviction and the potential to reform opinion. "A Dog's Tale," for example, was first published in *Harper's Monthly* in 1903 and was reissued as a pamphlet by the National Anti-Vivisection Society in London a few months later. Particularly in his later years, the fierceness of Twain's anti-imperialist convictions disturbed and dismayed those who regarded him as the archetypal American citizen who had somehow turned upon Americanism itself. "To the Person Sitting in Darkness" was reprinted as a pamphlet by the Anti-Imperialist League, which distributed well over a hundred thousand copies. Twain's angry indictment in this essay, as elsewhere, is unrelenting; he would have as the new flag for the Philippine Province "just our usual flag, with the white stripes painted black and the stars replaced by the skull and cross-bones." But for all his forthrightness he remained something of a curiosity, nevertheless, even for those who without reservation claimed him as somehow theirs. What was to be made, for example, of the creator of Huckleberry Finn and Tom Sawyer complaining in an interview in 1907 that we are educating our children to be patriots instead of citizens?

This turn to serious invective should never have been a surprise, of course. Even in the first published volume of his tales and sketches in 1867, Clemens's friend Charles Henry Webb introduced the collection with the observation that Mark Twain is principally known as "The Moralist of the Main" and only secondarily as "The Wild Humorist of the Pacific Slope." Nearly forty years later, Twain himself reaffirmed the distinction: "I have always preached. . . . If the humor came of its own accord and uninvited, I have allowed it a place in my sermon, but I was not writing the sermon for the sake of the humor. I should have written the sermon just the same, whether any humor applied for admission or not." Maybe so. But Samuel Clemens was too shrewd a man to think that his popular appeal resided in his earnestness alone. His reputation depended upon his wit, not his wisdom.

One is rather more tempted to believe that, more often than not, these competing tendencies worked in concert. In 1907, Twain announced that "Every man is in his own person the whole human race, with not a detail lacking. I am the whole human race without a detail lacking; I have studied the human race with diligence and strong interest all these years in my own person; in myself I find in big or little proportion every quality and every defect that is findable in the mass of the race." However, he repeatedly insisted in such essays as "James Fenimore Cooper's Literary Offenses" or "What Paul Bourget Thinks of Us" that the chief interest and duty of a writer is observation, not introspection. If Twain cherished his role as advocate, he made a point of serving as court stenographer as well. This insistence upon minute and keen attention cuts against the grain of abstract principle and philosophic credo. The literary critic Kenneth Burke, who had some gifts for humor and satire himself, once remarked upon his own paradoxical role as observer and analyst:

> I speak in my role as Wandering Scholar,
> which is to say:
> half experimental animal,
> half control group.
> I am mine own disease.

The terms of this implicit contradiction appear in Twain in many forms, and at times his desire for independence and his troubled awareness of his complicity in a social order he often despised constituted his own special disease. However much he played the role of rambunctious outcast, Twain never—or hardly ever—denied his membership in a community whose attitudes, laws, and policies he might repudiate but whose responsibilities and guilt he shared. Twain might invoke dreams of drift and absolute freedom from constraint, but he typically carried a portion of his troubled conscience along with him in the flight. As often as not, he made himself the butt of his own joke and thereby spared the reader the full force of his complaint. He might satirize all manner of hypocrisy, sham, and cruelty and yet sound some quiet note of forgiveness. For all his anger, invective, and simple cantankerousness, Twain rarely allows his satire to degenerate into the merely sanctimonious or self-righteous.

Twain might delightfully ridicule political rhetoric in such early sketches as "Barnum's First Speech in Congress" or "Cannibalism in the Cars," but his contempt was for the sin, not the sinner. In Twain's depiction, P. T. Barnum is a lovable fraud, after all, and Barnum's decision to run for Congress in 1867 automatically suggested the possibilities of conflating shameless and crass self-promotion with political bombast. "Cannibalism in the Cars" is far more grotesque and was likely based on his recollection of a group of Illinois legislators who were snowbound in 1855 and who ate dogs to survive. Still, the nervous laughter provoked by the recollection of several acts of cannibalism conducted according to democratic procedure is ultimately diluted by our sympathies when we learn that we have been listening to the "harmless vagaries of a madman, instead of the genuine experiences of a bloodthirsty cannibal."

The crude detachment of a western humorist looking as if for the first time at ancient and historically sponsored institutions provided its own sort of comedy. This was the essential joke of the highly episodic travel narrative *The Innocents Abroad* (1869), though Twain insisted in his preface upon a certain representative perspective—that his reader, too, would be likely to see Europe and the East in the same way if "he looked at them with his own eyes instead of the eyes of those who traveled in those countries before him." Even a casual glance at "The Tomb of Adam," however, discloses the nearly insurmountable gap between Twain's democratic sympathies and the individuality of his expression. His comic adventures in the Holy Land may cleanse the vision of the large burden of history or the timid attachment to pious sentimentality, but the wonderful bifocal illogic of his reactions and phrasing is apt to bind us just as forcibly to his genial narrative presence. At his best Twain not only speaks for us but phrases our thoughts in ways that, quite improbably, we instinctively feel are available to us, as though the language as well as the sentiment were our own.

If one reads, say, Henry James or Gertrude Stein, William Faulkner or Ernest Hemingway, for any length of time, the cadences, repetitions, and circumlocutions infect one's thoughts and impart their idiom. No matter how long one reads Twain, however, one cannot acquire his peculiar and antic way of looking at the world or his verbal facility in rendering that world. Twain, as Howells once observed, wrote as though English were a "primitive and not a derivative language, without Gothic or Latin or Greek behind it, or German and French beside it." This linguistic freedom of view is partly the source of his unpredictable vitality; it also helps to explain why Twain, in many fundamental ways a derivative and unexceptionable writer, has outlasted so many of his contemporaries.

But this same commitment to vernacular expression and oral tradition is also the source of a value: the unamazed recognition that people from every region and social condition have the verbal resources to speak for themselves. For much of Twain's genius derives from the simple transcription of voices. Sometimes this talent results in a delightful comedy of misunderstanding, as in the sketch "Buck Fanshaw's Funeral"; at other times the narrator displays an affectionate and engrossed attention to the cadence and poetry of dialect itself. This is certainly the case with two notable sketches told largely in African American dialect: "Sociable Jimmy" ("I took down what he had to say, just as he said it") and "A True Story, Repeated Word for Word as I Heard It." Twain may have played the part of vernacular ventriloquist at times, but in "A True Story," at least, there is a sudden seriousness to events that catches the narrator off guard, for it is "Misto C—", not Aunt Rachel, who is the dummy in this tale.

Clearly, the device of the innocent observer or the new man in the Old World he had employed in *The Innocents Abroad* worked in reverse as well. The persona of the tenderfoot, as he represented himself in *Roughing It* (1872), provided Twain with a dramatic frame for some his most hilarious sketches such as "The Story of the Old Ram" and "Buck Fanshaw's Funeral." When his personal indignation and cynicism outstripped his ability to satirize sanctioned custom or received opinion, however, the persona that was "Mark Twain" provided no defense against the world or the irascible sensibility that was Samuel Clemens. He expressed this sort of incapacity to W. D. Howells when he was struggling with his account of his travels in Europe, *A Tramp Abroad* (1880): "I wish I *could* give those sharp satires on European life which you mention, but of course a man can't write successful satire except he be in a calm, judicial good-humor—whereas I *hate* travel, & I *hate* hotels, & I *hate* the opera, & I *hate* the Old Masters—in truth I don't ever seem to be in a good enough humor with ANYthing to *satirize* it; no, I want to stand up before it & *curse* it, & foam at the mouth,—or take a club & pound it to rags and pulp." Such moods were temporary, however, and he eventually hit upon the joke that permitted him to satirize European custom and coordinate his episodic adventures abroad. It should be remembered, as well, that "Jim Baker's Blue Jay Yarn" came out of this same period of composition.

It may well be true, as some have suggested, that Twain was motivated to travel abroad by the profound resentment and shame he felt when the "Whittier Birthday Speech" he had given in 1877 appeared to offend rather than to please the literary worthies of New England. It may also be true that the blue jay yarn, interpolated into a book about those travels, was an indirect commentary on the humorlessness of Boston Brahmins who, like the incurious owl from Nova Scotia that ends the tale, are immune to the magnificent delights of anything western, either the tall tale or a redwood forest. If this tale is some form of muted revenge for earlier feelings of embarrassment, however, it seems equally true that the author was on the happiest terms with its composing and that he had acquired the "calm, judicial good-humor" that was the requirement of satire and the prerogative of the humorous yarn.

Clemens's reaction to the apparent displeasure with the "Whittier Birthday Speech" was predictable enough, particularly so since he was known as a popular and delightful speech maker. A couple of years later he delivered his brief speech "The Babies" before some six hundred Civil War veterans, and it was hugely successful, even though he gave it at three-thirty in the morning after several hours of wearying oratory. And on his seventieth birthday, it was Twain himself who was the literary figure to be celebrated. He delivered this birthday speech at Delmonico's in New York before a considerable number of literary worthies who had turned out for the occasion. But the failure of the much earlier "Whittier Birthday Speech" probably rankled for other reasons as well. Twain had been more than a little tentative and self-conscious about his identity as a frontier humorist virtually from the beginning of his literary career, and he sometimes desperately wanted to be taken for a serious moralist instead of as the nation's "phunny phellow." He often vigorously pursued the approval or at least the recognition of those who were more apt to reject or ignore him than otherwise; for there was more than a little of Tom Sawyer and Huck Finn in Mark Twain himself.

Like Tom Sawyer, he was always tempted to transgress the stated limits of propriety or social usage and to offer up his own boyish good nature as bond for the crime. He had courted the daughter of a well-respected New York family with a sincerity and amiability that finally outweighed his future father-in-law's objections to Clemens's coarse origins and doubtful occupation. Many years later, Twain horrified Howells when he appeared before Congress to testify on behalf of an international copyright law wearing his familiar white serge suit out of season, though his serious testimony was influential nonetheless. In "The Private History of a Campaign That Failed," ironically and quite deliberately published in the *Century Magazine* as part of its series on "Battles and Leaders of the Civil War," Twain told the story of his desertion from the Marion Rangers in 1861. The memoir is only superficially an attempt at self-recrimination and extenuation, however; for he claims that he was not "rightfully equipped" for the awful business of war and that he deserted in order "to save some remnant of my self-respect." In a word, he offered as excuse for his apparent cowardice nothing more substantial than a natural revulsion toward violence and his own blameless moral nature. Whether or not he actually possessed them himself, these were qualities Twain had attributed to one of the noblest of his fictional creations, Huckleberry Finn.

The antic mischief that was his genius was also cause for ready apology or extenuation—the half of him that was experimental animal reproved by the other half that was his internal control group. In a letter home written in January 1866, he described the jumping frog story as a "villainous backwoods sketch" and depreciated the artistic craft that had gone into it, describing it as a mere "squib." Yet in 1894 he hilariously defended the story against French translators and its absorption into an alien European culture, while at the same time locating the origin of the tale in Boetia, a tale that was both old and new—"for it was original when it happened two thousand years ago, and was again original when it happened in California in our own time."[1] Again and again Twain burlesqued polite and genteel sensibility and the several literary forms it adopted, but he was very pleased when his work at last appeared in the *Atlantic Monthly,* for the *Atlantic* meant literary respectability. He publicly maintained that *Personal Recollections of Joan of Arc* (1896) was his favorite creation, though privately he must have known that he had a greater emotional investment in *Huckleberry Finn* and *Tom Sawyer* (1876).

This is but to say that Twain was tugged and pulled by competing forces within him: an impulse to escape, rebel, or condemn and a desire for recognition and approval; an impulse to delight and amuse and a desire to be recognized as an earnest moralist and responsible citizen. The emotional costs of this double bind were sometimes high. His comic dissection of the force and ironies of conscience in "The Facts Concerning the Recent Carnival of Crime in Connecticut," for example, may serve as some form of comically grotesque sociological analysis. But it is also a record of the sufferings his own constitutionally tender conscience had exacted from him from early childhood on, for Twain was inclined toward self-accusation and apt to feel guilty about events over which he had little or no control.

He wished, as well, to belong to his own age and at times fancied himself something of an entrepreneur—a tendency that got him into more than a little financial trouble. Twain celebrated progress but yearned for the simplicity of an earlier time, and something of this deep ambivalence found its

---

1. Actually, Twain was mistaken in his belief that the tale had its origins in Boetia. As he was to learn later, the ancient Greek tale that Professor Van Dyke mentioned and that was published in the textbook Van Dyke sent Twain was in fact his own yarn. It had been adapted by Arthur Sidgwick for inclusion in his volume *An Introduction to Greek Composition.* At the time he wrote the "Private History of the 'Jumping Frog' Story," however, Twain was acting in good faith and genuinely happy to discover the story had ancient antecedents.

way into *A Connecticut Yankee in King Arthur's Court* (1889). He was perpetually fascinated with inventions, such as the bicycle, the telephone, and
the typewriter, and often lampooned his own awkward attempts to master
them. If Twain detected in his own person every quality and defect that is
"findable in the mass of the race," the comic incongruities he discovered
within himself were ready-made for humorous treatment. Much of his comedy, in fact, derives from a capacity, even an appetite, for self-parody, crafti-
ly combined with the sort of ignorance in his created persona that allows
one to see the familiar in altogether new ways.

This sort of comedy that thrives on pretended ignorance is frequently
generated out of Twain's own private confidence in his abilities and mastery of the subject at hand rather than out of some deep-seated anxiety or
insecurity. In "An Encounter with an Interviewer," for example, he pretends to be ignorant of a relatively new form of journalism, the interview.
This was a vehicle of self-representation Twain would later come to know
all too well, but even in 1874, when he wrote the sketch, he regarded the
practice with the amused skepticism of a practiced journalist. Burlesque
and parody are grounded in easy and familiar acquaintance with the conventions to be scrutinized and lampooned, and in this imagined encounter
of only a few pages Twain manages to mangle biography, history, memory, identity, even simple arithmetic with comic and generous charm. Much
of the comedy of situation in "Old Times on the Mississippi," to cite another familiar example, comes out of the dramatized ignorance, cockiness,
and ineptitude in this young man from Hannibal, Missouri. Yet Horace
Bixby, under whom Clemens served as an apprentice riverboat pilot, once
observed that this "cub" eventually came to know the river as well as anyone alive. In his "Map of Paris," the visual joke is founded on the narrator's absolute ignorance of printing and engraving, an unlikely premise for
a man who was a very capable typesetter from an early age.

A rather more tender version of self-parody is observable in "A Cat
Tale," which dramatizes the narrator's strained attempts to improvise a
children's story and at the same time conveys some sense of Twain's deep
affection for his daughters, Susy and Clara, and the quality of his domestic life. It was written in 1880, the same year his third daughter, Jean, was
born, and may adequately render the depth of parental feeling, the sort of
daily fun, and the reassurances of quiet family attachments that Twain cherished; "A Cat Tale" offers a glimpse of Twain's private life and personal af-
fections that he rarely shared with his reading public. By the end of the

1880s, however, things had begun to fall apart and his domestic and personal peace was threatened. All of the family members, including Twain himself, were plagued by chronic ill health. At least as early as 1891, it was clear that his publishing company, Charles Webster and Company, was going under. At about the same time it became apparent that his confident and prolonged investments in the Paige typesetting machine (sometimes averaging around three thousand dollars a month for years at a time) were unrecoverable. By 1900, he had become disillusioned with U.S. involvement in the Philippines and eventually became ashamed of his country and his race. In 1896 his daughter Susy died; in 1897 it was his brother Orion; in 1904 his wife, Livy; in 1909 his daughter Jean.

The personal consequences of these losses, it should go without saying, were feelings of bitterness, resentment, guilt, and outrage. For some fifty years after Twain's death, the darker portions of his late writings and particularly the notion that life may be at once a cruel dream and a Providential deceit (whether hatched by God or Satan hardly matters) were adequately represented in anthologies and collections by *The Mysterious Stranger*. Since 1963, however, it has been known that this story, as interesting as it is, is in fact a hybrid made up of portions of three different texts and amounts to editorial fraud concocted by Twain's literary executor and an editor from the Harper's publishing house and published by them in 1916. *The Mysterious Stranger* clearly does not represent Twain's literary intentions. There is no single and tidily representative text for these late years, one that would sufficiently convey the quality of Twain's sense of personal despair, angry cynicism, and injured hope.

Even so, there is nothing sinister in Twain's black humor and his fables of despair. He often suppressed or deferred the publication of the bitterest of his disclosures, and he insisted that the bulk of his "Autobiography" and other of his writings should not be published until after his death, in part because he deemed them too shocking for public consumption, but also because he believed that by adopting a persona who spoke from the grave he might speak with absolute frankness. Still, his final thoughts and convictions were hardly as scandalous, even in his own day, as the author himself believed they would be. Their interest for us now resides less in their intellectual skepticism or in the articulation of a materialist determinism, on the one hand, and a philosophical solipsism, on the other, than in their capacity to evince the quality of pity for the human condition the author so obviously felt. However much Twain might rant and rave about "the damned human race," his sympathy lingers around the edges of his dark tales and polemical essays and is registered in the voice of a man who would, and did, side with his kind against God and the angels. At all events, what has been jocularly described as Twain's "bad mood" period seems to have had divergent if somewhat overlapping effects upon his late writings.

His political commentary became more comprehensive and unrelenting and betrays little of the calm judicial humor he required for the sort of satire that meant to laugh out of court human foible and duplicity. Whatever political outrages may have motivated him in his late years, he seemed determined that he would not commit what he called the "lie of silent assertion," that he would not become a mute accomplice to deplorable events by virtue of his silence or his cowardice. In 1867 he could imagine Barnum's speech to Congress as an amalgam of political posturing and the promotion of his own museum of curiosities, a sideshow barker in the rotunda: "Help! help! for the stricken land! I appeal to you—and to you, sir—to every true heart in this august menagerie! Demagogues threaten the Goddess of Liberty!— they beard the starry-robed woman in her citadel! and to you the bearded woman looks for succor!" In the opening years of the twentieth century, however, he saw the starry robe of liberty as besmirched with blood and was writing such essays as "To the Person Sitting in Darkness," "The United States of Lyncherdom," "As Regards Patriotism," and "King Leopold's Soliloquy."

As Twain said of himself, he sermonized as he pleased, whether humor applied for admission or not; in most cases the humor (or at least the strategies of humor) was there, but not the hilarity. Earlier in his life he had confessed that he was "humiliated" by the fact that he was born a Southerner and that his relatives had owned slaves; now, in his unwanted recognition of U.S. policies of oppression, exploitation, and massacre, he was ashamed to be an American. He concluded his "Battle Hymn of the Republic (Brought Down to Date)," for example, with these lines set to a familiar tune:

> In a sordid slime harmonious, Greed was born in yonder ditch,
> With a longing in his bosom—and for others' goods an itch—
> As Christ died to make men holy, let men die to make us
>   rich—
> Our god is marching on.

Another consequence of his sense of loss and disillusionment was to become the despairing philosopher. Actually, that role may be too elevated a conception of his achievement, despite what Twain himself thought of the scandalous force of his convictions. In a way, he may be regarded as the village atheist for the nation. As in "Little Bessie," for example, he often chose to speak his disbelief through the uncomprehending sensibility of a child. Though the adult cynicism of Hollister probably represents Twain's mature convictions, the author was content to keep this malcontent offstage and let the child do the talking. Bessie pesters her mother with questions about pain, suffering, and death and wonders why an all-powerful God would create a depraved human race and then punish them for their frailty. Twain's cynicism here is unmistakable, but there is sympathy too—sympathy for a mother who cannot answer her daughter's questions or spare her from the doubts and pain of merely being alive; and sympathy for a child whose life in such a world is just beginning.

Twain's embrace of a mechanical determinism, latent since the late 1870s, may have served to alleviate the pain and disillusionment that are implicit in Little Bessie's questions; for if the human being is merely a machine, then one has little use for a moral sense and still less for feelings of guilt and doubt. At any rate, Twain's philosophical determinism entered more and more into his thought and expression and reached its most extensive if not its most engrossing expression in a philosophical dialogue titled *What Is Man?* and published anonymously in 1906. This exchange between a young idealist and a seasoned old man patiently demolishes cherished beliefs in personal merit, human freedom, and moral heroism and argues for the notion that man is a machine functioning mechanically according to habit and mere self-interest. This feature of Twain's thinking, however, is also expressed by a few shorter and in many ways superior pieces: "My First Lie and How I Got Out of It," "The Turning Point of My Life," and "Corn-Pone Opinions."

From very early in his literary career, Twain had measured public morality against the way things actually happen in life as he found it, and he got a lively humor out of the contrast. In the 1860s and '70s such tales as "The Christmas Fireside," "The Story of the Good Little Boy Who Did Not Prosper," and "Life as I Find It" were meant to ridicule the way popular sentiment assigned the fates of good and bad little boys to some superintending and wise power. At the end of his life he was asked to recall the most important influences upon him. Twain had the opportunity to portray himself as a good little boy come at last to well-deserved prosperity and fame. To his credit, he resisted.

In "The Turning Point of My Life," Twain traced the origin of his successful literary career not to early acquaintance with scripture or the wise counsel of the town patriarch or even to a patient and attentive mother, but to a case of measles he had contracted when he was twelve years old. Circumstance and temperament rule our lives and carve our fates, he argued, not character and virtue. At the very moment when he might easily indulge his own strong yearning for public approval and make himself the hero of his own life, he wrote instead: "And so I do not admire the human being— as an intellectual marvel—as much as I did when I was young, and got him out of books, and did not know him personally." Similarly, in "Corn-Pone Opinions," he elaborated upon the remembered remark of a slave he had known as a child: "You tell me whar a man gits his corn-pone, en I'll tell what his 'pinions is." Out of this bit of folk wisdom he worked up a succinct but full-blown mechanistic account of human behavior. Our most precious convictions and our most original thoughts have their source in the base human desire for self-approval and look to public opinion and other forms of outside influence for their justification.

Finally, Twain's comedy, if not altogether nihilistic, addressed ponderous themes and perennial subjects that outstripped the resources of satire and humor and addressed them in ways that choked off laughter. In *The Innocents Abroad* he represented himself as a buffoon standing before the tomb of Adam and weeping at the loss of this family relative he had never known. Thirty-five years later, his wife and one of his daughters already in the grave, he imagined Eve standing over the body of her son Abel. This original parent is a true innocent, slightly amazed by the audacity of her situation. There is no hilarity in the imagined loss of a child or in Eve acquiring for us all the first knowledge of death: "We cannot wake him! With my arms clinging about him I have looked in his eyes, through the veil of my tears, and begged for one little word, and he will not answer. Oh, is it that long sleep—is it death?" This moment is affecting, but it is Satan who has the last word: "Death has entered the world, the creatures are perishing; one of the Family is fallen. . . . The Family think ill of death—they will change their minds."

Satan was right. Clemens moved to his new house in Redding, Connecticut, with such family as remained to him in 1908. He wanted to name the house "Innocence at Home," but his daughter Clara persuaded him to name it "Stormfield," after Twain's sympathetic sea captain who had sailed to heaven but entered at the wrong port. Clara spent little time at Stormfield and would be married and removed to Europe by the end of the next year. What innocence was left in the home of Samuel Clemens consisted almost entirely in the person of his daughter Jean, but she died of an epileptic seizure the day before Christmas in 1909. Twain wrote "The Death of Jean" sitting close by her body, "writing, busying myself, to keep my heart from breaking," he said.

"The Death of Jean" is an inventory of the subtractions from life that come with old age. There is deep grief in the essay, but not a loss of perspective. Twain knows he must learn to live alone and without love, and he knows as well that his sorrow is self-indulgence. But he does not wish his daughter back, even to satisfy his sense of emptiness: "In her loss I am almost bankrupt, and my life is bitterness, but I am content; for she has been enriched with the most precious of all gifts—that gift which makes all other gifts mean and poor—death." The following April, Samuel Clemens himself died at Stormfield.

It was peace and innocence, a final innocence, that Clemens detected in the face of his dead daughter: "How lovable she looks, how sweet and how tranquil! It is a noble face, and full of dignity; and that was a good heart that lies there so still." Only a few months later, William Dean Howells would read the features of a dead friend and detect in Clemens that same dignity of expression, and something more: "I looked a moment at the face I knew so well; and it was patient with the patience I had so often seen in it: something of puzzle, a great silent dignity, an assent to what must be from the depths of a nature whose tragical seriousness broke in the laughter which the unwise took for the whole of him." We can never have the whole of him now, but it would be truly unwise to neglect those unequal portions Samuel Clemens left behind under an assumed name—"Mark Twain."

VIII

The Short Stories of Ambrose Bierce

Herman Melville once complained that he would likely be known to posterity, if at all, as the man who had lived among cannibals. The substance and interest of his fiction insured him against such a fate. Ambrose Bierce has not been so fortunate. He is popularly known as the man who in old age walked into Mexico to accompany Pancho Villa's army and was never heard from again, only incidentally known as the author of *The Devil's Dictionary* and several exquisite short stories, and hardly known at all as a prolific writer whose collected works filled twelve substantial volumes. His final, and presumably fatal, gesture is romantic, I suppose, but it is also absurd. Besides, no one really knows where and how Bierce died. He might well have been engineering one last literary hoax; some scholars think so, and he was capable of such deception. The mystery of his last days is at least vividly obscure, but it has tended to eclipse the steadier certainties of the life he did lead.

The final image of him is ridiculous; he becomes something of an inverted Don Quixote—a seventy-one-year-old asthmatic huffing and puffing through the Mexican deserts chasing after an army whose politics, if he ever considered them, he would have deplored, more intent on putting himself in harm's way than tilting at windmills, to be sure, but perversely idealistic nonetheless. But Ambrose Bierce was not a ridiculous man, and the life he lived was more interesting and more substantial than its flamboyant and perhaps imagined conclusion. Though his fiction is not autobiographical in the way that Melville's is, Bierce's actual life does shed light on the themes and techniques of his imaginative writing. For that reason, it is worthwhile to linger over his biography before commenting on the achievement of his short fiction.

It was Gen. William Tecumseh Sherman who observed that "War is Hell." Ambrose Bierce, who had seen much of the same war and often closer at hand than Sherman himself, defined the subject somewhat differently in *The Devil's Dictionary:* "War, *n.* A by-product of the arts of peace. The most menacing political condition is a period of international amity. . . . War loves to come like a thief in the night; professions of eternal amity provide the night." The authority of Sherman's remark, we must suppose, derives from sad experience. Bierce's is founded on the jaundiced coupling of abstractions uttered in a tone of weary urbanity and says a great deal more about the persona of the cynical lexicographer than it does about war or peace. This is to be expected of a man who has acquired (among other sinister sobriquets) the title "Bitter Bierce."

Despite ample and fine biographical treatment of the man, Ambrose Gwinett Bierce remains, and will perhaps always remain, something of a mystery. It is not at all clear, at any rate, how much of his supposed bitterness was temperamental and how much contrived, and it is easy to overestimate the depth of his resentment. We know, for example, that, apart from his devotion to his brother Albert, Ambrose was not particularly attached to or even fond of his family. We know as well that in his *Collected Works* he reserved a section of one volume for stories gathered together under the title "The Parenticide Club." Whether these two facts, taken together, make a third is less certain. Judging from the tone of two stories from that section ("My Favorite Murder" and "Oil of Dog"), the thought of parenticide provided the occasion for tall-tale humor and grisly fun and nothing more. And as the reader will soon discover, much of the shock and affecting pathos of his serious short fiction derives from the loss of some family member—a wife, a twin brother, a father, a mother. Bierce knew how to play to his reader's sensitivities, even though he did not necessarily share them himself.

Though the narrator of "My Favorite Murder" is accused of murdering his mother, his legal defense is that that crime pales in comparison with the way he murdered his uncle. This is purely antic fiction, and we know, as yet another fact, that Ambrose preferred his successful and relatively worldly uncle Lucius to his pious and bookish father, Marcus, and certainly bore his uncle no ill will. Lucius Versus Bierce had come west to Ohio from Connecticut in 1815, and his younger brother Marcus had followed him a few years later. He had almost immediately embarked on plans for self-improvement, adventure, and self-advancement. He participated in the illegal Patriot's War to rescue Canada from British domination and thereafter was known as "General Bierce." He escaped conviction for violating U.S. neutrality laws and, in fact, was eventually elected the mayor of Akron.

The writer's father, Marcus Aurelius Bierce, by contrast, came west to a religious settlement known as "Horse Cave" in Meigs County, Ohio, and it was there that Ambrose was born on June 24, 1842. While the uncle enjoyed a flamboyant popularity, the father eked out an obscure living on farms, first in Ohio and, after 1846, in Indiana. It is not surprising that Ambrose might attempt to emulate the uncle and scorn the father.

Bierce attended a poor country school in Indiana and apparently from an early age rejected the dour religious conviction of his family and surrounding community. Many years later he would define *faith* as "belief without evidence in what is told by one who speaks without knowledge, of things without parallel." However, in his youth he had neither the opportunity nor the literary sophistication to express this sort of contempt. His uncle paved the way to both, perhaps, when he sent his nephew to the Kentucky Military Institute in 1859, for the curriculum there was a demanding one and the previously recalcitrant boy proved to be an able student.

Like another supposedly rebellious spirit, Edgar Allan Poe, with whom he is so often compared, Bierce seems to have responded to—even liked— soldierly discipline and decorum. Surely it was at the military institute that he acquired the military bearing that characterized him for the remainder of his life. It appears that he also received more than adequate training in topographical engineering; the surviving maps that he made during the Civil War reveal either a natural talent for or thorough training in draftsmanship. In either case, Bierce's alert responsiveness to natural contours and spatial relationships, so necessary to map making, would serve him well in the war and also in his short fiction.

Bierce returned to Indiana from the military institute later the same year. He was eager for the sort of adventure and experience that was unavailable to him there, however, and spent his time performing odd jobs with little enthusiasm. A national emergency supplied him with a personal opportunity. When the Civil War broke out, the young man enlisted as a private in the Indiana Ninth Brigade for three months' service, ample time, it was believed, to put down the insurrectionists to the south. His entrance into the conflict does not seem to have been prompted by a principled political interest in preserving the Union so much as by the sort of fiery idealism that motivated his uncle to "liberate" Canada. Even so, during his first brief tour of duty, which consisted mostly of skirmishes or minor battles, Bierce established his courage by risking his life to rescue a fallen comrade.

After the three-month term had expired, the Ninth Brigade was reorganized for a three-year tour of duty (the revised estimate of the time necessary to end the war) and Bierce reenlisted as a sergeant. His brigade returned to the Cheat Mountains of western Virginia, where he again saw minor action. When his brigade was assigned to the Army of the Ohio, Bierce was destined to experience the horror of battle on a grand scale. The Army of the Ohio, under the command of Gen. Don Carlos Buell, was ordered to join Grant's Army of the Tennessee for assault on the Confederate railroad center in Corinth, Mississippi. However, the Confederate General A. S. Johnston launched his own offensive against Grant on April 6 at Pittsburg Landing, Tennessee, a day before the Army of the Ohio arrived. The engagement became known as the Battle of Shiloh, after the name of a small chapel in the area. In an essay, "What I Saw of Shiloh," Bierce remarks upon the irony: "The fact of a Christian church . . . giving name to a wholesale cutting of Christian throats by Christian hands need not be dwelt on here; the frequency of its recurrence in the history of our species has somewhat abated the moral interest that would otherwise attach to it."

As the war progressed, Bierce rose through the ranks, eventually to first lieutenant, and he was present at many of the fiercest engagements of the war. In the Battle of Shiloh, the Ninth Indiana alone lost 170 men. The total figures are staggering: Federal soldiers killed or wounded, 13,047; Confederates, 10,694. Other engagements in which Bierce saw action were at least as brutal. The Battle of Stones River (January 1863): Federal soldiers killed or wounded, 9,532; Confederates, 9,239. The Battle of Chickamauga (September 1863): Federal soldiers killed or wounded, 16,170; Confederates, 18,454. He was also present at other bloody encounters, as violent if not so epic: Missionary Ridge; Pickett's Mill (which he later described as "criminal" for its mismanagement); much of Sherman's campaign for Atlanta, which, as the army moved southward, produced a steady torrent of death (in a single month, over twenty thousand men from both sides were killed); a skirmish at Kennesaw Mountain (where Bierce himself received a near fatal injury from a sniper's bullet requiring three months' convalescence); and the Battles of Franklin and Nashville.

Bierce had entered the war a boy of nineteen. When it was over he was still young; though, as his Civil War memoirs repeatedly lament, he had also left his youth somewhere behind him. He had witnessed the grotesqueries of war, but he had also observed the fear, spite, arrogance, and stupidity of human conduct, alongside transcendent acts of valor and self-sacrifice. He had dutifully followed orders from on high, though he at times privately thought them ill-informed or misguided. He had been seriously wounded, and, briefly, he had been a prisoner of war. He acquired a lifelong respect for Generals Buell and William Hazen, under whom he had served and who in Bierce's estimation had been unfairly rebuked, and something less than respect for Generals Sherman and Grant, who enjoyed the nation's favor.

And he had experienced the unthinkable. In the Cheat Mountains of western Virginia, for example, he witnessed an event that would find its way into the disturbing tale "The Coup de Grâce." One day his column passed the repulsive bodies of fallen soldiers, "their blank, staring eyes, their teeth uncovered by the contraction of lips." The next day, they passed the same bodies, which seemed to have altered their positions, to have shed part of their clothing, and to have lost their faces. They had been eaten by pigs. In the fiction, Bierce describes the scene this way: "Fifty yards away, on the crest of a low, thinly wooded hill, [Captain Madwell] saw several dark objects moving about the fallen men—a herd of swine. One stood with its back to him, its shoulders sharply elevated. Its forefeet were upon a human body, its head was depressed and invisible. The bristly ridge of its chine showed black against the red west. Captain Madwell drew away his eyes and fixed them again upon the thing which had been his friend." The point to be made here is that the macabre quality of Bierce's imagination often consisted in humanizing the unimaginable, not in adding contrived or ghastly detail to his fictions.

After the war, Bierce found employment but he remained without occupation. It would be years before he resolved to become a writer, but he seems to have already acquired one of the indispensable requirements, which he would declare in his essay "To Train a Writer" (1899): To the aspiring writer "a continent should not seem wide, nor a century long. And it would be needful that he know and have an ever present consciousness that this is a world of fools and rogues, blind with superstition, tormented with envy, consumed with vanity, selfish, false, cruel, cursed with illusions—frothing mad!" The peace at Appomattox, it would appear, had not abolished the depravity of his species.

For a time Bierce served as an aide for the Treasury Department in Alabama, having the unenviable duty of seizing and protecting southern cotton that the government had decided was federal property. Though evidently blameless himself, Bierce saw several instances of roguery, opportunism, and venality among his northern colleagues, and he continually faced the possibility of retributive justice of one sort or another from resentful and frustrated southerners.

Along with a deepening cynicism, he acquired at this time the asthmatic condition that plagued him for the rest of his life. For these and other reasons, Bierce may have welcomed the unexpected opportunity to join General Hazen in Omaha for a fact-finding expedition of the west. Besides, the offer carried with it the promise of a captaincy. Through no fault of Hazen's, the commission eventually offered him was for a second lieutenancy, but by the time Bierce received this news he was in San Francisco. Bierce indignantly refused the commission and left the army for good, but he was to remain in California for many years.

He took a job as a night watchman at the subtreasury building in 1867, and it was about this time that he undertook to transform himself into a professional writer. Bierce approached the project with the sort of discipline he would years later advise in "To Train a Writer"—reading widely, especially in the classics, sharpening his perceptions and attempting to think clearly, and, if any were left to him, "dispelling his illusions and destroying his ideals." His literary debut was the publication of a poem in the *Californian*. Though he continued to write poetry for the rest of his life and published two volumes of satirical verse, *Black Beetles in Amber* (1892) and *Shapes of Clay* (1903), he concluded early that his métier was not as a poet and directed his energies toward the writing of prose.

Apart from the novel, which Bierce considered a "short story padded," he proved to be capable in a variety of genres—the essay, the sketch, the fable, the satire, the tall tale, and of course the short story. He was soon publishing pieces in local periodicals, and when he was offered the opportunity to edit the *San Francisco News Letter* he gave up his job at the Treasury and began to write the "Town Crier" column. Later, he offered Bret Harte some of his essays that were rather more serious than the satiric journalism he was contributing to the *News Letter*. They were published in the *Overland Monthly*, and it was in that periodical that Bierce published his first piece of short fiction in 1871. It was in that year, too, that he married Mollie Day, the daughter of a prosperous miner.

In a relatively brief time, Ambrose Bierce had found his calling, trained himself as a writer, infiltrated San Francisco literary circles, and married above his station. For a man who, by all odds, should have lived out his days as the village atheist of Elkhart, Indiana, Bierce had succeeded mightily. His "Town Crier" column had acquired some reputation as far east as

New York and London, his popularity in Britain rivaling that of Bret Harte and Joaquin Miller. This was propitious, for the bride's father promised to send the newlyweds to England as a wedding present. Bierce resigned from the *News Letter* and the couple left the city in the early spring of 1872.

He instantly became so fond of the mother country, and perhaps of the English fondness for him as well, that he remained there for three years. Often using the pen name "Dod Grile," he wrote for *Figaro* and *Fun*. Bierce began to socialize with the Fleet Street crowd and established a close friendship with the humorist Tom Hood. Bierce's first three books were published in England—*The Fiend's Delight* (1873), *Nuggets and Dust* (1873), and *Cobwebs from an Empty Skull* (1874)—and the first two of his three children were born there. His expatriation, in other words, was altogether agreeable, and he might have remained in England indefinitely, but his wife, who had returned home for a visit, wired him that she was pregnant with their third child. Somewhat reluctantly, he sailed for America in September 1875.

Now a father with three children, Bierce was faced with beginning to build a career once again, and he seems to have taken a more calculated interest in the project than he had when he first arrived in San Francisco. He became the associate editor of the *Argonaut,* a periodical with a definite political agenda in mind, and to write his "Prattle" column, which sometimes contradicted the purposes of the owners. Under the pseudonym "William Herman," Bierce and T. A. Harcourt published *The Dance of Death* (1877), which purported to condemn the waltz on moral grounds, but did so in suggestive, almost lurid detail. Whether this literary hoax was intended to succeed in commercial as well as antic terms is unclear, but it became something of a best-seller, and Bierce himself helped sales along by damning the book in the *Argonaut.*

In 1879, Bierce abruptly retired from the literary life and removed to the Black Hills of the Dakota Territory. Perhaps his move can be explained because he did not get along with Frank Pixley, the founder of the *Argonaut;* perhaps it was because the San Francisco of the 1870s had become in the words of his biographer Carey McWilliams "magnificent, dull and empty"; or perhaps it was because Bierce, with three young children to support, was seeking a more stable financial future. In any case, he served as a mining engineer in Rockerville and planned to have his family join him there in the not-too-distant future. This undertaking ought to have been immensely profitable to Bierce and to the company for which he worked, but ineptitude, spite, and knavery worked together to spoil the venture. Despite charges of corruption and mismanagement, Bierce, as he had done in Alabama after the war, performed his duties honestly and honorably. According to Paul Fatout, who has exhaustively charted Bierce's experience in the Dakotas, he was the ablest businessman and miner in the entire company. For a man whose motto was "Nothing matters," it is nevertheless apparent that his personal sense of integrity mattered deeply to him. Whether Bierce's conduct proceeded from principled idealism or from a feeling for what he owed himself is not clear.

Back in San Francisco, or rather nearby, since his asthma troubled him there more than at higher elevations, the journalist worked five years for the *Wasp,* where he resumed his "Prattle" column. By 1886 he was out of work once again, however. The entrance into his life of the young publisher of the *San Francisco Examiner,* William Randolph Hearst, was fortuitous. Bierce suddenly had a regular income, a certain autonomy that allowed him to work out of the city, and, though the two men were often in decided disagreement, considerable freedom from editorial intervention. From 1887 until 1899, when he left to live in the east, Bierce worked for Hearst in, if not absolute contentment, at least productive stability.

Unfortunately, it was during this period also that his domestic life disintegrated. He separated from his wife in 1888; the next year his son Day was killed in a gun duel. How much or little the combination of hard-won professional success and personal disappointment and grief installed within him the productive tensions necessary for his art is impossible to say. Regardless, it is a fact that these same years saw the creation of much of his best work. He continued to fashion what would become his notorious *The Devil's Dictionary* (1911), though it first appeared as *The Cynic's Word Book* (1906). More important, Bierce wrote a remarkable number of short stories in a relatively brief time, enough, in fact, to publish two volumes in successive years. *Tales of Soldiers and Civilians* was published simultaneously in England as *In the Midst of Life* in 1892; his tales of the supernatural, *Can Such Things Be?* was published in 1893.

The titles of these two collections are perhaps indicative of the high literary ambitions the author had for them. No doubt a British audience for his volume of Civil War stories would possess neither the fund of fairly recent memories of a national conflict nor a casual acquaintance with the place, occasion, or seriousness (both political and symbolic) of the war. It was likely for that reason that the English edition was published under the title *In the Midst of Life,* though it is unclear whether the change was the decision of Bierce or his publishers, Chatto and Windus. In any event, the phrase is taken from the funeral service in the Anglican Book of Common Prayer: "In the midst of life, we are in death." The change in title gave his volume of tales the force of spiritual parable and freed it from the historical associations it would have had for an American audience. His collection of supernatural tales, on the other hand, took its title from *Macbeth.* Shortly after the appearance of Banquo's ghost, Macbeth exclaims to Lady Macbeth:

> Can such things be,
> And overcome us like a summer's cloud,
> Without our special wonder? You make me strange
> Even to the disposition I owe,
> When now I think you can behold such sights
> And keep the natural ruby of your cheeks,
> When mine is blanch'd with fear. (*Macbeth* 3.4)

Whether or not the Shakespearean allusion also conveys something of the misogyny that is sometimes attributed to him, Bierce at least meant to suggest the moral dilemma that is implicit in much of his supernatural writing as well as to insist upon the literary merits of the genre.

Circumstances did not immediately conspire in favor of the author's ambitions, however. Though both collections of short fiction were favorably reviewed in America and England, the failures of publishing houses deferred at least in financial terms the success he may have anticipated. The reissue of an enlarged edition of *In the Midst of Life* in 1898 did something to correct the imbalance. Meantime, he enjoyed being the center of San Francisco literary circles. He gave a great deal of time and energy to aspiring young writers without compromising his severe critical standards; in return he typically received unqualified admiration from his pupils. In rather altered terms, Bierce occupied the position of a Dr. Johnson, whom he respected and admired, or a William Dean Howells, whom he did not. Still, the satisfaction he had once taken in the San Francisco literary life had diminished considerably by the end of the century. Bierce seemed to welcome the change Hearst provided by sending him east. He moved to Washington, where prior experience had demonstrated to him that he was relatively free from his asthmatic condition.

Bierce's duties there were not onerous, and he made several short trips to nearby cities, including New York where his remaining son lived. He moved in military circles now, and he visited more than once the Civil War battlefields he had known in an earlier life. When Bierce indulged himself in the memoir, and in dramatic contrast to his war fiction, he could become romantic. He concludes "What I Saw of Shiloh" in a tone of dismay and nostalgic grace: "Is it not strange that the phantoms of a blood-stained period have so airy a grace and look with so tender eyes?—that I recall with difficulty the danger and deaths and horrors of the time, and without effort all that was gracious and picturesque? Ah Youth, there is no such wizard as thou! Give me but one touch of thine artist hand upon the dull canvas of the Present . . . and I will willingly surrender an other life than the one that I should have thrown away at Shiloh." It is not so very surprising that Bierce should seek out one last battlefield, this time in Mexico, and to throw away his life.

No doubt the debate about whether Bierce was suicidal will continue. It is rather more certain that in the beginning years of the new century he was contemplating final things. He was several times seriously ill and, it seemed, surrounded by death and sickness. His remaining son, Leigh, died of pneumonia in 1901; soon after, his daughter, Helen, contracted typhoid fever and nearly died herself; and his estranged wife, Mollie, died the same year. As for Ambrose Bierce, he was busily tying up loose ends. Thanks to the admiring support of the publisher Walter Neale, Bierce was able to bequeath to anyone who remained interested a handsome edition of *The Collected Works of Ambrose Bierce*. For four years, from 1908 to 1912, he worked diligently on what eventually became a twelve-volume set. He transferred his cemetery plot in California to his daughter in 1913 and soon thereafter announced to a friend in a letter, "I'd hate to die between two sheets, and, God willing, I won't." In October 1913 he left Washington. Once again he toured the battle sites of his youth and then moved on to New Orleans, San Antonio, Laredo, and finally El Paso. Apparently he acquired in Juarez the necessary papers that would permit him to accompany Pancho Villa's army (though this is by no means certain), and by late December he was in Mexico. He was never heard from again; this much is certain.

When we turn to Bierce's short fiction, it is wise to make some necessary distinctions. First, there is an organizing principle inherent in the tables of contents of his *Collected Works*. Ambrose Bierce did not make the sorts of confusions that some of his later anthologizers have. "A Tough Tussle," for example, though it takes place on a Civil War battlefield, is not really a war story. It was first published in *Can Such Things Be?* and because he kept it in that volume in the *Collected Works*, we must conclude that he always considered it a tale of the supernatural. "Jupiter Doke, Brigadier-General" is not a war story, either, but a pointed comic satire, and one of his best in that vein. I do not pretend to know what Bierce had in mind when he grouped this and other stories together under the rubric "Negligible Tales," but Bierce was as capable of false modesty as he was of audacious and fierce independence. Finally, tales of the supernatural ("The Realm of the Unreal," for example) should not be confused with ghost stories (such as "An Arrest"). Again, I am not sure that I always recognize the distinctions he was making, but the perils of contradicting a man who insisted that he knew what he was doing and why remain long after the threat of his lacerating wit has vanished.

Ambrose Bierce was such a deliberate maverick that other distinctions that may not at first seem momentous or even real are also in order. As a critic, he was not critical but opinionated (as the title of volume 10 of the *Collected Works, The Opinionator,* clearly indicates). In his essay "On Literary Criticism," he demonstrates just how little patience he has for those critics who "read between the lines," discover in this vacancy the author's true "purpose," and present it as a "problem" that the author has attempted to "solve." He had labels for such critics—"microcephalous bibliopomps," "strabismic ataxiates," and the like. (Is it any wonder that H. L. Mencken should find the man so appealing?) Bierce was not a humorist, either, but a satirist (though he freely acknowledged that a republican form of government could not sustain or encourage satire). He was not a comedian, but a wit (though his tall tales are sometimes extremely funny and his wit often more wry than biting). "Wit," he wrote, "may make us smile, or make us wince, but laughter—that is the cheaper price that we pay for an inferior entertainment, namely humor." So self-defined, he proclaims his superiority over and prohibits comparisons to men he knew and more or less liked—Bret Harte and Mark Twain.

Bierce professed to despise the novel and novelists. Following Poe, he argued that because a novel could not be read at a single sitting it could not achieve a single, unified aesthetic effect. Curiously, he held the romances of Scott and Hawthorne to no such standard. As for the novel, however, he believed that the legitimacy of the form died (depending on his mood) with Fielding and Richardson and surely survived no later than Thackeray. (By fiat, down go Howells and James.) More specifically, he had no use for realism and realists. He defined *realism* in *The Devil's Dictionary:* "The art of depicting nature as it is seen by toads. The charm suffusing a landscape painted by a mole, or a story written by a measuring worm." (Nevertheless, Stephen Crane and Ernest Hemingway responded to the disturbing realism of Bierce's war stories.) He was neither regionalist nor local colorist, though he sometimes acted as apologist for California writers and was capable of at least competent dialect writing. Still, he objected to the "corn-fed enthusiasm of the prairies" and thus dismissed Hamlin Garland with finality.

Bierce was American to his fingertips and trafficked in that national identity when he was in England, but he also announced that a "'distinctively American literature' has not materialized, excepting in the works of Americans distinctively illiterate." He scoffed at the idea of originality and exalted excellence in established forms, but his own fiction is often rightly described as experimental, and he rang some interesting changes on familiar genres. Like so many other writers of his day, Bierce was not above indulging in the formulaic plot twists of O. Henry or the fantastic but dramatic dilemmas of Frank Stockton. But he claimed to despise popular magazine fiction and thought its highest function was to "stir up from the shallows of its readers' understanding the sediment which they are pleased to call sentiment, murking all their mental pool and effacing the reflected images of their natural environment." He also objected to the didactic in fiction, but this was easy for someone to say who had at his disposal for most of his writing life a column in which he could be as vituperative and as didactic as he pleased.

What are we to make of these snarled and snarling convictions, and what is left standing once this freewheeling iconoclast is done smashing the false idols of his day and of the next? Not much, I suppose, but some awfully interesting fiction, interesting and distinctive enough to make the adjective *Biercean* meaningful. Besides, many of the idiosyncrasies of the man are not so very perplexing. Like many, perhaps most, autodidacts, his self-education was disciplined but not systematic, and he wears his erudition a bit too gaudily at times. Having achieved such an exacting style through severe training and determination, he could be as unforgiving as the recruit who has just made it through boot camp. His mature prose is stately and polished to an almost Augustan sheen. For that reason, perhaps, he could not resist publishing a minutely prescriptive book of usage, intended mostly for journalists and editors and rather indignantly called *Write It Right* (1909). At all events, the verbal precision he eventually acquired was brought into the service of the grotesque, the unreal, and the unthinkable, and the combination frequently resulted in superb fiction.

In his essay "The Short Story," Bierce rebels against the laws of realism, the laws "Cato Howells has given his little senate." Among those laws is that of probability. In point of fact, he insisted, life itself is improbable—motives are impenetrable, occurrences unpredictable and strange, moral imperatives perversely insufficient to human emergencies: "It is to him of widest knowledge, of deepest feeling, of sharpest observation and insight, that life is most crowded with figures of heroic stature, with spirits of dream, with demons of the pit, with graves that yawn in pathways leading to the light, with existences not of earth, both malign and benign—ministers of grace and ministers of doom." The fiction writer has no use for probability "except to make what is related *seem* probable in the reading—*seem* true." This essay was published under the heading "The Controversialist." Of course Bierce's position here is deliberately contrary and, if nothing more, serves to authorize what he had already achieved in his short fiction.

Part of the author's special competence in creating the seemingly true probably derives from his training in topological engineering, in map making, for he was capable of the dramatic rendering of spatial relations in ways that few writers of much greater talent would even attempt. The suspense and terror of "One of the Missing" or "The Man and the Snake," for example, are built up out of analogous situations. In both instances, the setting is soon organized around the fearful consciousness of a single (and supposedly fatal) focal point—the barrel of a rifle and eyes of a snake. Whether the protagonist is pinned down, as in the first instance, or transfixed, as in the second, the relation of hands, feet, furniture, and the like are depicted with the sort of minute precision that have led some critics, quite mistakenly, to label Bierce a realist. His imagination was vivid, but it was not realistic. He located the figures of his fiction in remarkably different environments with exacting attention, and he moved effortlessly from broad expanses to constricting human predicaments in ways that took the gothic out of doors or made suspense out of the stuff of sometimes accidental, sometimes providential operations.

In an autobiographical sketch that recounts his early experience of the war entitled "On a Mountain," Bierce wrote of his aesthetic appreciation of the Cheat Mountains of western Virginia. For a "flatlander" such as himself, who had grown up on the plains of Ohio and Indiana, "a mountain region was a perpetual miracle. Space seemed to have taken on a new dimension; areas to have not only length and breadth, but thickness." This same territory became the site for one of his most popular stories, "A Horseman in the Sky," and likewise depends on a talent for topographical rendering:

> The country was wooded everywhere except at the bottom of the valley to the northward, where there was a small natural meadow, through which flowed a stream scarcely visible from the valley's rim. This open ground looked hardly larger than an ordinary door-yard, but was really several acres in extent. . . . Away beyond it rose a line of giant cliffs similar to those upon which we are supposed to stand in our survey of the savage scene, and through which the road had somehow made its climb to the summit. The configuration of the valley, indeed, was such that from this point of observation it seemed entirely shut in, and one could but have wondered how the road which found a way out of it had found a way into it, and whence came and whither went the waters of the stream that parted the meadow more than a thousand feet below.

Except for the self-consciously correct prose in which this scene is cast, it might have served as one or another actual report Bierce gave his commanding officers after a reconnaissance of the territory ahead. Into this picturesque fictional scene, however, Bierce introduces an improbable moral dilemma, once again related to patricide and specific to a drowsy Union sentinel named Carter Druse. The young sentinel shoots the horse of a mounted enemy soldier perched on a cliff across the way. The still mounted soldier plummets through the air into the valley below. This horseman in the sky supplies an image both for the reader and a Federal officer below that is at once horrifying and noble, as though this "equestrian statue of impressive dignity" were ushering in some "new Apocalypse."

Bierce's talents for mapping the territory of the imagination were combined with others. Those talents, too, perhaps derived from his experience in the war. The landscape he antiseptically charts with the detachment of a surveyor often takes a subjective turn and is typically colored by the limits of perception or invested with fear and dread. The war, at least as he remembered it when he came to write short fiction, was a world apart. "How curiously we had regarded everything! how odd it all had seemed!" he wrote in "A Son of the Gods." "Nothing had appeared quite familiar; the most commonplace objects—an old saddle, a splintered wheel, a forgotten canteen—everything had related something of the mysterious personality of those strange men who had been killing us." In "A Tough Tussle," he put it another way: In the soldier's nighttime vigil, "There are sounds without a name, forms without substance, translations in space of objects which have not been seen to move, movements wherein nothing is observed to change its place. Ah, children of the sunlight and the gaslight, how little you know of the world in which you live!"

At his best, Bierce is able to synthesize these two worlds—the precisely measurable and the uncertain and unnameable—with stylistic grace. A single, clear image sometimes conveys the tension: "This night was bright enough to bite like a serpent." More often, he establishes an atmospheric apprehension. In "An Occurrence at Owl Creek Bridge," the Confederate spy about to be hanged is invested with especially acute senses, so keen that they "made record of things never before perceived": "He noted the prismatic colors in all the dewdrops upon a million blades of grass. The humming of the gnats that danced above the eddies of the stream, the beating of the dragon-flies' wings, the strokes of the water-spiders' legs, like oars which had lifted their boat—all these made audible music."

By contrast, for the child in "Chickamauga," the "haunted landscape" is vivid with light and color but eerily silent as well: "Through the belt of trees beyond the brook shone a strange red light, the trunks and branches of the trees making a black lacework against it. It struck the creeping figures and gave them monstrous shadows, which caricatured their movements on the lit grass. . . . It sparkled on buttons and bits of metal in their clothing." "An Occurrence at Owl Creek Bridge" and "Chickamauga" are very nearly perfect tales, and these descriptive passages, along with many others, serve simultaneously as clues to the final narrative disclosure and as evocations of a mental world so vividly pictured that its mysterious reality is strangely compelling.

Bierce is masterfully adroit in his management of point of view as well and carefully circumscribes how much or little he will or can share with the reader. In "One Kind of Officer," the noise of battle makes communication nearly impossible, and when a lieutenant tries to convey some urgent information to his captain, we are told in a unnervingly formal narrative voice:

"His gestures, if coolly noted by an actor, would have been pronounced to be those of protestation." "A Son of the Gods" is subtitled "A Study in the Present Tense" and takes a rather different narrative tack. It quickly becomes a form of on-the-spot reporting, the narrative perspective on a distant rider limited by his field glasses and a general uncertainty: "One moment only and he wheels right about and is speeding like the wind straight down the slope—toward his friends, toward his death! . . . [H]e is down. No, he recovers his seat; he has but pulled his horse upon its haunches. They are up and away! . . . They are down at last. But look again—the man has detached himself from the dead animal. He stands erect, motionless, holding his sabre in his right hand straight above his head. . . . It is a sign to us, to the world, to posterity. It is a hero's salute to death and history." In the voice of a ringside radio announcer (though such an analogy would necessarily be obscure to the author), Bierce has given a blow-by-blow narration in the present tense and yet before our very eyes he has converted the momentary bravery of a "military Christ" into a tale of the "pitiless perfection of the divine, eternal plan."

Bierce had a seemingly endless variety of points of view at his disposal—one narrator has received his story secondhand; another suffers from a lack of memory; another apologizes that he is "no storyteller"; others, for one reason or another, cannot hear or see. He sometimes prolongs moments and compresses eons. In "One of the Missing," we learn that "it was decreed from the beginning of time that Private Searing was not to murder anybody that bright summer morning. . . . For countless ages events had been so matching themselves together . . . that the acts which he had in will would have marred the harmony of the pattern." A few pages later, we are immersed in Searing's perilous present. He is trapped beneath a collapsed building, his own rifle barrel staring him in the face, the reader held tight to the figure's tortured consciousness: "Here in this confusion of timbers and boards is the sole universe. Here is immortality in time—each pain an everlasting life. The throbs tick off eternities."

For Bierce, the world of war is a disturbing mix of the chaotic, random, and destructive events confronted by the ordered arrangements of military rank, decorum, and protocol. The combination provides ample opportunity for irony. In many of his short stories, for example, there is the drama of a conflict of duty, and in every instance the observance of duty has its destructive consequences. In "The Story of a Conscience," Captain Hartroy orders the immediate execution of a man who had once saved his life and then quietly commits suicide. In "A Horseman in the Sky," the father commands his son to "do what you conceive to be your duty"; his duty, it so happens, requires him to kill the father. In "An Affair of Outposts," Captain Armisted saves the life of the man who has made him a cuckold, and as a consequence loses his own. Most affecting of all, in "The Affair at Coulter's Notch," the artillery officer Captain Coulter complies with the command to fire upon his own house; within are his wife and child. Related to these are stories of false pride: of the witty stoic, Parker Adderson, who borrows his courage from what he takes to be strict military observance; of Lieutenant Brayle in "Killed at Resaca," a man "vain of his courage"; or of Captain Ransome, whose wounded pride causes him to knowingly fire upon his own men, in "One Kind of Officer." These are rank offenses against the law of probability, to be sure, but they do not feel that way in the course of reading.

Bierce's tales of the supernatural, as well as his tall-tale humor, are in this sense continuous, both tonally and morally, with his war fiction, and he sometimes bent existing comic forms to match his cynicism. More than once, he wrote in the mode of the condensed novel popular among the San Francisco bohemians, including Bret Harte and Mark Twain. By reducing their "novels" to five hundred to twenty-five hundred words, complete with chapter titles, intricate plots, and thwarted love affairs, these humorists meant to burlesque the sentimental romance. Bierce used the same form, but he was not very much interested in parodic comedy. Instead he used chapter titles to deepen the irony of the events or to give them the effect of sinister parable. One chapter title reads, "How to Play the Cannon without Notes"; another advises, "When You Have Lost Your Life Consult a Physician"; yet another observes, "One Does Not Always Eat What Is on the Table," followed by a description of the local coroner examining a corpse.

Nor was Bierce the only California writer known for irreverence and verbal assault. Western journalism was notoriously fierce and coarsely comic, but his invective had little of the mischievous or the antic in it, and his comedy was so outlandishly grotesque (as in "Oil of Dog" or "A Revolt of the Gods") that it makes one a little bit ashamed to laugh. Bierce seemed intent on outdoing the competition, if only to maintain a cranky independence from the rest. He did not altogether succeed in keeping his admirers at bay, however. He disdained the role of humorist, but Mark Twain included several of his animal fables in his *Library of American Humor*

(1888). He pilloried William Dean Howells, and when he learned that Howells had declared him one of America's three greatest writers, Bierce's acceptance of the compliment was less than gracious: "I am sure Mr. Howells is the other two." Nevertheless, Howells saw fit to include "An Occurrence at Owl Creek Bridge" in his *Great Modern American Stories* (1920).

At times Bierce even distanced himself from the terms of his own fiction, and of his own experience. In the 1870s, Bierce and Tom Hood made a pact, probably as a gesture of the depth of their friendship, that the first to die should attempt to contact the other. Shortly after Hood died in 1875, Bierce reported that he met the spirit of his old friend and had the "evidence of my own senses" as affirmation of the fact. A few years later, in the *Argonaut* he dismissed the experience by saying that "the senses fool one another," that "sight is translated into sound, or sudden and strong mental impressions are mistaken for tactual ones."

This brush with the world beyond would provide the basis for his story "The Damned Thing." However, there he gave yet another account of the presence of a spirit—the malevolent presence was of a color that the human eye is unable to discern. Bierce was fond of explaining his mysteries away by scientific or quasi-scientific theory, only to repudiate that explanation in its turn. In "A Tough Tussle," Second-Lieutenant Byring decides that his fear of the supernatural is not unusual; superstitious dread has been passed on generation after generation since the beginning of the human race and will require yet another ten thousand years to outgrow. But the final disclosure in the tale casts doubt on this view. In "Moxon's Master," Bierce uses Herbert Spencer's mechanistic definition of *life* as the intellectual rationale for the creation of an automaton chess player, but that theory cannot quite explain why the machine is a sore loser.

Ambrose Bierce may have deserved every epithet applied to him—"wicked," "bitter," "cynical," and the like. I rather suspect he enjoyed his reputation, however; notoriety is for certain temperaments more fun than fame. He seemed to seize upon every opportunity for an irony, at any rate, as if it were some delicious morsel to be savored. He seemed to delight in his ability to make us squirm. If he preferred wit to humor, it was because he preferred to make his readers wince, not laugh. "Haïta the Shepherd" and "A Bivouac of the Dead" are rare examples of what can be described as poignant. Most of his short stories are shocking, horrifying, or unnerving; they are sometimes moving, but on the author's terms, not our own.

Despite all the disconcerting grotesqueries in his short fiction, composed it would appear with malice aforethought, I doubt we are ever tempted to think of Bierce as despairing. There is too much self-evident care and attention given to the style and cadence of his prose to really believe that nothing mattered to him, and there is too much fierce indignation for us to really believe he was beyond being morally offended. In keeping with his cynical persona, Bierce once defined *happiness* as "An agreeable sensation arising from contemplating the misery of another." Given the world he knew, or thought he knew, and the myriad ways he so vividly pictured that world for his readers, I suppose Bierce must have had his share of happiness.

IX

Realism, the "Real," and the Poet of Reality

Some Reflections on American Realists
and the Poetry of Wallace Stevens

I

American realism, as Edwin H. Cady pointed out some time ago, has "nothing special to do with 'reality' as such."[1] Rather, it is founded on what he terms a "Common Vision," is rooted in and takes its authority from some shared sense of experience. That experience, democratically available to innumerable readers who look on life directly and bring their knowledge of it to literature, invests the common man and woman, so Howells believed, with a true standard for the arts. The task and achievement of the realist writer in these terms is to render faithful expressions of life, and the literary results are recognized to be "realistic" fictions by a kind of unspoken consensus or mean averaging of individual experience; or rather, to speak a bit less sociologically, we as readers acknowledge the "realistic" by means of close and repeated acquaintance with those intersecting interests and internal adjustments to life that make cooperative living possible.

The "real" of American realism, therefore, is somehow mysteriously available and communicable in ways that are tied to, yet strangely independent of, individual experience and private perception. So understood, realism enjoys a privilege akin to what philosophers call apodictic certainty, akin to but not identical with such certainty because realism does not rest so much on logical demonstration as on repeated familiar experience. Two minds may be found to be coterminous and coalesce in the same world of objects, observed William James, and he named this commonsense view

1. Edwin H. Cady, *The Light of Common Day: Realism in American Fiction* (Bloomington: Indiana University Press, 1971), 15.

a "natural realism."[2] Jones blows on his candle, and my candle goes out; Jones pulls on one end of a rope and I on another—our hands and the rope also are mutual objects in this experience. I find "over and over again" that your objects are the same as mine and am constantly reassured that our minds meet in a shared world (*RE*, 38–39).

It is only in this way that Henry James's observation that the real "represents to my perception the things we cannot possibly *not* know, sooner or later, in one way or another" makes much sense. So defined, the "real" is merely one of the "accidents of our hampered state."[3] The language of James's familiar definition is typically precise and discrete. The *real*, those things we cannot not know, is nevertheless *represented to his perception*; it is the by-product of being alive, an accident. It is, alas, what we all have somehow agreed to settle for, to act upon and be actuated by. The real, so considered, may be subsumed under the large category of impressions James once insisted he would fight for.

The other *real*—that is, the reality philosophers, psychologists, and scientists, each in his or her own way, pursue and attempt to define or to manage—always outruns us. At hazard in such a pursuit, as Cady remarks, and in the very attempt to possess it, is the possibility that we may forfeit a common vision, lose all "sense of direct connection to experience."[4] This was the danger William James detected in the philosophical atmosphere of the day; the debate between "tenderminded" idealists and "toughminded" materialists left most men and women caught in the cross fire. This is "your dilemma," he told his readers in "The Present Dilemma in Philosophy": "you find the two parts of your *quaesitum* hopelessly separated. You find empiricism with inhumanism and irreligion; or else you find a rationalistic philosophy that indeed may call itself religious, but that keeps out of all definite touch with concrete facts and joys and sorrows."[5] Pursued to one side, the side of Berkeleyean idealism, and our lives may become what William James elsewhere called a "congeries of solipsisms" (*RE*, 37–38),

2. William James, "A World of Pure Experience," in *Essays in Radical Empiricism,* ed. Frederick H. Burkhardt et al. (Cambridge: Harvard University Press, 1976), 39–40. Citations from this volume are hereafter cited in the text with the abbreviation *RE*.

3. Henry James, preface to *The American,* in *The Art of the Novel: Critical Prefaces* (New York: Charles Scribner's Sons, 1962), 31.

4. Cady, *Light of Common Day,* 16.

5. William James, *Pragmatism, and Four Essays from "The Meaning of Truth,"* ed. Ralph Barton Perry (Cleveland: World Publishing, 1955), 26–27. Citations from this volume are hereafter cited in the text with the abbreviation *P.*

or at best remote from actual experience and living interests; pursued to the other, as Henry James observed, and we risk having our impressions "impaled" on the naturalist's pin.

The stance American realism took, like pragmatism itself, was a "meliorist" position, halfway between brute fact and hovering ideal, the place where most men and women conduct their lives. Nestled in the heart of realism, and to some degree constituting its "problem," however, was "the real." This, to anticipate my conclusion, is really the only point I wish to make here, that the real was the worm in the heart of realism. American realism, in its minute attention and careful loyalty to experience as lived, prepared the way for its own succession. As realism moved in the direction of the psychologism of Henry James, it prepared for some versions of literary modernism. But there was another path it might take, one mapped out by William James. As the psychologist/philosopher contemplated the nature of what he termed "pure experience," he advanced upon the real, moving from his pragmatism to his pluralism and on to his radical empiricism, moving ever more closely to a neoromantic attitude.[6]

It was this second path that Wallace Stevens took, and it helps to explain why Stevens could claim to be a poet of reality but cannot without some distortion be called a realist poet. Moreover, in his insistence that poetry helps us "to live our lives," he held on to the Howellsian belief in the practical value of imaginative literature and attacked the sentimental and the positivistic with a "poetry of the earth." Stevens's aesthetic program was an attempt to keep the connections to experience, to resist the dangerous "pressure of an external event or events on the consciousness to the exclusion of any power of contemplation."[7]

Something of the same peril is represented by Henry James in *The American Scene* (1907). In the midst of his witnessing the aspects of "our vast, crude democracy of trade" there are momentary violations of the usual mad activity that make them "really precarious and rare," "lonely ec-

6. By placing emphasis on and giving metaphysical weight to "affectional facts," or feelings, James was aware of the romantic implications of his notion of "pure experience." The New Realists, including his former student, Ralph Barton Perry, urged the link between his pragmatism and "natural realism," but James himself did not see or was not interested in the connection. See Herbert W. Schneider, *Sources of Contemporary Philosophical Realism in America* (Indianapolis: Bobbs-Merrill, 1964), 15–16.

7. Wallace Stevens, *The Necessary Angel: Essays on Reality and the Imagination* (New York: Vintage, 1942), 20. Hereafter cited in the text with the abbreviation *NA*.

stasies" that often make up for the hustle and bustle and altogether too hasty quality of American life.[8] Throughout *The American Scene* it sometimes seems as though James might really have to "go to the stake" (*AS*, xxv) for his impressions, that he stands "upon a builded breakwater against the assault of matters demanding a *literal* notation":

> I walked, at the best, on the breakwater—looking down, if one would, over the flood of the real, but much more occupied with the sight of old Cambridge ghosts, who seemed to advance one by one, even at that precarious eminence, to meet me. (*AS*, 68)

There should have been no surprise for James that he was thus caught between his memories of the country he had left (memories now some twenty years old) and his immediate perceptions, and that both had somehow been rendered at once apposite and yet indifferent one to the other. That is the stance he takes in his book and that constitutes part of the value of his depiction of American life. His memories are discontinuous with the experience of the real, and his perceptions, to borrow the language of his brother, are as a rule neither warm nor intimate. Worse, both the common vision and the private impression are perpetually at risk. The continuity of experience dissolves in the fluxional character of American life and asks for, at best, "literal" notation rather than imaginative rendering. But a few authentic moments may be retrieved: In the United States,

> where the pleasure of contemplation is concerned, discretion is the better part of valour and insistence too often a betrayal. It is not so much that the hostile fact crops up as that the friendly fact breaks down. If you have luckily *seen*, you have seen; carry off your prize, in this case, instantly and at any risk. . . . These things demand that your exposed object shall exist; and to exist for exposure is to be at the best impaled on the naturalist's pin. (*AS*, 411)

James's recommendation here is almost if not quite for a retreat from public understanding and a common possession of shared experience, a retreat from realism to the real.

---

8. Henry James, *The American Scene* (Bloomington: Indiana University Press, 1968), 67. Hereafter cited in the text with the abbreviation *AS*.

James, as the "restless analyst" of American life in the first years of the twentieth century, in the final, scolding passages of *The American Scene,* delivers himself of his final "big" impression—that the "leaps and bounds" of the American spirit are motivated by an inward impatience and realized in an outward clumsiness. While he is seated beside the large square of plate glass in a "missionary Pullman," the occasion itself prompts the observation. The Pullman is "the great symbolic agent" for "all the irresponsibility behind it" and the great expanse of the level floor of the land outside is the "material opportunity" on which Americans have contrived a "devil's dance" of prosperity in the service of the superficial and the raw. As he rides over the land, the irony of his situation is complete. He is forced to "'slang' it for relief of the o'erfraught heart":

> "Oh, for a split or a chasm, one groans beside your plate-glass, oh for an unbridgeable abyss or an insufferable mountain!"—and I could so indulge myself though still ignorant of how one was to groan later on, in particular, after taking yet further home the portentous truth that this same criminal continuity, scorning its grandest chance to break down, makes but a mouthful of the Mississippi. (*AS,* 465)

It is nicely convenient to leave Henry James seated within a symbolic agent of the times and to have his nose thus pressed against the glass, or rather to have others join him in his Pullman. For it allows me to consider, in shorthand so to speak, and in an amateur way, the relation of realism to the real and to do so by contemplating several passages that also take as their vantage point observations made from a moving railroad car. Joined as they are by a common point of view, these passages provide a context, at once historical and epistemological, that may in turn make possible a few observations about the "realism" of Wallace Stevens. Those several passages are:

> At one point, they [Clifford and Hepzibah Pyncheon] were rattling through a solitude;—the next, a village had grown up around them;— a few breaths more, and it had vanished, as if swallowed by an earthquake. The spires of meeting houses seemed set adrift from their foundations; the broad-based hills glided away. Everything was unfixed from its age-long rest, and moving at whirlwind speed in a direction opposite to their own.
>
> *The House of the Seven Gables* (1851)

"Do you see how the foreground next the train rushes from us [Basil and Isabel March] and the background keeps abreast of us, while the middle distance seems stationary? I don't think I ever noticed that effect before. There ought to be something literary in it; retreating past, and advancing future, and deceitfully permanent present—something like that?"

A Hazard of New Fortunes (1889)

The great Pullman was whirling onward with such dignity of motion that a glance from the window seemed simply to prove that the plains of Texas were pouring eastward. Vast flats of green grass, dull-hued spaces of mesquit and cactus, little groups of frame houses, woods of light and tender trees, all were sweeping into the east, sweeping over the horizon, a precipice.

"The Bride Comes to Yellow Sky" (1898)

They were nearing Chicago. Signs were everywhere numerous. Trains flashed by them. Across wide stretches of flat open prairie they could see lines of telegraph poles stalking across the fields toward the great city. Far away were indications of suburban towns, some big smoke-stacks towering high in the air.

Sister Carrie (1900)

The train was racing through tree tops that fell away at intervals and showed the sun standing very red, on the edge of the farthest woods. Nearer, the plowed fields curved and faded and the few hogs nosing in the furrows looked like large spotted stones.

Wise Blood (1952)

There is hardly need to comment upon the technological violation of the pastoral ideal as it is presented in these passages; that subject has been fully explored by Leo Marx.[9] (Though it is worth noting that these passages take as their vantage point a seat *within* the technological instrument itself and are therefore separated from the natural context it so gracelessly intrudes upon. Such artificial perspective and smooth progress, as Henry James knew, could only be halted by the most dramatic terrain, the "unbridgeable abyss," the "insuperable mountain"; no sentimental attachment to the pastoral ideal could halt its momentum.) Nor is there need to re-

9. See Leo Marx, *The Machine and the Garden: Technology and the Pastoral Ideal* (New York: Oxford University Press, 1964).

hearse the enormous social, technological, and political changes that attended the age of American realism and made the perception of change something of an assault on sensibility; that too has been amply discussed by Jay Martin, Howard Mumford Jones, Warner Berthoff, and others.[10] (But, again, it is perhaps significant to note that the movement of the locomotive, the primary symbolic agent of the dramatic alterations of American life, allows in this instance for the peculiar perception of change and motion in the landscape.)

What is more important for our purposes is the fact that these passages address a verifiable phenomenon, but each writer in a different way interposes a rhetorical veil between the pure experience of perception (the "real") and their privileged point of view. Which is to say that each passage gives the reader ideas about things, not the thing itself. Or perhaps it is better to avoid the language of Wallace Stevens for the moment and to rely, once again, on William James.

To be radically empirical about this so-called optical illusion one must right away admit it to be real, for all that is experienced, including the relations available in the experience itself, is constitutive of reality. Moreover, while we may admit that our experiences may terminate in a "nucleus of common perception," we must also admit that our individual experiences "float and dangle" around a common center and for the most part remain "out of sight and irrelevant and unimaginable to one another" (RE, 24). The warmth and intimacy of perceptions insist that, though they are perhaps shared, they nevertheless are related to us and remain ours in this familiar sense, continuous with the experience that has preceded them and full of the expectancy we bring to them. "The holding fast to this relation," says James, "means taking it at its face-value, neither less nor more; and to take it at its face-value means first of all to take it just as we feel it and not to confuse ourselves with abstract talk about it, involving words that drive us to invent secondary conceptions in order to neutralize their suggestions and to make our actual experience again seem rationally possible" (RE, 25).

And what is that "thing" that these five writers mutually observe? It is

10. See Jay Martin, *Harvest of Change: American Literature, 1865–1914* (Englewood Cliffs: Prentice-Hall, 1967); Howard Mumford Jones, *The Age of Energy: Varieties of American Experience, 1865–1915* (New York: Viking Press, 1970); and Warner Berthoff, *The Ferment of Realism: American Literature, 1884–1919* (New York: Free Press, 1965).

a piece of reality, available to anyone who is willing, say, to drive across Kansas. It is an optical illusion of motion in the landscape, partly explainable by perceptual psychology and partly by the laws of physics. The land circles counter-clockwise round a focal point in the middle distance, and this whirling disk advances across the landscape, biting into the land ahead, relinquishing a portion to that left behind. As such, the phenomenon provides an analogue to William James's description of the "field of experience": "Our fields of experience have no more definite boundaries than have our fields of view. Both are fringed forever by a more that continuously develops, and that continuously supersedes them as life proceeds" (*RE*, 35).

One may adjust this deception to other sorts of extraperceptual relations, of course, but, as Henry James so rightly saw, to insist upon the existence, which is to say the nonempirical reality, of this impression is to instantly have it explained and explained away by the naturalist. It is true, of course, that the perception of the twisting, bending round of the landscape is an ocular deception; moreover, such a perception is dependent on the speed of the moving train—the "reality" of this percept could not have come into existence, or at least would have remained imperceptible, without the technological accomplishment of a certain velocity in the locomotive, which is both the emblem of large cultural changes and in this case the enabling agent for the experience of motion and change "out there." But the privileged access to this impression requires a holding fast to it, a refusal to abandon it to transcendental or extraperceptual explanations.

The fictional formulations of this phenomenon are so perfectly adapted to the larger purposes of these five texts that one could almost believe the works were themselves elaborations of the image. Hawthorne's *The House of the Seven Gables*, which as Eric Sundquist has pointed out has special affinities with the concerns of American realists,[11] is in part a rumination on the nature of time and the consequences of progress and change, and the scene from the window serves as symbol for the consciousness "unfixed" from its age-long rest. For Hepzibah, the railway journey is both phantasmagoric and familiar; at first, she mistakes the experience for a dream but then an accustomed commonplace—"Sleep; sport; business; graver or lighter study;—and the common inevitable movement onward!

11. Eric J. Sundquist, "Introduction: The Country of the Blue," in *American Realism: New Essays* (Baltimore: Johns Hopkins University Press, 1982), 7–9.

It was life itself!" For Clifford, it is an escape from crime and condition and promotes his philosophy of a future "nomadic" state; all human progress may be described as an "ascending spiral curve." For Hawthorne himself, it seems, it is one of many figures for the perennial mistake that the "tattered garments of Antiquity" can be so completely exchanged for a new suit.[12] The description serves his literary purpose to show the folly of a world set free from history, but the reality of the scene as perceived movement is lost in his extrapolations.

The same may be said for Howells. *A Hazard of New Fortunes* is another and more complicated examination of change and progress, and Howells demonstrates his proportionating intelligence in rendering the description. For he identifies the phenomenon as an "effect" and has his semi-autobiographical narrator claim that there might be something "literary" in it, not that the reality of the perception might itself be the subject of literature. Howells's aesthetic program demanded an intervening and balancing judgment; to supply a correcting sense of proportion is the role of the artist: "The artist sees a dog down the street—well, his eye instantly relates the dog to its surroundings. The dog is proportioned to the buildings and the trees. Whereas, many people can conceive of that dog's tail resting upon a hill top." The realist novel serves as a corrective, but it does so by making actual experience seem commonly possible. For those whose noses are "tight against life,"[13] a common vision, a natural realism, displaces the naive impression. Realism drives out reality.

As one might expect, the literary impressionism of Stephen Crane comes closer to an active confrontation with this restricted piece of reality we have been considering. The opening paragraph of "A Bride Comes to Yellow Sky" is an attempt to paint in words. He uses masses of pure colors—vast flats of green, spaces of mesquite, groups of houses—and quickens them with broad liquid verbs—*pouring, whirling, sweeping.* Still, there is no attempt to steal the prize and carry it off, no mistaking that this is an impression. The glance from the window "seemed" to prove (and this is the rhetorical point of the whole story) that "the plains of Texas were pouring eastward." Crane's descriptive imagination is happily and effectively converted into cultural criticism—the frontier has been tamed, and all but un-

12. Nathaniel Hawthorne, *The House of the Seven Gables,* ed. Seymour L. Gross (New York: W. W. Norton, 1967), 257, 180.
13. Quoted in Cady, *Light of Common Day,* 4.

consciously, by the great Pullman, an anonymous seamstress in New York, and a shy bride from San Antonio. This is the idea Crane sets before the whirling reality he so vividly describes. No more than Howells or Hawthorne does Crane take reality at face value.

It is no surprise that Dreiser seems altogether blind to the "effect" (to use Howells's word) we have been contemplating. Nothing in the passage suggests (now to borrow from Henry James) that he has "seen" at all. Instead he brings a double-consciousness to our piece of reality, a consciousness that is at once so susceptible to mockery and yet so strangely powerful. "Signs were everywhere numerous." This is not so much a redundancy as a double seeing—they are "everywhere" in the sense of being bewildering to the untutored sensibility of Carrie Meeber, and "numerous" in the sense that they are mathematically exact, countable. Smokestacks were "towering high in the air." (Where else, pray tell, would they tower?) But they are at once ominous and located in public space. Dreiser embraces both the tough- and tender-minded positions. The world his characters live in is naturalistically decipherable, but their fates are raised to the pitch of melodrama. For them, telegraph poles are "stalking across the fields" and smokestacks loom threateningly above them. For the author, there is no holding fast to the relation, and "secondary conceptions" (because they are antithetical) not only preclude the real but provide their own special tension.

The passage from Flannery O'Connor's *Wise Blood* perfectly prepares for the upside-down world of Hazel Motes, Christian *"malgré lui"* and prophet of the Church without Christ. He is the preacher of a church "where the blind don't see and the lame don't walk and what's dead stays that way" but Hazel Motes's life mysteriously contradicts his announced purposes. His landlady tells him that "time goes forward, it don't go backward and unless you take what's offered you, you'll find yourself out in the cold pitch black,"[14] but his self-imposed martyrdom to a church without redemption moves "backwards to Bethlehem" in a way that finally converts even the landlady's understanding. Our piece of reality corroborates O'Connor's fictional world, but she, as author, does not hold fast to the relation. The perception of the movement is tempered with a modernist irony and serves to advance her own theme. Fixed objects (trees and fields) fall

---

14. Flannery O'Connor, *Three By Flannery O'Connor: Wise Blood, A Good Man Is Hard To Find, The Violent Bear It Away* (New York: New American Library, 1962), 60, 124.

and curve and fade away, and hogs are transformed into stones; the forward rush of events bends round and is handed over to the past; the territory ahead is always the territory behind.

The consideration of this perceptual phenomenon now fans out like a hand of cards, from New England romantic to southern modernist. And it may be said that I have stacked the deck by so restricting myself to this little piece of human reality, as in a sense I have. The whole of fictions, much less of literary periods and methods, cannot be so circumscribed. My procedure is made out of convenience, and my object is meant to be little more than suggestive. But by so focusing upon a shared reality and examining how perception recoils upon the consciousness of the artist (for each writer appropriates that reality and makes it serve a literary purpose quite distinct from the pure experience that discloses the phenomenon) we have provided, however strained and tentatively, a Pullman car of fiction, having not many windows, but one.

These brief and limited considerations do at least call into question the mimetic quality of fiction, and particularly of realist fiction. For the authors represented here display little interest in the *real* as the subject of their description, and if they have some correspondence theory of truth or relation in mind, the correspondence between pure experience and fictional rendering is not essential to it. These writers do not dramatize a world so much as they render their own sense of the world appropriate to the fictions they are creating. Like Henry James's figure of the house of fiction in his preface to *The Portrait of a Lady*, our passengers are "watching the same show" and our piece of reality is "as nothing without the posted presence of the watcher."[15] It is a matter of convenience, too, to have Wallace Stevens join the others in this Pullman car and to argue that he was more intent than the rest to press his nose to the glass, to take reality at face value, to see and carry off the prize.

II

The figure of a Pullman car of fiction (or, now, because we add Wallace Stevens to the equation, a Pullman car of literature) is an ungainly one. But it does have one advantage over James's image of a house of fiction. For the

15. Henry James, *The Art of the Novel*, 46.

first years of the new century had resolutely "unfixed" stable realities and permanent truths. Men and women no longer witnessed the effects of change so much as they rode within the car of the imagination that was itself in motion. William James's world of pure experience was a shifting mosaic of perception and interest; and it was, he said, a mosaic without any transempirical cement to bind experiences to some transcendent order of understanding. Thought, he had argued in his *Psychology* (1890), occurs in a stream, and his friend Henri Bergson promoted the idea that the fundamental reality of the universe was change and becoming. For Bergson, true metaphysics was the attempt to do away with symbols (whether verbal or numerical) and enter into a living reality of duration. Process philosophers such as Dewey and, later, Whitehead articulated a world of constant becoming. Even physicists and mathematicians began to admit that the stuff of the world was a very unstable compound and that the "laws" of nature might themselves be susceptible to alteration over time.[16]

Culturally, it would no longer do to say that change happened to individuals; life itself was change. But as Hawthorne so plainly and so early saw, life in motion would not interrupt the regular occupations or diversions:

> A party of girls, and one young man, on opposite sides of the car, found huge amusement in a game of ball. They tossed it to-and-fro, with peals of laughter that might be measured by mile-lengths; for, faster than the nimble ball could fly, the merry players fled unconsciously along, leaving the trail of their mirth afar behind, and ending their game under another sky than had witnessed its commencement.[17]

But by the end of the century Americans had developed what Daniel Boorstin calls a "statistical consciousness" and had accommodated themselves to a world in flux by all manner of standardizing processes.[18] The invention of measuring cups and spoons and hence of recipes, the introduction of interchangeable parts, standards of measurement, ready-made clothing, scientific management, standard time, all these and other attempts

16. I have dealt with some of these aspects of cultural change in America prior to World War I in "Bergson in America," in *Prospects: An Annual Journal of American Cultural Studies*, vol. 11, *Essays* (Cambridge University Press, 1987), 453–90.

17. Hawthorne, *House of the Seven Gables*, 257.

18. See Daniel Boorstin, *The Americans: The Democratic Experience* (New York: Vintage, 1974), particularly parts 2 and 3, pp. 89–244.

to economize effort and to regularize and homogenize activity and experience had as their necessary complement what Kenneth Burke calls the "bureaucratization of the imaginative" and fostered a debilitating alienation from the world as world. Considered in these terms, commonly shared experience did not enlarge the sympathies so much as it constricted consciousness. As William James remarked in the early years of the new century, in his *Pragmatism* (1907), only the smallest part of experience comes to us without the "human touch," "we can hardly take in an impression at all, in the absence of a preconception of what impressions there may be":

> When we talk of reality "independent" of human thinking, then, it seems a thing very hard to find. It reduces to the notion of what is just entering into experience and yet to be named, or else to some imagined aboriginal presence in experience, before any belief about the presence has arisen. . . . We may glimpse it, but we never grasp it; what we grasp is always some substitute for it which previous human thinking has peptonized and cooked for our consumption. (*P*, 162)

Ironically, shared experience and a common vision were to become the bugbears of the imagination. For cliché and formula were too often laid over experience; reality came in premeasured scoops and doses and was therefore stable, and therefore socially if not personally familiar. Most people, observed Bergson, develop a very useful and highly artificial socialized self to the hurt and exclusion of an authentic self, a *"moi fondamentale,"* and acquire ready-made responses to and ideas about life that float upon the consciousness like "dead leaves on a pond." For Robert Frost, the new poetic project (and he may have had Bergson's image in mind here) was to "clean the pasture spring," "to rake the leaves away" and wait "to watch the water clear." For Wallace Stevens, it was to do away with the "masquerade of thought" and serve "Grotesque apprenticeship to chance event." He, like his figure Crispin in "The Comedian as the Letter C," would throw off

> . . . fictive flourishes that preordained
> His passion's permit, hang of coat, degree
> Of buttons, measure of his salt. Such trash
> Might help the blind, not him.[19]

19. *The Collected Poems of Wallace Stevens* (New York: Alfred A. Knopf, 1968), 39. Hereafter cited in the text with the abbreviation *CP*.

Stevens's poetry, early and late, is to a degree a continuation of Howells's literary project to have literature serve the uses of life, to draw its subjects from the common and the ordinary, to rebel against sentimental idealism and desiccating positivism. But proportion and balance, because they typically eclipsed the real and acted as impersonal substitutes for experience, were for Stevens so many "fictive flourishes." Instead, he would contrive a poetry not out of accommodation and adjustment but out of excess; he would commend his art to the "real." He would, by striking comic poses and delivering ever more lavish metaphors, avoid literal notation and yet keep the connections with experience. In a word, he would play the clown if necessary, in a search for the "blissful liaison, / Between himself and his environment" (*CP*, 34).

Stevens's partly autobiographical figure Crispin makes his several journeys toward a poetry of reality. His personal discontent might have kept him a "prickly realist." Instead, he attended to "things within his actual eye, alert / To the difficulty of rebellious thought" (*CP*, 40). Crispin recognizes that individual rather than shared experience may underwrite his project, but that nature outlives the poet and the poem, nevertheless:

> He first, as realist, admitted that
> Whoever hunts a matinal continent
> May, after all, stop short before a plum
> And be content and still be realist.
> The words of things entangle and confuse.
> The plum survives its poems. (*CP*, 40–41)

But the "real" was the only remaining undiscovered continent for a poet, and one worth "crossing the seas to find." Crispin came to believe that "his soil is man's intelligence":

> Crispin in one laconic phrase laid bare
> His cloudy drift and planned a colony.
> Exit the mental moonlight, exit lex,
> Rex and principium, exit the whole.
> Shebang. Exit omnes. Here was prose
> More exquisite than any tumbling verse:
> A still new continent in which to dwell. (*CP*, 36–37)

Crispin's new purpose is to "drive away / The shadow of his fellows from the skies," to be released from their "stale intelligence" and "to make a new intelligence prevail" (*CP*, 37). The poet as "florist" would ask the aid of "cabbages" in order to drive out the ideal and to celebrate the "rashest trivia" of experience in the service of the real.

The eleventh of some thirteen ways of looking at a blackbird is this:

> He rode over Connecticut
> In a glass coach.
> Once, a fear pierced him,
> In that he mistook
> The shadow of his equipage
> For blackbirds. (*CP*, 94)

I take the "glass coach" to be a railroad coach and not a carriage, but I don't insist on it. This is an assumption made simply out of the convenience of having Stevens join the others in our figurative Pullman car.

Like the other twelve ways of looking at a blackbird, this haiku-like poem is in part a specimen of Wallace Stevens's experimentation in an imagist poetic. But only in part, because it possesses, as do most of the poems in his first volume, *Harmonium* (1923), something of the doctrinal, the theoretic, the satirical. In the poem "Theory" Stevens expressed one of those doctrinal points quite succinctly:

> I am what is around me.
>
> Women understand this.
> One is not a duchess
> A hundred yards from a carriage. (*CP*, 86)

The Connecticut man who rides over the state in his glass coach is not so astute as the duchess. He is, one supposes, one of those "thin men of Haddam" whose idealized sense of himself, his assumed immunity to chance event and pretense to aristocratic invincibility (his "equipage"), is threatened by the movements of his own shadow. When he mistakes the moving shadows of his coach for blackbirds, as Joseph Riddell remarks, the man is made suddenly aware of his own mortality, of a world of death and change indifferent to his station or estate.[20] As with so many of the poems in *Har-*

---

20. Joseph Riddell, *The Clairvoyant Eye: The Poetry and Poetics of Wallace Stevens* (Baton Rouge: Louisiana State University Press, 1965), 87.

monium, though by no means so explicitly, "Thirteen Ways of Looking at a Blackbird" playfully and punningly renders the assault of the *real* upon the *ideal.* And to the extent that this is characteristic of his poetry, Wallace Stevens may be considered, as he wished to be considered, a "poet of reality."

"There is nothing in the world greater than reality," Stevens wrote in his book of aphorisms, *Adagia.* "In this predicament we have to accept reality itself as the only genius."[21] Stevens, at least, took reality as his genius, and his poetry and prose writing are filled with variations on this statement or with a gathering of the implications of it: "The real is only the base. But it is the base" (*OP,* 160); "Poetry increases the feeling for reality" (*OP,* 162); "Reality is the object seen in its greatest common sense" (*OP,* 178); "Reality is a cliché from which we escape by metaphor" (*OP,* 179); "Metaphor creates a new reality from which the original appears to be unreal" (*OP,* 169); "Reality is not what it is. It consists of the many realities which it can be made into" (*OP,* 178). This sampling of aphorisms from *Adagia* communicates, if only telegraphically, Stevens's preoccupation with the "real" as the proper subject of poetry. And if some of the statements seem at variance with one another, it is because he indiscriminately uses the same word to represent two distinct conceptions of reality. There is the real of realism—that is, the natural realism of a common vision—and there is the naive realism of pure experience before secondary conceptions have been interposed between that experience and our appropriation of it as thought.

It is this second form of reality to which Stevens, as poet, committed himself. For he wished "To live in the world but outside existing conceptions of it" (*OP,* 164), and to write a kind of poetry that would return to his readers a sense of the world, and of reality, before it had been peptonized and cooked. Like Henry James, Stevens recognized that the artist's truest subject is his perspective, his own creative temperament. A poet's only subject, he said, is his "sense of the world" (*NA,* 121), and, for the poet, "Conceptions are artificial. Perceptions are essential" (*OP,* 164). Reality is the "central reference" (*NA,* 71) for poetry. Stevens did not believe, any more than Howells, that literature could be made out of the literary. It had to be made out of life, and life meant acting and existing in a physical world.

---

21. In Wallace Stevens, *Opus Posthumous: Poems, Plays, Prose,* ed. Samuel French Morse (New York: Vintage, 1982), 177. Hereafter cited in the text with the abbreviation *OP.*

The "real" for Stevens is not a "'collection of solid, static objects extended in space' but the life that is lived in the scene that it composes; and so reality is not that external scene but the life that is lived in it. Reality is things as they are" (*NA*, 25). To capture that portion of the real that constantly eludes the common experience and that we may perpetually grasp at but never quite hold is, for Stevens, both the joy and the duty of the poet. When a renewed sense of the real can be conveyed to the reader, when "reality is returned," it is as though "a shadow had passed and drawn after it and taken away whatever coating had concealed what lay beneath it." This, says Stevens, is the "revelation of reality," and the phrase is significantly like James's notion of pure experience:

> There is inherent in the words the *revelation of reality* a suggestion that there is a reality of or within or beneath the surface of reality. There are many such realities through which poets constantly pass to and fro. . . . The most provocative of all realities is that reality of which we never lose sight but never see solely as it is. (*OP*, 214)

It was this sort of reality that Stevens attempted to reveal in his poetry, believing as he did that an available freshness and renewal of sensibility were always near at hand. In "Notes toward a Supreme Fiction" he defined the difficulty of rendering this "real":

> But the difficultest rigor is forthwith,
> On the image of what we see, to catch from that
> Irrational moment its unreasoning,
> As when the sun comes rising, when the sea
> Clears deeply, when the moon hangs on the wall
> Of heaven-haven. These are not things transformed.
> Yet we are shaken by them as if they were.
> We reason about them with a later reason. (*CP*, 398–99)

Which is to say that Stevens resisted the proportionating intelligence of Howells, though he perpetuated, in their essentials, the aesthetic and moral aims of realism. And, perhaps taking his cues from William James, whom he much admired,[22] he refused to neutralize the suggestions of perception in order to make experience seem "rationally possible." Instead, he en-

22. Margaret Peterson, in her *"Harmonium* and William James," *Southern Review*

dorsed that same suggestiveness as the constantly renewable resource for metaphoric transformation, for a poetry of the earth.

In "Metaphors of a Magnifico" Stevens contemplates the "old song / That will not declare itself," whether two minds can know the same object:

> Twenty men crossing a bridge,
> Into a village,
> Are twenty men crossing twenty bridges,
> Into twenty villages,
> Or one man
> Crossing a single bridge into a village.

His, appropriately, is a poet's not a philosopher's answer. For he loses hold of the question in the perception of the approaching village:

> The boots of the men clump
> On the boards of the bridge.
> The first white wall of the village
> Rises through fruit-trees.
> Of what was it I was thinking?
> So the meaning escapes.
>
> The first white wall of the village . . .
> The fruit-trees. . . . (*CP*, 19)

For Stevens the imagination is part of reality, it is that power that enables us to compose the scene in which we live. The unreal "fecundates" the real, he insisted, and his intent in this, as in so many of his poems, is to reaffirm the power of pure perception over unsolvable problems or acquired conceptions and forms.

The poems of Stevens's first book, *Harmonium,* give evidence of his ambition to be a poet of reality, an ambition he clung to throughout his poetic career. Several of them satirize the tendencies of both realists and materialists to stabilize and idealize an essentially unreifiable world, and thereby to remove it from the concrete relations of living experience. In a poem like

---

7 (summer 1971), 658–82, argues the profound influence of James on Stevens's first volume of verse, claiming James to be the "philosophical father of *Harmonium.*" Her essay and this one have many overlapping concerns; however, were I to argue a case of influence rather than analogue, I think I would instance Bergson as having the more profound influence upon Stevens's poetry, including the poems of *Harmonium.*

"Gubbinal" he pretends to relinquish an individual's account of experience to the positivist:

> That strange flower, the sun,
> Is just what you say.
> Have it your way.
>
> The world is ugly,
> And the people are sad. (CP, 85)

But more often he is aggressively satirical. The Doctor of Geneva foolishly stamps the sand and tugs his shawl and feels no "awe" before the "visible, voluble delugings" of a world of incessant change (CP, 24); "Gloomy grammarians in golden gowns" meekly keep their "mortal rendezvous," indifferent to the world around them (CP, 55); for the "homunculus," an artificial and shrunken man, it is better that he keep monastic vigil and "think hard in the dark cuffs / Of voluminous cloaks," for the beauty he sees may not be a "gaunt, fugitive phantom" but a "wanton, / Abundantly beautiful, eager" (CP, 26); the "high-toned old Christian woman" builds a "haunted heaven," but a vital reality close by, "unpurged by epitaph," comes in "squiggling like saxophones" (CP, 59). Stevens picked his quarrel with any who would displace the physical world of change and growth and experience with idealized conceptions of it. For him, every sort of "intellectualist" (to use William James's term) was potentially a figure of fun:

> Rationalists, wearing square hats,
> Think, in square rooms,
> Looking at the floor,
> Looking at the ceiling.
> They confine themselves
> To right-angled triangles.
> If they tried rhomboids,
> Cones, waving lines, ellipses—
> As, for example, the ellipse of the half-moon
> Rationalists would wear sombreros. (CP, 75)

Stevens wanted no cardboard substitutes for the life of experience, and his satire of dogged, even sentimental attachment to ideas about things rather than things as they are has both a negative and a positive function. As with literary realists, such scorn and ridicule deflate pretense and re- store, or perhaps insist upon, some sense of the common lot, but they also delimit notions of the real. There is a hemming-in and redirection of at- tention away from the exalted, remote, and idealized and toward perceived actualities. More numerous than his satirical poems in *Harmonium* are his special pleadings for the real.

Sometimes those pleadings occur as lyric celebrations. In "Jasmine's Beautiful Thoughts underneath the Willow" he speaks of an "idiosyncrat- ic music" that is like a "vivid apprehension"

> Of bliss beyond the mutes of plaster,
> Or paper souvenirs of rapture,
>
> Of bliss submerged beneath appearance,
> In an interior ocean's rocking
> Of long capricious fugues and chorals. (*CP*, 79)

In "The Place of the Solitaires" he insists that

> There must be no cessation of motion,
> Or of the noise of motion,
> The renewal of noise
> And manifold continuation. (*CP*, 60)

In "O Florida, Venereal Soil," he asks that "a few things for themselves" be disclosed to the lover of the world. And in "Tea at the Palaz of Hoon" the poet becomes the "compass of that sea" he has perceived:

> I was the world in which I walked, and what I saw
> Or heard or felt came not but from myself;
> And there I found myself more truly and more strange. (*CP*, 65)

As often, Stevens offers simple renderings of the real. In poems such as "Earthy Anecdote," "Life Is Motion," or the familiar "Anecdote of the Jar," he speaks of an immanent world of unceasing change, only glimpsed by the senses but formalized and composed by the imagination. In "De- pression before Spring" the hair of his blonde lover

> Is dazzling,
> As the spittle of cows
> Threading the wind. (*CP,* 63)

And one of his "Six Significant Landscapes" is this:

> The night is of the color
> Of a woman's arm:
> Night, the female,
> Obscure,
> Fragrant and supple,
> Conceals herself.
>
> A pool shines,
> Like a bracelet
> Shaken in a dance. (*CP,* 74–75)

It would be possible to multiply examples from *Harmonium* or elsewhere, but these samples are sufficient to demonstrate that Wallace Stevens attempted to carry off the prize of his impressions and to forge that attempt into an aesthetic value. He wished to dispense with an intermediate intelligence that adjusts perceptions to conceptions, even if those conceptions might be of a commonly shared reality. The metaphors of a strand of hair as spittle threading in the wind or of a pool shining like a bracelet were intended to cleanse the vision, to see the earth again, as he said in a later poem, "Cleared of its stiff and stubborn man-locked set" (*CP,* 497). In "excess there is cure for sorrow" he once wrote, and the excess of metaphoric transformation of the real was meant to provide an analogue to the reader's experience, not identical with the poet's but shared by virtue of the "strange rhetoric" of the parallel that always exists between nature and the imagination. This is the function of poetry; it is "a rhetoric in which the feeling of one man is communicated to another in words of exquisite appositeness that takes away all their verbality" (*NA,* 118).

There is neither space nor need, really, to rehearse the epistemological foundations of Stevens's aesthetic. It is enough to say that, for him, the imagination is a value and a power. The imaginative may acquire social forms (as, for example, in the ceremony of weddings or funerals or in the fashions of the day), but the imagination as a power over events is ultimately personal and keeps the connections between individual perception and actual experience. The "real," for Stevens, is always ready at hand if one can somehow manage to get outside preexisting conceptions of it. "We live in concepts of the imagination before the reason has established them," he wrote; and if we indulge the imagination, we establish a privileged access to "the instantaneous disclosures of living." Such disclosures, he continued, are "disclosures of the normal" (*NA,* 154).

So understood, Stevens's poetry is the poetry of reality and of the normal. Like Howells, he attempted to keep a fidelity to experience, but he raised the ante. His view from the Pullman car window was not an "effect" but a living reality, and there was definitely something literary in it. In an age of disbelief, the imagination made belief possible. In a world in which the abnormal (that is to say, the artificially stabilized and homogenized) passes for the normal, the excesses of the imagination restore a sense of normality. Stevens tried to keep the connections, to give his readers "things as they are," not as we would have them. "The earth of things," observed William James, "long thrown into shadow by the glories of the upper ether, must resume its rights" (*P,* 86). This was a plea that realists and the poet of reality alike might rally around. By committing himself to a poetry of the earth, and by abandoning realism for reality, Stevens meant to show that the earth had clear title.

X

In the Shallow Light of the Present

The Moral Geography of *Death Comes for the Archbishop*

There are two aspects of *Death Comes for the Archbishop* (1927) that have long perplexed me, though so far as I know they have not bothered others sufficiently to have become established critical issues subject to debate and interpretation. The first problem is a textual one, for in the final pages of this novel there is a puzzling episode that threatens to subvert the achieved spiritual grace and final wisdom of the central character and to complicate the direction and interests of Cather's narrative, and one naturally wonders why Cather should make such a perilous artistic gesture.[1] The second problem is an extratextual one and concerns the genesis of the novel, for what we know of the compositional history of the book contradicts the author's statements about the happy mood in which she wrote her novel and the easy and uninterrupted progress she made in composing it. In fact, she did interrupt her writing in order to return to the Southwest, specifically to visit Canyon de Chelly, and the experience of that trip figured importantly in the final direction her narrative would take. Both problems are finally related to one another and ultimately bear upon the author's ambitions for and achievement in this, her favorite work. It is my purpose here, then, to consider these problems separately, as a way of preparing for a few summary comments about the final accomplishment of the novel and the character and quality of the author's final spiritual affirmations in the closing sections.

---

1. In "Willa Cather's Subverted Endings and Gendered Time," *Cather Studies* 1 (1990): 68–88, Susan Rosowski has shown just how important and subversive Cather's endings tend to be.

I

In the final book of *Death Comes for the Archbishop,* Bishop Latour knows that Death is coming for him. There is no dramatic resolution to events in this novel, but rather the playing out of inevitabilities, and there is, in the narrator, at least a tonal reassurance and security present that quietly and without haste brings the story to its close. Latour's work is done—his cathedral is complete, his diocese secure. His friends are gone—Father Joseph, dead; Olivares, dead; Kit Carson, dead. The long background to this moment is the novel itself, the story of a life given over to God, a country, and a people, and it is the strong lingering aftertaste of a life lived, not thoughts of blessed peace and salvation, that now preoccupies Latour. For we are told the Archbishop is leaving his past; the future, he knows, will take care of itself. He sits in the middle of his own consciousness and his memories have lost their perspective: "None of his former states of mind were lost or outgrown," we are told. "They were all within reach of his hand, and all comprehensible."[2] In the midst of this most spiritual of occasions he has a secular revelation—that the earthly interests and uses of life are for the living and that Death is the final and most intimate of friends. Latour enjoys what Whitman called in "When Lilacs Last in the Dooryard Bloom'd" the "sacred knowledge of death":

> Then with the knowledge of death as walking
>   one side of me,
> And the thought of death close-walking the other
>   side of me,
> And I in the middle as with companions, and as holding
>   the hands of companions. (ll. 120–22)

Bishop Latour, in his final days, judges conduct differently—mischance, doubt, mistake, resistance, and rebuke, these seem unimportant to him now. His life is thick with memory and an understanding that brings contentment. Into this final perspective, however, a figure from his past comes

---

2. *Death Comes for the Archbishop,* Willa Cather Scholarly Edition, ed. John J. Murphy, Charles Mignon, et al. (Lincoln: University of Nebraska Press, 1999), 305. Subsequent references to this edition will be incorporated parenthetically into the text.

back to him "not in memory, but in the flesh, in the shallow light of the present" (305). It is the Navajo, Eusabio. He has heard that Latour is failing and has traveled from the Little Colorado River to Santa Fe. A trip that once would have taken two weeks has been accomplished in a matter of days, and the last leg of his trip from Gallup to Santa Fe, thanks to the railroad, has taken only a few hours. However urgent his need to reach the Archbishop, Eusabio is nevertheless skeptical of the railroad and the changes it has brought about: "Men travel faster now, but I do not know if they go to better things," he says. Latour's response is in keeping with his new-found patience and wisdom: "We must not try to know the future, Eusabio. It is better not" (306).

However, it is precisely at this moment, when the Archbishop seems above earthly care, that, instead of bringing her narrative to a serene and well-earned close, Cather introduces new subjects and new dimensions to the character of her lighted figure. Latour asks after Manuelito, the steadfast Navajo warrior who opposed Kit Carson and refused the Long Walk to Bosque Redondo by hiding out until the U.S. government restored the Navajo to their land, and who at last is an old man growing still older in his ancestral home. Latour is glad that he has lived "to see two great wrongs righted; I have seen the end of black slavery, and I have seen the Navajo restored to their own country" (306). He remembers the violence and greed and politics that kept the Indian wars going and that imposed the policies that deprived the Navajo of their sacred land.

The penultimate section of the final book of *Death Comes for the Archbishop* is a set piece that fills in a neglected portion of Latour's background—his meeting with Manuelito in Zuni and his refusal of Manuelito's request that he travel to Washington to argue the Navajo cause before the government; his travels with his French architect to Canyon de Chelly in 1875 after the Navajo people have returned to till their crops, graze their sheep, and grow their peaches in the canyon's sandy bottom. Canyon de Chelly is an "Indian Garden of Eden" (313), and it is apparent that Latour has come to a fuller understanding of this people who, far more than Pueblo tribes, have resisted the incursions of the Church and for whom the land and their faith are inseparable. Canyon de Chelly and Shiprock are kind parents to the Navajo; they are places "more sacred to them than churches, more sacred than any place is to the white man" (310–11).

Here, as everywhere in the novel, Cather merely "touches and passes on." But artistically, as well as in other ways, this is a perilous gesture in her narrative. She introduces facts about Latour's history that may well serve to discredit him in the reader's eyes, and she suggests a more primitive and in many ways more holy faith than the religious faith of missionaries who build churches and say benedictions. For part of the Archbishop's memories are of Kit Carson's brutal devastation of the Navajo's orchards and crops in Canyon de Chelly, of a long stream of survivors of the Long Walk, and of a Navajo woman suckling a lamb until a ewe can be found. And there is the image of Manuelito himself, a great warrior in hiding, whose wealth has been reduced to a mere thirty sheep and a few starving horses, and whose children must eat roots to survive. Yet Latour had refused to plead the Navajo cause to the government. Cather introduces as well the legend of Shiprock, a craggy peak that once sailed in the air until the divine parents set it in the desert as a sign that this was to be the Navajo homeland. Shiprock is rugged holy architecture; the church at Santa Fe, as we know by this point in the novel, is a human construction symmetrically built out of human frailty.

Willa Cather was too deliberate an artist to risk subverting her fiction with an afterthought, and her placement of this brief episode just prior to her record of Bishop Latour's passing in the final section is not so much a rupture in her text as it is a reaffirmation of what I believe was her original artistic ambition for her novel. That ambition was stated succinctly not about her own narrative but that of her friend Sarah Orne Jewett. In February 1925 she wrote her famous preface to *The Country of the Pointed Firs and Other Stories,* and there she disclosed her admiration for three American novels: *The Scarlet Letter, Huckleberry Finn,* and *The Country of the Pointed Firs.* She could think of no other American books that have the promise of a long, long life and that "confront time and change so serenely."[3]

This is a curious grouping, more curious still the quality she believes unites these three novels as masterpieces of American fiction. One understands instantly how her remark applies to Jewett's work; one knows as well how deeply and permanently Jewett influenced Cather's art. But how the other two fulfill her single and rather impressionistic criterion for artistic greatness is somewhat problematic. Whether or not Cather consciously strove to emulate the examples of Jewett, Hawthorne, and Twain, *Death*

3. Reprinted in *Willa Cather on Writing* (New York: Alfred A. Knopf, 1949), 58; hereafter incorporated parenthetically within the text.

Comes for the Archbishop departed radically from the spirit of her own most recent fiction.

Willa Cather interrupted her work on *The Professor's House* (1925) to write her preface to her collection of Jewett's fiction, and shortly after she had completed the story of her professor she would turn her attention to her novella, *My Mortal Enemy* (1926). Neither of these novels possesses the poise and serenity of her *Archbishop*. Godfrey St. Peter's final understanding is that he has fallen out of love and that he must learn to live out his life without "delight." Father Fay may think of Myra Henshawe as a "saint," but we as readers never do; she too has lost the power of love and clings to Catholic rite as fiercely and as desperately as to her ebony crucifix. These characters enlist our sympathy, but they do not compel our admiration.

If, in fact, Cather wished to create a novel that might have some claim to the sort of serenity she discerned in *The Country of the Pointed Firs*, *The Scarlet Letter*, and *Huckleberry Finn*, her acknowledged models were the murals of Puvis de Chavannes and the lives of the saints, *The Golden Legend*. Together, these five objects of her attention and admiration provide a basis for speculation about the ambition and achievement of the novel that, above all her others, Cather found most satisfying.

"Miss Jewett," Cather observed in her preface, "wrote of the people who grew out of the soil and the life of the country near her heart, not about exceptional individuals at war with their environment" (*On Writing*, 55). Jewett's "instinctive preference" for the common life was combined with a devotion to form that has "an organic, living simplicity and directness." Certainly some of this same instinct moved Cather to write a novel of the Southwest, but its people were not her own and in many ways must have remained permanently mysterious to her. Moreover her chosen setting was too grand and vast to invite the intimate treatment Jewett could bring to Dunnet Landing. There were daunting technical difficulties in coping with such a subject. The area was simply too large and various, and its people were varied, too, and had little to do with one another.[4] Jewett may have supplied Cather with the trusting spirit to attempt her project, and she also may have learned from her how to amplify and encompass her subject through the bonds of kinship and goodwill, the recourse to local history, the recounted tale, the intricate chambers of fond memory, even the am-

---

4. Reported in James Woodress, *Willa Cather: A Literary Life* (Lincoln: University of Nebraska Press, 1987), 392.

plifications of folklore and legend. But Jewett would not have solved this most basic of problems for her.

On the other hand, Twain might have. After all, he had written a picaresque novel in *Huckleberry Finn* and evidently felt no obligation to follow the requirements of the picaresque form but merely to indulge in its narrative opportunities. Twain launched his young hero down some four hundred miles of river territory and surveyed the manners and customs of all manner of folk. Huck is mischievous, of course, but he is no picaro. Though Huck's adventures are diverse, the author had achieved an emotional coherence in his novel by means of the adolescent consciousness of his young narrator (too shrewd to be entirely victimized by events; too innocent to be cynical about human wickedness). Twain had taken some of his cues from Cervantes in creating his own novel, and Cather, too, had made Bishop Latour and Father Joseph into rough analogs of Don Quixote and Sancho Panza. But, unlike Cervantes, Twain had submerged his own adult satirical impulses in the language and feelings of a child. The result is a novel that simultaneously dramatizes duplicity, snare, and cruelty and yet renders these same evils through a consciousness that, miraculously, seems undiminished and uncompromised by them. This is the quality Cather admired in *Huckleberry Finn,* the capacity in the author to confront time and change serenely, and she herself more nearly approached it in the *Archbishop* than in any other of her works.

In her open letter to the editor of *The Commonweal* on how she came to write *Death Comes for the Archbishop,* Cather confessed that writing the book "was like a happy vacation from life, a return to childhood, to early memories" (*On Writing,* 11). It was Twain, as she well knew, who found tonic relief from adult aggravation in the nostalgic indulgences of early memory. But *Huckleberry Finn* is also a prickly book and an excessive one—at times an escape from the disillusionment that comes with age; at times angry satirical attack on the sources of despair and disappointment. It was not Twain but Hawthorne who might have provided her with a more reliable model of serenity and artistic restraint.

Virtually every nineteenth-century reader of Hawthorne would have been responsive to his remarkable achievement in tone. Poe identified Hawthorne's originality in his "tranquil" and "subdued" manner and named it "repose." Margaret Fuller commended his "tranquil elegance." Herman Melville detected in Hawthorne's tales a "blackness ten times black," but he responded foremost to "the still rich utterance of a great intellect in repose." Henry James said of Hawthorne that "there has rarely been an observer more serene, less agitated by what he sees and less disposed to call things deeply into question." Though she was a twentieth-century writer, Cather was in most ways a nineteenth-century reader and apt to be more responsive to Hawthorne's tranquility than to his irony and ambiguity.

But there is another quality in Hawthorne that Cather admired. In "The Novel Démeublé" she notes that the "material investiture" of *The Scarlet Letter* is rendered as if it were all but unconscious; and she recalls the "twilight melancholy" of the book. In the enchantment of its "consistent mood, one can scarcely see the actual surroundings of the people; one feels them, rather, in the dusk." The high school student, she said, will learn very little about Puritan life from *The Scarlet Letter*; similarly, she confessed in her letter to *The Commonweal* that, however flattering it was to her for her readers to think otherwise, she had not "soaked" herself in Catholic lore. Instead, like Hawthorne, she had imaginatively entered into that spiritual condition without confounding her task with a superabundance of information and therefore without risking the "deadening" pompousness that typically attends such an acquisition of fact at the expense of an intuitive sympathy. And it is rarely mentioned that the most famous statement in "The Novel Démeublé" grows out of a paragraph on *The Scarlet Letter*: "Whatever is felt upon the page without being specifically named there— that, one might say, is created. It is the inexplicable presence of the thing not named . . . that gives high quality to the novel or the drama, as well as to poetry itself" (*On Writing*, 41–42).

That these three works played any part in Cather's creative approach to *Death Comes for the Archbishop* is mere surmise. It is a fact, nevertheless, that this narrative is Cather's first attempt at a historical novel, and the three books she marks for longevity and greatness are in their odd ways also historical novels of the sort Cather approved.[5] Of course, *The Golden Legend* and the frescoes of Puvis de Chavannes are the works Cather herself identifies as epitomizing what she was striving for in her novel. She identifies quite precisely the qualities she responded to in them and wished to emulate. Both avoid "accent" and possess nothing of the sense of being

---

5. Cather distinguished between the sort of historical narrative that contemplates the past from the secure position of one's own present (Flaubert's *Salammbó* is her example) and the sort that seeks to get behind the historical epoch and to look forward (Thomas Mann's *Joseph* novels are examples). Her preference is clearly on the side of the latter, and each of the American masterpieces she names is historical in just this sense.

artificially composed. The lives of the saints are rendered with such an even-
ness of treatment that there is the enviable indifference to "situation" and
the confident allegiance to "mood." "The essence of such writing," she
adds, "is not to hold the note, not to use an incident for all there is in it—
but to touch and pass on" (*On Writing*, 9).

Puvis de Chavannes's frescoes have that same quality—always, it seems,
ready to risk the sort of monotony that typically attaches to the assurances
and remote confidence of faith and spiritual vision. His paintings are the
arrangements of spare lines, uneventful flat surfaces, quiet colors; the figures are in precise yet somehow indefinite relation to the scene. Viewed
close at hand, these paintings appear realistic; a few paces back and they
become romantic.[6] Cather claimed that since she first saw these frescoes
she had wanted to attempt this effect in prose, and at least at the level of
the sentence she is remarkably successful.

Most imaginative writing, she says, is the conjunction of the general and
the particular. *The Golden Legend* was remarkable to her for its steady and
unaccented joining of actual existence and spiritual condition. Ethically
and spiritually, this is the condition of sainthood—martyrdom and suffering and trivial incident equally measured against one "supreme spiritual experience" (*On Writing*, 9). But Cather's conjunctions are achieved at the
conscientious level of style and form and do not mysteriously grow out of
some simple devotion, however much she would have us believe that the
book was composed quickly and in a uniformly happy mood. After all, the
likely readers of the lives of the saints are a community of believers, as are
those mostly French believers who come to admire Chavannes's depictions
of the patron saint of Paris. Theirs is an immense and largely historically
conditioned advantage that the imaginative writer, and especially the American writer, rarely enjoys. For Cather (as for Hawthorne, Twain, and Jewett) the writer's problem is that one must simultaneously create the fiction
and the conditions for fiction itself; one may not assume belief but compel
it. And this difficulty is particularly acute in historical fiction.[7]

---

6. Clinton Keeler, in his "Narrative without Accent: Willa Cather and Puvis de Chavannes," *American Quarterly* 17 (spring 1965): 119–26, makes this point without elab-
oration when he insightfully enlists Ortega's distinction between "proximate" and "distant" vision to explain the nature of this effect in Chavannes's frescoes.
7. Terrence Martin's discussion of Hawthorne's creative method and quality of imagination in *Nathaniel Hawthorne* (New York: Twayne Publishers, 1965) is particularly
instructive on this point, as is James Cox in "*The Scarlet Letter:* Through the Old Manse
and the Custom House," *Virginia Quarterly Review* 51 (summer 1975): 432–47.

Here, by way of clarification of this point, is a specimen passage from book 1 of her novel:

> As the wagons went forward and the sun sank lower, a sweep of red carnelian-coloured hills lying at the foot of the mountains came into view; they curved like two arms about a depression in the plain; and in that depression was Santa Fé, at last! A thin wavering adobe town . . . a green plaza . . . at one end a church with two earthen towers that rose high above the flatness. The long main street began at the church, the town seemed to flow from it like a stream from a spring. The church towers, and all the low adobe houses, were rose colour in that light,—a little darker in tone than the amphitheatre of red hills behind; and periodically the plumes of poplars flashed like gracious accent marks,—inclining and recovering themselves in the wind. (21–22; ellipses Cather's)

The passage is designed to convey a definite impression; every verbal gesture instills in the reader a mood of relief and elation. The location and relation of "things" in space and light are definite and exact—far and near, above and below, before and behind—but they dissolve in curves and thin wavering lines, plume and flash, sweep, incline, and recovery. And the rhythms of time are largely marked by interruption (note her use of dashes and ellipses), relaxation ("came into view"), and assault ("Santa Fé, at last!"). These are the rhythms of the arrival of a confused and weary traveler who, after nearly a year of misadventure, has reached his destination. What Cather wants to disclose here is the "exaltation of an hour," nothing more; an hour sunk in history and revived by human feeling and anticipation. As she observed in the essay, "Light on Adobe Walls," and as she displays here, the writer cannot paint the light but only the tricks shadows play with it. Finally all the writer can truly do is to paint the emotion that the inexhaustible relation of light and shade give her.

For the purposes of comparison only, I quote first a passage from *The Scarlet Letter*, followed by one from *The Country of the Pointed Firs*:

> It was a little dell where they had seated themselves, with a leaf-strewn bank rising gently on either side, and a brook flowing through the midst over a bed of fallen and drowned leaves. The trees impending over it had flung down great branches from time to time, which choked up the current and compelled it to form eddies and black depths at

some points, while, in its swifter and livelier passages, there appeared a channel-way of pebbles, and brown, sparkling sand. . . . Continually, indeed, as it stole onward, the streamlet kept up a babble, kind, quiet, soothing, but melancholy, like the voice of a young child that was spending its infancy without playfulness and knew not how to be merry among sad acquaintance and events of sombre hue.[8]

It had been growing gray and cloudy, like the first evening of autumn, and a shadow had fallen on the darkening shore. Suddenly, as we looked, a gleam of golden sunshine struck the outer islands, and one of them shone out clear in the light, and revealed itself in a compelling way to our eyes. Mrs. Todd was looking off across the bay with a face full of affection and interest. The sunburst upon that outermost island made it seem like a sudden revelation of the world beyond this which some believe to be so near.[9]

What is so obvious in these three passages (and I might have included also Huck's famous description of the river at daybreak at the beginning of chapter 19 of Twain's novel) is the glad acceptance of the very conditions of art as Cather succinctly described them in "Light on Adobe Walls": "No art can do anything at all with great natural forces or great elemental emotions. No poet can write of love, hate, jealousy. He can only touch these things as they affect the people in his drama and his story, and unless he is more interested in his own little story and his foolish little people than in the Preservation of the Indian or Sex or Tuberculosis, then he ought to be working in a laboratory or a bureau" (*On Writing,* 124–25). In all three passages, the scenes wear the mood as a garment. The conditions of the reader's belief and rapt attention derive not from the facts of description but from the reflected light of lived experience. And in the case of *Death Comes for the Archbishop,* the little people that inhabit Cather's novel appear to be involved with something great precisely because the author concentrates so exactly on how they are deeply affected by local events and small things; these are the natural forces and passions at work in her narrative. Cather was of course supremely interested in her little story and her

8. Nathaniel Hawthorne, *The Scarlet Letter* (New York: New American Library), 178.

9. Sarah Orne Jewett, *"The Country of the Pointed Firs" and Other Stories* (New York: Doubleday and Company, 1955), 33.

foolish little people, but the particular interest she had in her Archbishop was both absorbing and complex.

II

One of the most obvious things to be observed about the story of Archbishop Latour is that, as a figure, he satisfied twin admiring impulses in Cather—he is the sort of adventuring pioneer who is moved by a vision, and in that sense resembles Captain Forrester of *A Lost Lady* (1923); but he is also a pioneer in the way that Alexandra Bergson of *O Pioneers!* (1913) is, someone who is not ambitious or restless but instead trusts to the instinct of place. Latour, too, is an adventurer; he has traveled far to reach his diocese, and he travels widely within it. After some forty years, his missionary activity behind him, he considers retiring to his college in Clermont, but, in the end, he prefers the aromatic air of a new country to his native France. Like Alexandra, Latour, by the end of the novel, belongs to the land. New Mexico first impressed him as a "geometric nightmare," but now he "aches" for the landscape when he is away from it.

But it is also clear that Cather did not wish to make her Archbishop an active hero but to disclose through him a rare sensibility. Latour had "accomplished an historic period," we are told; the most conspicuous accomplishment of the era, however, is not his church but the locomotive, whose high thin whistle amuses rather than disturbs him. Unlike Father Haltermann, the Belgian priest Cather had met in New Mexico and who had quit the Southwest during the war to return to Europe and become a chaplain in the French army, Willa Cather had something quite different in mind for her Catholic priest. Latour would somehow become immune to the pressures of contingency and transcend the felt urgency of duty and religious vocation. He would rather more resemble the Shakespeare she imagined in "Light on Adobe Walls." Shakespeare did not have to learn how to grow old, but even so she detected in his last work that he had outlived the necessities of his own creative impulse. He might have turned from his art "to enjoy with all his senses that Warwickshire country which he loved to weakness—with a warm physical appetite. But he died before he had tried to grow old, never became a bitter old man wrangling with abstractions or creeds" (*On Writing,* 126). Jean Latour, however, was to grow old, and he would be more successful at it than Godfrey St. Peter and Myra Henshawe had been; for he would indeed turn his attention to a country he had learned to love.

What struck Cather most about the statue of Bishop Lamy, the original for Latour, was that he appeared distinguished and fearless and, above all "very, very well-bred": "What I felt curious about was the daily life of such a man in a crude frontier society" (*On Writing,* 7). Here is a telling remark about what interested Cather about her created character and her self-evident love for him.[10] However, even the admirable qualities Cather identifies in Lamy could in her fictional rendering of them degenerate into fastidiousness or cold reserve. That is to say, Latour might easily have become an old man on the frontier wrangling with creeds and abstractions, or he might have returned to France and perhaps have become as aloof and complacent as those cardinals in her prologue who argue Latour's case over a prolonged evening dinner.

The situation is a familiar one in Cather's fiction: It is the old problem she had identified in *The Troll Garden* (1905) by quoting passages from Christina Rossetti and Charles Kingsley. Inside the walls of the garden is the temptation and satisfaction of beauty and with it an inevitable dissipation and feebleness. Outside the precinct of art and culture are rude "forest children," healthy and vigorous but also barbaric and ignorant. Here, to borrow a phrase from Henry James, was the "beautiful difficulty" of her narrative. For it was apparently settled from the beginning that her character would transcend the terms of this paradox. On the one hand, Latour is a narrative device, a Jamesian register upon whom are inscribed and through whom are transmitted the effects of a country dense with mystery, legend, and fable. On the other, he is a living character, a sensibility; the landscape and the people of this country will transform his initially narrow spiritual commitments and mere delicacy of feeling into actual qualities, transform them, that is, into a larger and more embracing spirituality. How that was accomplished invites another line of inquiry and further speculation.

Though Cather claimed inspiration for her novel at a single moment, she knew that, subconsciously, she had been acquiring for many years the perceptions, tales, and memories for such a book. Besides, inspiration may

10. On January 11, 1926, while she was writing *Death Comes for the Archbishop,* Cather wrote to Irene Miner Weisz and there confessed her love for her Archbishop. The letter is in the Cather/Weisz Collection at the Newberry Library in Chicago.

supply motive, but it rarely supplies technique as well. Cather claims in her letter to *The Commonweal* that the composition of her novel took only a few months and that the happy mood in which it was conceived persisted throughout. In fact, Cather worked on the novel sporadically for well over a year, and two experiences subsequent to the moment of its inspiration contributed something important to the design of her book.

Edith Lewis is not always accurate in her chronology of events, but she seems to be faithful to the impressions and moods conveyed to her by her long-time companion.[11] Two episodes in the genesis of *Death Comes for the Archbishop* are of special interest here. In *Willa Cather Living,* Lewis recalls that in the summer of 1925, when the two traveled to Ácoma, they took the train as far as Laguna pueblo, intending to hire a driver to take them the remaining thirty or forty miles. However, the journey was delayed by about a week due to summer cloudbursts, and they stayed in what Lewis remembered as the dirtiest and roughest hotel she had ever seen. "Behind the hotel was a wretched 'tourist's camp,'" she writes, "where families in old cars crusted with mud, and with mattresses tied to them, often stopped for the night. Sometimes they would try to leave before dawn, so as not to have to pay the 50 cents fee." Despite these deplorable conditions, it was during this week, Lewis continues, that "Willa Cather often said afterwards she got the most constructive ideas for her story that she had in the whole course of writing it."[12]

Again, the episode invites speculation—what were those constructive ideas that supplemented and clarified her original inspiration? In part, there was in the situation itself not only the revealing intersection of two cultures but, perhaps, for Cather herself something of a self-revelation. In the tourist's camp there is the image of the restless American, stalled by the mud, pinching pennies, and cursing the inconvenience. Then there is Laguna pueblo, not so old as Ácoma, but steadfastly resistant to change and opportunity. And on the hill, the mission church—immaculately white, somewhat imperious, yet, inside, the walls are decorated with native art.

11. In Edith Lewis, *Willa Cather Living: A Personal Record* (New York: Alfred A. Knopf, 1953), Lewis cannot recall when they visited Canyon de Chelly (it was the summer of 1926) and remembers mistakenly that they went to Acoma in July 1926 (they had visited the mesa the summer before). It is true that Cather had to return to the Southwest to verify details and get firsthand impressions of places she had not yet visited, but Lewis mixes up the years and the places. See Woodress, *Willa Cather,* 364–65, 392–94.
12. Lewis, *Willa Cather Living,* 145.

Cather must have felt within herself something of the same tensions and paradoxes that were all about her—balked by the rains, anxious to get on with the trip; repulsed by the accommodations, generally discontented with events, yet temporarily within a community, like Ácoma, that compelled her admiration and that had long outgrown the desire to master events.

Something of the irony of her situation must have contributed to whatever Cather meant when she confided that her most constructive ideas came from that week's delay. At least the basis for many of the thematic contrasts in the novel were acted out in Laguna that week. For example, the Ácomas, the Bishop observes, share that universal yearning for something "permanent, enduring, without shadow of change" (98) and in their literal-mindedness have satisfied that yearning by living on their Rock. Atop this mesa, Latour is homesick for his own kind, "for European man and his glorious history of desire and dreams" (103). The Ácomas have endured by sheer "immobility" and have mysteriously achieved "a kind of life out of reach." Cather's treatment of the legend of Fray Baltazar on Ácoma further dramatizes this contrast—the despotic European priest's desire to master environment through artifice and indulgence is measured against an antediluvian people who had increased "neither in number nor desires" (109) for several centuries.

And of the mesa country itself, she writes that it appeared as if the Creator had walked away from the Creation, diverted by some more pressing claim upon His attention and had merely "left everything on the point of being brought together. . . . The country was still waiting to be made into a landscape" (100). This, essentially, is the dramatic situation of Alexandra Bergson in *O Pioneers!*; through her the shaggy beast of the prairie will be brought under control and made to yield a harvest for the world. But the southwestern desert is not the Nebraska Divide. Only reluctantly does it yield up a scanty corn crop and twisted peach trees. Cather had felt the vast indifference of the southwestern landscape for some time. Elizabeth Sergeant reports that an early impression Cather had had of the desert reminded her of the passage from Balzac: *"Dans le désert, voyez-vous, il y tout et il n'y rien—Dieu, sans les hommes."*[13] There is not in this perception, however, the sort of understanding that might encompass the condi-

13. Elizabeth Sergeant, *Willa Cather: A Memoir* (Lincoln: University of Nebraska Press, 1963), 84.

tion of the enduring Ácomas or other Native American tribes, for obviously in this desert there is God and man, though a species apart from the European man Latour so obviously is.

For Cather, the southwestern deserts and mountains, like the Nebraska prairie, possess the natural force of personality independent of human desire, but they are as well a grand stage upon which many generations of human stories have taken place. Latour has come to claim this land for the Church, and he explores it with curiosity and purpose. His own adventures in this land gather together the several customs and legends of place, and those, in turn, are filtered through and located in Latour's desire to comprehend the mysteries that surround him. Cather solved the purely technical difficulty of encompassing the broad reach of the territory by fusing the picaresque example of *Huckleberry Finn* with the allegorical mode of *The Divine Comedy.* She populated this desert country with human legend, incident, and passion, and she animated her hero with the desire to accept and understand, not to subdue or condemn. Whether or not the setting for these human dramas, that is, the natural landscape itself, became something more than a vast stage is a question we will hold in abeyance for the moment.

Of particular interest, though, is the way she achieves a structural coherence by making several of her interpolated tales illustrative of sin and thus bringing them into sharp contrast with the living landscape upon which they are enacted. D. H. Stewart and, more recently, John J. Murphy have shown how much Cather owed to Dante in the construction of her narrative.[14] My interest here is less in whether or how profoundly *The Divine Comedy* influenced Cather than in simply noting how she achieved the impress of an atmospheric quality, that is, a "material investiture," in her narrative by means of an almost typological drama of human sinfulness.

The seven deadly sins are personified in as many characters, and that feature of the novel may be rehearsed succinctly: Buck Scales, with his snakelike head, his malevolent glances, and his murderous past is the epitome of Wrath; the stout and despotic Fray Baltazar, whose "sensuality went no further than his garden and table" (112), is clearly a representative of Gluttony; Padre Martinez, known for his several debaucheries, is an emblem of

14. See D. H. Stewart, "Cather's Mortal Comedy" *Queen's Quarterly* 73 (1966): 244–59, and John J. Murphy, "Cather's New World Divine Comedy" *Cather Studies* 1 (1990): 21–35.

Lust; Trinidad, likely Martinez's son, is stupefied by every sensual distur-
bance and is manifestly a figure of Sloth; Manuel Chavez, in whose "disdainful features" Latour detects "the fierceness of some embitterment"
(192), is a jealous man and a fitting emblem for Envy; and Lucero, the
"miser," is a symbol of the sin of Avarice. Interestingly, Cather is most tol-
erant of the sin of Pride, the sin the Church itself reckons the most damning. For it is embodied in the sympathetic figure of Doña Isabella, whose
vanity and amusing resistance to the necessity of disclosing her true age for
her inheritance are more comic than deplorable.

These human dramas, along with the multiple legends and fables that
inhabit Cather's narrative (the legend of the holy family at the cotton-
woods, the appearance of the Virgin in Mexico, the huge serpent kept in
the mountains by the Indians) coordinate a largely episodic narrative that
surely threatened to come apart by virtue of its sheer diversity. But there is,
throughout *Death Comes for the Archbishop,* an emotional coherence and
a certain moral geography to events. If this were all, however, if Latour
were allowed merely to preside over his diocese without being profoundly
implicated in it, something would be missing, too. That Cather thought
something was missing may be inferred from the fact that she felt compelled
to return to the Southwest in the summer of 1926.

Cather and Edith Lewis traveled by train to Gallup, New Mexico, where
they hired a car to take them to the rim of Canyon de Chelly, and from
there they descended into the canyon by horseback. Apparently this trip of
two thousand miles was undertaken with some deliberation. Something
was lacking in her developing narrative, something that could not be supplied by her considerable reading in the history of the Southwest or retrieved from the fund of memories she had of the landscape and its people.
It is impossible to know with any precision what that trip provided her,
whether the novel was reconceived within the frame of a reinvigorated impetus or, perhaps, invested with a set of new directives. In any event, she
did not wait to return home to New York to take up her novel again; instead, within days she was writing, presumably under the stimulus of fresh
perceptions. Nor can one know, exactly, what she did write after that trip,
but, according to James Woodress, a significant portion of the book had
yet to be written. Certainly, the next to the last section of the book, in which
she describes Canyon de Chelly, was the direct result of her trip. And, giv-
en the tapestry-like quality of the narrative, whole sections could have been
interpolated virtually anywhere within the novel.

After the visit to Arizona, Cather and Lewis went to Santa Fe, and at the invitation of Mary Austin who was away, spent a few weeks in her house. How much actual writing Cather did in Santa Fe is uncertain (she had left the manuscript of what she had already written in New York), but she was grateful for this show of hospitality and took advantage of the uninterrupted quiet. Later, however, more than a little put out by Austin, Cather claimed that she had written only letters there.[15] Undoubtedly she wrote some portion of the novel and probably letters as well.

Perhaps, when she still felt the flush of gratitude to Austin, she wrote parts of the book "The Great Diocese." In section 3 of that book, "Spring in the Navajo Country," Latour visits Eusabio; his friend provides him with a hogan and leaves him alone. "Navajo hospitality is not intrusive," the narrator says (234). Most of the three days spent there are given over to reflections upon his first meeting with Vaillant and to writing letters. This and the next section, "Eusabio," narrate the Bishop's deep feelings for Joseph and the Indian people, most particularly the Navajo. The placement of "Spring in the Navajo Country" is interesting as well, for it follows the section "December Night," in which Latour has his deepest and most troubling spiritual doubts. These are relieved by his simple nearness to Sada, who conveys to him "the holy joy of religion" (227) and makes him recognize that his cathedral is to be Sada's house, not his own.

Latour's own "holy joy," however, is not so much a transcendent Christian joy as it is an invigorated acceptance of the immanent natural world as a theater of the spirit, and it is rendered in the two following sections. Traveling with Eusabio was "like traveling with the landscape made human"; it "was the Indian manner to vanish into the landscape, not to stand out against it" (245). The Navajo, we are told, possess nothing of the "European desire to 'master' nature, to arrange and re-create" (247), and this is something of a revelation for Latour. We are told in the prologue that it is part of the French character to "arrange," and Cather's novel is itself an arrangement, a "composition." But Eusabio obliterates any trace of human occupation; for it was the Navajo way "to pass through a country without disturbing anything; to pass and leave no trace, like fish through the water,

---

15. Austin criticized Cather's Francophila and yet at the same time bragged that the novel had been written in her home and went so far as to point out the chair in which Cather had written her novel. These impertinent demonstrations led to an immediate breakup of their friendship. See Woodress, *Willa Cather*, 394–95.

or birds through the air" (246). What is left, and is the more sacred for this lack of interference, is the landscape itself: "the sky was as full of motion and change as the desert beneath it was monotonous and still. . . . The landscape one longed for when one was far away, the thing all about one, the world one actually lived in, was the sky, the sky!" (245).

How much Latour has changed since he first entered this country. At first dismayed and distraught by the featureless monotony of a country he had come to claim for the glory of God, the story of his own spiritual growth is not the story of bringing the gospel to an alien land but of finding his own faith made more comprehensible in a country that had once impressed Willa Cather as lastingly indifferent to human desire and occupation, a place for God, not man. Latour once smiled at his own "mixed theology" when the whiteness of angora goats reminded him of sheep washed in the "blood of the Lamb" (32), but in his old age Latour has become something of the pagan himself. His spiritual condition has become a physical craving, not to be satisfied by abstraction or creed. He is willing to die in exile for the sake of that southwestern sky. Somehow his spirit is released "into the wind, into the blue and gold, into the morning, into the morning!" (288), and he feels young again.

III

The deathbed memories of Archbishop Latour are of the Navajo country, but his final memory is of his own land and his efforts in the French countryside to forge a new "Will" in young Joseph Vaillant, who was "being torn in two before his eyes by the desire to go and the necessity to stay" (315). All of these memories are retrievals from episodes recorded in sections of "The Great Diocese." At his dying, Latour's thoughts are not on final things, but beginnings, not on absolution and eternity, but perpetual change and accommodations to the shifts of time. Ultimately, the serenity with which Latour confronts time and change are founded not so much on religious conviction as on the active spiritual kinship he has had with his friend Father Joseph and a physical appetite for this southwestern country. His revelation that life is an experience of the Ego, but not the Ego itself, is "apart from his religious life; it was an enlightenment that came to him as a man, a human creature" (304).

From the beginning, Cather's literary ambitions for her novel were high ones. Two years before she began *Death Comes for the Archbishop,* she had succinctly defined the quality that made a work of fiction a "masterpiece": the capacity to confront change with serenity. She sought to emulate those American writers whose best work possessed this quality, and she applied her artistic purpose to a southwestern land and people that had long attracted her. She chose for the hero of her narrative a man who fascinated her and whose fine personality was preserved in the face of what must have been a crude and difficult existence. However, she was little interested in the threadbare story of the individual at war with his environment. Besides, the historical record of the life of Bishop Lamy did not conform to this pattern. Instead, her narrative would be about a religious man whose own faith was altered by his experience with the people he sought to convert and eventually was transformed into a larger spiritual vision.

Cather had indeed written her narrative in "the manner of legend" as she claimed she had in her letter to *The Commonweal,* and legend, as opposed to folklore, she told Fanny Butcher, is a sort "of interpretation of life by faith."[16] Legend does not require belief, and it does not speak to the wish to transcend an earthly existence; on the contrary, it is an enhancement of life. "The greatest poverty is not to live / In a physical world," wrote Wallace Stevens, "to feel that one's desire / Is too difficult to tell from despair":

> The adventurer
> In humanity has not conceived of a race
> Completely physical in a physical world . . .
> This is the thesis scrivened in delight,
> The reverberating psalm, the right chorale.[17]

Latour is himself an adventurer in humanity and dimly recognizes in the shallow light of the present—in his companionship with Eusabio and in his visit to Canyon de Chelly—the holiness of a physical race in a physical world.

Stevens comes close to the sort of affirmation Cather makes in the con-

16. Fanny Butcher, *Many Lives—One Love* (New York: Harper and Row, 1972), 358.

17. *The Collected Poems of Wallace Stevens* (New York: Alfred A. Knopf, 1954), 325–26.

cluding sections of her novel. It is Miguel de Unamuno, however, who provides apt and prayerful comment on the sort of faith this is. In *The Tragic Sense of Life,* he writes: "Do not destroy time! Our life is a hope which is continually converting itself into memory and memory in its turn begets hope. Give us leave to live! The eternity that is like an eternal present, without memory and without hope, is death. Thus do ideas exist, but not thus do men live. Thus do ideas exist in the God-Idea, but not thus can men live in the living God, in the God-Man."[18]

The last thoughts of Latour are not ideas of the God-Idea but tangible memories of beginnings, full of the poise and serenity of achievement, full of the excitement of hope. And Cather has nicely prepared us for this final moment. For we as readers become the privileged "watchers" of the scene —and in the nineteenth century, we have been told, to watch at a deathbed was considered a "privilege," "in the case of a dying priest it was a distinction" (180). When the church bell tolls the Archbishop's death, the people pray; in their hearts, Latour himself has become an item of faith, a legend. In the hearts of men and women who in some ways may be more holy than he, certainly men and women whose faith is more simple, the Archbishop is at once a memory and a hope. He joins that sustaining and common store of folklore and legendary belief; through the memory of him they face the future.

Father Joseph had predicted this for his friend: "Perhaps it pleased [God] to grace the beginning of a new era and a vast new diocese by a fine personality. And perhaps, after all, something would remain through the years to come; some ideal, or memory, or legend" (266). Outside, the people pray for the soul of their Archbishop. But Jean Latour's own tranquil final thoughts are of a very human future; they are the recollection of a moment of decision and possibility. Jean Latour and Joseph Vaillant stand at a roadside in France, and even then the *diligence* from Paris "was already rumbling down the mountain gorge" to take them to a New World (315).

18. Miguel de Unamuno, *The Tragic Sense of Life,* trans. J. E. Crawford Fitch (New York: Dover, 1954), 256.

XI

Fitzgerald and Cather

The Great Gatsby

Shortly after *The Great Gatsby* was published in 1925, F. Scott Fitzgerald received a letter from Willa Cather complimenting him on his achievement.[1] Fitzgerald was understandably excited about the letter, so much so that he woke up Christian Gauss and his wife at one o'clock in the morning to celebrate.[2] His behavior was extravagant, for Gauss was a dean at Princeton and much Fitzgerald's senior, but extravagant behavior was not unusual for Fitzgerald. Nevertheless, there is reason to suppose that the excitement Cather's letter generated in the young author was authentic and that it somehow verified his own ambitions for his new novel. For he had consciously striven to emulate Cather's literary technique; but, more importantly, she had exerted a greater influence upon him than even he seems to have realized, in matters of incident and story as well as style and technique.

Maxwell Geismar, in his book *The Last of the Provincials,* was the first to suggest the influence of Cather upon *The Great Gatsby*. He perceived a similarity of theme and tone in the concluding passages of *My Ántonia* and *Gatsby*. The novels bear a special similarity as well, he argued, in their first-person narrators, Jim Burden and Nick Carraway, both of whom possess

1. This letter is in "Scrapbook IV (The Great Gatsby)," p. 21, in the Firestone Library, Princeton University, and is dated April 28, 1925. Cather's letter was actually written in response to a letter from Fitzgerald in which he confessed to writing a passage in Gatsby that he thought reminiscent of a passage from *A Lost Lady*. Fitzgerald's letter is reprinted in Matthew Bruccoli's "'An Instance of Apparent Plagiarism': F. Scott Fitzgerald, Willa Cather, and the First *Gatsby* Manuscript," *Princeton University Library Chronicle* 39 (1978): 171–78; stipulations in Cather's will prohibit quotation from her letter.
2. Reported in Arthur Mizener's *The Far Side of Paradise: A Biography of F. Scott Fitzgerald* (Boston: Houghton Mifflin, 1965), 202.

a remembered association with someone unique and unexampled yet who embodied something precious, if lost, "like the founders of the early races," as Cather had phrased it.[3]

James E. Miller augmented and fortified the Cather/Fitzgerald connection considerably in his *The Fictional Technique of F. Scott Fitzgerald*. He suggested the possibility that Fitzgerald might have been acquainted with Cather's essay "The Novel Démeublé," in which Cather urged novelists to throw all of the furniture of fiction out the window; and, in contrast to Geismar, Miller speculated that Fitzgerald might have learned more about literary form from reading *A Lost Lady* (another first-person narrative) than from *My Ántonia* because the first is more compact, less "furnished." At any rate, Miller is surely correct in arguing that *Gatsby* represents Fitzgerald's movement away from the heavily furnished novel of "saturation," which swarms with detail, and toward the unfurnished, refined novel of "selection." And *A Lost Lady* does display greater artistic restraint than *My Ántonia*. Miller further identified the nature of Cather's influence on Fitzgerald as essentially one of technique, and especially that Fitzgerald learned from her a great deal about "point of view and about form and unity."[4]

Henry Dan Piper went even further in arguing Cather's influence on Fitzgerald when he contended that she was "almost as important as" Conrad in contributing inspiration to Fitzgerald's developing literary craftsmanship. And he additionally speculated that the young author might have responded to Edmund Wilson's review of *A Lost Lady* in January 1924, in the *Dial*. There, Wilson had argued that that novel achieved its dramatic intensity through the skillful management of its first-person point of view. This review, Piper suggested, "may even have had something to do with Fitzgerald's decision three months later to abandon the third-person approach to his story."[5] But I would argue that Cather's influence upon Fitzgerald was not restricted to matters of technique alone and that his affinity with her was even more extensive than Geismar, Miller, and Piper have suggested.

3. Maxwell Geismar, *The Last of the Provincials: The American Novel, 1915–1925* (Boston: Houghton Mifflin, 1943), 166.

4. James E. Miller Jr., *The Fictional Technique of Scott Fitzgerald* (The Hague: Martinus Nijhoff, 1957), 78. rev. ed. as *F. Scott Fitzgerald: His Art and His Technique* (New York: New York University Press, 1964).

5. Henry Dan Piper, *F. Scott Fitzgerald: A Critical Portrait* (New York: Holt, Rinehart, and Winston, 1965), 133–34.

There is no doubt that Fitzgerald thought highly of Cather's achievements (he identified himself in a letter to her as one of her "greatest admirers"), and her work was in his mind during and after the composition of *The Great Gatsby*. He was familiar enough with *A Lost Lady* (though he consistently misremembered the title as "The Lost Lady") to recognize that he had written a paragraph in *Gatsby* that "strangely paralleled" a paragraph in that book and conscientious enough to write Cather directly before the publication of his novel and inform her of this accidental plagiarism.[6] Additionally, in a letter to Charles C. Baldwin, again before the completion of *Gatsby*, he proudly announced that his book would be an "attempt at form," an attempt "to convey the feel of scenes, places and people directly—as Conrad does, as few Americans (notably Willa Cather) are already trying to do."[7] After the publication of his novel, however, despite his conscious ambitions to write a novel of form rather than a rambling chronicle of the jazz age, Fitzgerald confessed to H. L. Mencken that his book was a "failure" compared to *My Ántonia* and *A Lost Lady*.[8] This may or may not have been false modesty on Fitzgerald's part; he had often bragged about his accomplishment in *Gatsby* and felt this book made him a novelist to be reckoned with. In fact, simply in terms of what he had attempted, a novel of form, he was probably correct in the comparison. Artistically, *A Lost Lady* is no doubt the better book—it is quiet and sure; its tone is steadier; its narrative persona more consistently drawn; it seldom yields to excitable variations of mood and tempo.

But, be that as it may, we know as well that Fitzgerald, while he recognized Cather as a fellow artist, equally recognized her as a fellow midwesterner. Somewhat mistakenly, however, he thought of her as a midwestern novelist whose pioneers were exclusively "Swedes."[9] He may have had Cather in mind, in fact, and was distinguishing his experience from hers, when he had Nick recall his return trips with fellow students from

6. *The Letters of F. Scott Fitzgerald*, ed. Andrew Turnbull (New York: Charles Scribner's Sons, 1963), 507. Hereafter cited as *Letters*.

7. Quoted in Miller, *Fictional Technique*, 73–74.

8. Letter to H. L. Mencken, May 4, 1925, *Letters*, 480–81.

9. Letter to Maxwell Perkins, c. June 1, 1925, *Letters*, 183–88. Fitzgerald provided Perkins with a "History of the Simple Inarticulate Farmer and His Hired Man Christy" in this letter. In his entry for 1918, he wrote: "Willa Cather turns him [the simple farmer] Swede." *My Ántonia* (1918) does not deal with Swedes but Bohemians. Fitzgerald was probably thinking of *O Pioneers!* (1913), which does deal with Swedish farmers.

Eastern schools at Christmastime. When they saw and breathed once again the snow in the air, Nick recalls, we became "unutterably aware of our identity with this country for one strange hour, before we melted indistinguishably into it again." "That's my Middle West—," says Nick, "not the wheat or the prairies or the lost Swede towns, but the thrilling returning trains of my youth, and the street lamps and sleigh bells in the frosty dark and the shadows of holly wreaths thrown by lighted windows on the snow. I am part of that." It is this reverie in the final chapter that triggers the recognition that his story has been a midwestern one: "I see now that this has been a story of the West, after all—Tom and Gatsby, Daisy, Jordan and I were all Westerners, and perhaps we possessed some deficiency in common which made us subtly unadaptable to Eastern life."[10] And it is the El Greco–like "distortions" (177–78) he perceives in Eastern life that justify his return home after Gatsby's death.

Although *My Ántonia* and *A Lost Lady* are the only Cather novels Fitzgerald mentions in his letters, he showed a special respect for one of her short stories, "Paul's Case," when he wrote that that story alone was worth more than anything Dorothy Canfield had to say in her fiction and had claimed in his letter to Cather herself that it was one of his favorites.[11] His mention of this story is suggestive because of certain similarities it has to *Gatsby* and its thematic similarity to one of Fitzgerald's own stories, "Absolution," which had been originally intended as a prologue to *The Great Gatsby* and which would fill in details about Gatsby's early life. Cather's story, as its subtitle, "A Study in Temperament," suggests, is clearly a case study.

It is the story of a young man living in Pittsburgh who leads two lives— a cramped, conventional one symbolized by the pictures of George Washington and John Calvin and the motto "Feed the Lambs" that hang above his bed, and the life of his romantic imagination, which thrives when he is at work as an usher at Carnegie Hall. Paul takes his courage to deal with the first from his romantic convictions about the second. He dresses flamboyantly and is disdainful of the conventional expectations placed upon him by his father and his school. In one episode, Paul follows the theater performers to their hotel after the performance and allows his imagination

10. *The Great Gatsby* (New York: Scribner's Sons, 1925), 177. Hereafter cited parenthetically in the text.
11. Letter to Dayton Kohler, March 4, 1938, *Letters,* 571–72.

to play upon the exotic possibilities that lay within. As he stood in the gravel drive in the rain, he looked up at "the orange glow of the windows above him. There it was, what he wanted—tangibly before him, like a fairy world of a Christmas pantomime"; but mocking spirits stood guard at the doors, and, as the rain beat in his face, "Paul wondered whether he were destined always to shiver in the black night outside, looking up at it."[12]

In a bold gesture, he steals three thousand dollars and travels to New York and lives in romantic splendor for a fortnight. His resources depleted and aware that his father is in New York looking for him, he opts to end his life rather than return to his home on Cordelia Street. Paul commits suicide by throwing himself in front of an onrushing train, and he drops back into the "immense design of things." Reminiscent as "Paul's Case" is of certain elements in *Gatsby*—Gatsby's flamboyant dress, his romantic imagination, and his sacred, late-night vigil in chapter 7 standing in a gravel drive in a pink rag of a suit, looking up at lighted windows—the emotional complex of boyhood, the imagined life that gives Paul courage, is closer to Fitzgerald's story of Rudolph Miller, which he called "Absolution."[13]

"Absolution," too, deals with a young man caught between the conventional expectations of him and his own romantic imagination, represented by his undaunted double, who neither observes convention nor is fearful of the consequences of his disregard. For Rudolph Miller, the imagined double has a name, Blatchford Sarnemington. Blatchford lives in "great, sweeping triumphs," but Rudolph is gnawed by conscience. And when he goes to his priest to admit that he had lied in confession, he is taken aback by Father Schwartz's rhapsodic speech about the seductive attractions of the world. The priest advises Rudolph to go to an amusement park, where "everything will twinkle." For Father Schwartz, like Rudolph, is attracted to the romantic world where "things go glimmering."

He eventually removed this episode from his novel and sold it separate-

---

12. "Paul's Case: A Study in Temperament," in *Youth and the Bright Medusa* (New York: Random House, 1975), 189. "Paul's Case" was first published in *McClure's* and later collected in *The Troll Garden* (1905) and *Youth and the Bright Medusa* (1920). Since Fitzgerald mentions "Paul's Case" and "Seduction," both of which are included in *Youth and the Bright Medusa,* in his letter to Cather as being his favorite stories by her, it is likely that he read the story in this last collection.

13. "Absolution" was first published in the *American Mercury* in June 1924, 136–51; it is reprinted in *Fitzgerald's The Great Gatsby: The Novel, the Critics, the Background,* ed. Henry Dan Piper (New York: Charles Scribner's Sons, 1970), 83–92.

ly as a short story, and in the novel he changed Rudolph's name to Jimmie Gatz and his alter ego's to Jay Gatsby, but the double life of his newly named character persisted. More than "Paul's Case," however, Cather's first novel, *Alexander's Bridge,* seems to have exerted the most suggestive influence upon Fitzgerald. The novel was serialized in *McClure's* under the title *Alexander's Masquerade* in 1912 and published as a book by Houghton Mifflin later the same year. It was well received and was reissued with an author's preface in 1922, at a time when Fitzgerald was contemplating the novel that would become *The Great Gatsby.*

As a first novel, *Alexander's Bridge* is understandably an apprentice piece in many ways—Cather herself was to claim her second novel, *O Pioneers!* (1913), her first spiritually and to confess that at the time of writing *Alexander's Bridge* she was too fascinated by the unfamiliar and was unmindful of the richness of the subject matter closest to her—her native Nebraska.[14]

In any event, *Alexander's Bridge* is the story of a middle-aged engineer named Bartley Alexander whose worldly success and marital happiness are vaguely insufficient for him. Living in Boston, his supervision of the construction of a cantilever bridge in Canada requires him to travel to London periodically in order to reacquaint himself with British building codes. It is in London that he attends a play in which Hilda Burgoyne, his first love of several years before, stars. He rekindles the flame against his better judgment, all the while recognizing that his marriage is the more valuable and durable relationship. But Bartley is not actually in love with Hilda so much as he is in love with a more youthful and vital image of himself, which he perceives to be slipping away from him and which he seeks to recapture through her. Repeatedly he resolves to put an end to the affair, but he is so obsessed with this idea of himself that his resolution weakens and he travels to London to be with her.

Toward the end of the novel, Hilda's troupe travels to New York and they meet in an apartment that he keeps for business purposes. It is the distraction of Hilda that prevents Alexander from attending to a telegram from Canada concerning a structural problem with the bridge. A second telegram reaches him and he rushes to the construction site. The lower

---

14. "My First Novels: There Were Two," part 6 of *The Colophon,* 1931; reprinted in *Willa Cather on Writing: Critical Studies on Writing as an Art* (New York: Alfred A. Knopf, 1949), 89–97.

beams are showing strain, and Bartley immediately orders the workers off the bridge. But his commands come too late; the bridge collapses and Alexander drowns along with dozens of workers.

The novel is principally interesting in that it reveals Cather's persistent concern with the doubleness of personality, though with the Catherian technique as yet unrefined. In particular, her symbolism is too obvious and heavy-handed. The cantilever bridge is a conspicuous analogue for Bartley's mental state—just as Bartley's personality is described as possessing a "weak spot where some day strain would tell,"[15] so is there a structural defect in the bridge he is building. The strain is tested, of course, in his maintenance of two lives, the secure domestic one with his wife and the youthful, romantic one with Hilda. Bartley longs for the days when he had a "single purpose and a single heart" (101), but in pursuing that dream in middle age he develops a "another nature," as if "a second man has been grafted into me," and "he is fighting for his life at the cost of mine" (102). The cantilever bridge, stretched halfway across the river, is explicitly identified as symbolic of Alexander's passion, and the river beneath as "death, the only other thing as strong as love. Under the moon, under the cold, splendid stars, there were only those two things awake and sleepless; death and love, the rushing river and his burning heart" (118).

The angles of this love triangle are roughly congruent with those in *Gatsby*, but the most suggestive similarities exist in a single passage that identifies Alexander's background and his developing desire to retrieve himself from the past through his passion for Hilda. He recognizes that he is afraid of the "dead calm of middle life which confronted him" (38) and longs for the days when he felt his own "wild light-heartedness":

> Such hours were the only ones in which he could feel his own continuous identity—feel the boy he had been in the rough days of the old West, feel the youth who had worked his way across the ocean on a cattle-ship and gone to study in Paris without a dollar in his pocket. The man who sat in his offices in Boston was only a powerful machine. Under the activities of that machine the person who, in such moments as this, he felt to be himself, was fading and dying. He remembered how, when he was a little boy and his father called him in the morn-

15. *Alexander's Bridge* (Lincoln: University of Nebraska Press, 1982), 12. Hereafter cited parenthetically in the text.

ing, he used to leap from his bed into the full consciousness of himself. That consciousness was Life itself. Whatever took its place, action, reflection, the power of concentrated thought, were only functions of a mechanism useful to society; things that could be bought in the market. There was only one thing that had an absolute value for each individual, and it was just that original impulse, that internal heat, that feeling of one's self in one's own breast.

When Alexander walked back to his hotel, the red and green lights were blinking along the docks on the farther shore, and the soft white stars were shining in the wide sky above the river. (39–40)

The parallels between the lives of Gatsby and Alexander as they are revealed in this passage are rather obvious. Both characters come from provincial western or midwestern homes and had worked aboard ships. Both studied abroad—Alexander in Paris, Gatsby for a few months at Oxford. And both observe green lights across the water, which serve as emblems of that image of themselves that they attempt to retrieve through reviving a lost love. This last parallel is the most significant because it is the green light at the end of Daisy's dock in East Egg that becomes the dominant symbol of Gatsby's emotional complex. At the conclusion of chapter 1, Nick returns home in the evening and observes his mysterious neighbor "regarding the silver pepper of the stars." He decides to call to him, but checks himself when he realizes Gatsby is "content to be alone—he stretched out his arms toward the dark water in a curious way, and, far as I was from him, I could have sworn he was trembling. Involuntarily I glanced seaward—and distinguished nothing except a single green light" (21–22). And Fitzgerald returns to this image in the lyrical conclusion of the book when he has Nick sum up Gatsby's motivation: "Gatsby believed in the green light, the orgiastic future that year by year recedes before us" (182).

The green light did not always occupy so central a position in the novel. Originally there were two lights at the end of Daisy's dock, and these were meant simply to convey a certain romantic intimacy, for they were introduced in chapter 5 when Daisy and Gatsby were reunited.[16] Through

16. Information concerning the composition of *The Great Gatsby* is primarily based on Kenneth Eble's "The Craft of Revision: The Great Gatsby," *American Literature* 36 (autumn 1964): 315–26; and supplemented by Piper, *F. Scott Fitzgerald,* 138–54, and Matthew Bruccoli's *Some Sort of Epic Grandeur: The Life of F. Scott Fitzgerald* (New York: Harcourt Brace Jovanovich, 1980), 195–219.

revision, Fitzgerald made the image central to his novel. He made it the dominant image of the concluding paragraphs and introduced it into the final paragraph of chapter 1. It became a symbol to which Gatsby devoted the last ounce of his "romantic readiness," "his extraordinary gift for hope." Fitzgerald's appropriation of this image and his transformation of it into a forceful symbol invites further speculation about how extensive the influence of *Alexander's Bridge* was upon the author.

Gatsby enacts his own masquerade and, like Alexander, at odd moments the strain of his dual life tells. Despite his "resourcefulness of movement," Nick notices that Gatsby was "never quite still; there was always a tapping foot somewhere or the impatient opening and closing of a hand" (64). There is also a fascinating division between Gatsby's public personality and his private, sinister business dealings which Fitzgerald wisely decided to keep mysterious. Jay Gatsby, as opposed to Jimmie Gatz, is an invention that Nick says, "sprang from his Platonic conception of himself" (99), and to this immutable conception, we are told, Gatsby was faithful to the end. His extravagant and obsessive designs to recapture Daisy's love are vain attempts to "repeat the past," an ambition to which Gatsby devotes all his energies.

Like Bartley Alexander, Gatsby pursues his own lost vitality and youth; Alexander is in his mid-forties, but Gatsby is much younger. He is, according to Nick, an "elegant young roughneck, a year or two over thirty" (48). Yet when Maxwell Perkins, Fitzgerald's editor, wrote the author after reading the manuscript, that Gatsby seemed to be a much "older man," Fitzgerald replied: "It seems of almost mystical significance to me that you thought he was older—the man I had in mind, half-unconsciously, *was* older."[17] This discrepancy is not one of detail—what we know of Gatsby's background numerically tallies with his actual age—it is rather a matter of the emotional quality of Gatsby's character. He is not so old as to possess Meyer Wolfsheim's tired sentimentality, who excuses himself at the restaurant because he belongs to "another generation" (73). But Gatsby is well into that "menacing" decade which Nick imagines for himself on his thirtieth birthday: "Thirty—the promise of a decade of loneliness, a thinning list of single men to know, a thinning briefcase of enthusiasm, thinning hair" (136). Gatsby's enthusiasms already have thinned to one, his enthusiasm for Daisy.

17. Letter to Maxwell Perkins, c. Dec. 20, 1924, *Letters*, 171–75.

Gatsby's obsessions are, as Nick speculates, with "some idea of himself": "He talked a lot about the past, and I gathered that he wanted to recover something, some idea of himself perhaps, that had gone into loving Daisy. His life had been confused and disordered since then, but if he could once return to a certain starting place and go over it all slowly, he could find out what that thing was." That "thing," in fact, probably never existed for Gatsby (or for Jimmie Gatz for that matter). For Nick renders Gatsby's recollections of his love for Daisy five years before in such romantic and distorted detail that we immediately recognize the futility of his dreams. The moonlit "blocks of the sidewalk" in Daisy's hometown really formed a ladder to a "secret place above the trees" where, once climbed, Gatsby could "gulp down the incomparable milk of wonder." As he kissed Daisy that autumn evening in Louisville, he listened "for a moment longer to the tuning-fork that had been struck upon a star. Then he kissed her. At his lips' touch she blossomed for him like a flower and the incarnation was complete" (111–12).

The "incarnation" of which Nick speaks, and which is unbelievable precisely to the degree that it is poetic, is that particularized moment, as it is sustained by memory, when Gatsby believed his own Platonic self had for an instant touched the earth; and it is that identity, which never actually existed, that he seeks and which is symbolized by the green light across the water. It is Gatsby's futile dream which Fitzgerald explicitly identifies with the American Dream in the conclusion of the novel and which thus makes a mythical figure of his character:

> I became aware of the old island here that flowered once for Dutch sailors' eyes—a fresh, green breast of the new world. Its vanished trees, the trees that had made way for Gatsby's house, had once pandered in whispers to the last and greatest of all human dreams; for a transitory enchanted moment man must have held his breath in the presence of this continent, compelled into an aesthetic contemplation he neither understood nor desired, face to face for the last time in history with something commensurate to his capacity for wonder. (182)

This is the age-old dream Gatsby seeks, but it is a vain striving: "He had come a long way to this blue lawn, and his dream must have seemed so close that he could hardly fail to grasp it. He did not know that it was already behind him, somewhere back in the vast obscurity beyond the city, where the dark fields of the republic rolled on under the night" (182).

These famous concluding passages of *The Great Gatsby* not only bear the weight of the novel and, in fact, transport Gatsby's story into the realm of myth, but they had informed it as well. The final paragraphs grew out of a single lyrical sentence that Fitzgerald had originally used to conclude the first chapter. He crossed that sentence out, worked up the paragraphs, and placed them at the conclusion. In doing so, he introduced the green light, which had before been confined to chapter 5, and then worked it into the concluding paragraph of chapter 1 as well. Thus, he gave Gatsby's yearnings a single and dramatic focus, for this green light, as symbol, is inextricably wed to Gatsby's consciousness of it. Through revision, Fitzgerald made his small-town boy from North Dakota a jaded and mysteriously sinister figure, for whom the world at large does not go "glimmering," as it had in "Absolution," but for whom a single and resolute purpose, existing in the free solution of his own imagined memory, of a possession five years past, is palpably located and symbolized in the green light at the end of Daisy's dock.

Fitzgerald's creative imagination, as Arthur Mizener has pointed out, was an instinctive rather than a calculating one. Despite his claims that he was attempting to write a novel of form, the author's relation to his material in Gatsby was probably felt rather than discerned. Surely Maxwell Perkins must have been dismayed by the reply he received after he had written Fitzgerald commending him on his achievement with this novel and making a few suggestions: "You once told me you were not a *natural* writer," he wrote, "—my God! You have plainly mastered the craft, of course; but you needed far more than craftsmanship for this." Fitzgerald's response included a curious remark: "My first instinct after your letter was to let [Gatsby] go and have Tom Buchanan dominate the book . . . but Gatsby sticks in my heart."[18] If we imagine what a small and trivial book his novel might have been with Tom Buchanan as the dominant character, we must realize how much we have to thank for Fitzgerald's "heart." But more than that, we can understand how, in his meticulous attention to individual sentences, his "craftsmanship," he was somehow blind to the larger successes of his novel except in the most instinctive way. This may help to explain why he might recognize a paragraph that "strangely paralleled" one

---

18. Perkins, Letter to Fitzgerald, Nov. 20, 1924, in *Editor to Author: The Letters of Maxwell E. Perkins*, ed. John Hall Wheelock (New York: Charles Scribner's Sons, 1950), 38–41; Fitzgerald, Letter to Perkins, c. Dec. 20, 1924, *Letters*, 171–75.

of Cather's in *A Lost Lady* and, at the same time, to have failed to re-member the title of that novel or to recognize the ultimately larger influ-ences which "Paul's Case" and *Alexander's Bridge* had exerted upon him.

Willa Cather had written Fitzgerald of her admiration of *Gatsby* in the spring of 1925; the next fall she would begin to write what she ultimately considered her finest novel, *Death Comes for the Archbishop* (1927). It would be written, she would recall a few years later, in "the style of leg-end," the essence of which is to lightly "touch and pass on." Such a cre-ative method would be a "kind of discipline," she wrote, "in these days when the 'situation' is made to count for so much in writing."[19] It was this sort of artistic detachment that Cather had cultivated since the beginning of her career and that gave rise to some of her finest work. In part, her dis-paragement of *Alexander's Bridge* in the preface to the 1922 edition of the novel proceeded from her belated recognition that she had relied too much upon "interesting" material and had tried to capitalize upon a situation. But, unlike Cather, the imaginative coherence Fitzgerald achieved in *The Great Gatsby* appears to have derived not from his detachment from but his involvement with his material. However much Fitzgerald may have learned from Cather about the writer's craft, however much *Alexander's Bridge* may or may not have contributed to his plot, one suspects that the real achievement of Gatsby had its sources in an intense emotional identi-fication with both his main character and his narrator in a way that was but half-conscious. If Fitzgerald responded to *My Ántonia* and *A Lost Lady* professionally, he probably responded to *Alexander's Bridge* personally, for it identified an emotional complex he found sympathetic, one indeed that may have tallied with his own.

In the opening chapter of *The Great Gatsby*, Nick Carraway confesses to his burgeoning expectations for his new career in the East: I was going to "become again that most limited of all specialists, the 'well-rounded man.' This isn't just an epigram—life is much more successfully looked at from a single window, after all" (4). His single-window ambitions prove untenable, however; soon after his arrival in New York his life becomes en-tangled with the careless, careening lives of others. Dragged to a New York City apartment by Tom Buchanan, Nick, Tom, Myrtle Wilson, and the rest

19. "On *Death Comes for the Archbishop*," an open letter to the editor of *The Com-monweal*, Nov. 23, 1927; reprinted in *Willa Cather on Writing*, 3–13.

drink, argue, and lament through the afternoon and into twilight, and Nick reflects upon his unwilling association with this crowd: "Yet high over the city our line of yellow windows must have contributed their share of human secrecy to the casual watcher in the darkening streets, and I was him too, looking up and wondering. I was within and without, simultaneously enchanted and repelled by the inexhaustible variety of life" (36).

Casual observer and reluctant participant, Nick brings a double vision to the story he tells, at once diffuse and exact. It is a simultaneous vision that, much like a stereopticon, lifts its figures from the page precisely because the images don't quite jibe, but are, instead, flat and lifeless without this discrepancy. How close this sort of double consciousness is to Fitzgerald's very sane assessment of his own "crack up" in an essay by the same name. "The test of a first-rate intelligence," he wrote a decade after the publication of *Gatsby*, "is the ability to hold two opposed ideas in the mind at the same time, and still retain the ability to function."[20] Fitzgerald's quiet and lucid self-diagnosis is a complaint not of the loss of his intelligence but of his ability to function, his artistic edge.

While he was writing *The Great Gatsby*, however, he retained the ability to function though he divided himself by identifying with both the jaded and obsessive Gatsby and the dazzled Nick, full of "interior rules" yet awestruck by the variety of life. Thus divided, he would divide his sympathies. Fitzgerald had of course identified with Gatsby; he wrote John Peale Bishop that that character "started out as one man I knew and then changed into myself—the amalgam was never complete in my mind." But he was Nick Carraway, too. For he could well remember his own first reactions to New York as being one "up from the country gaping at the trained bears. . . . I had come only to stare at the show. . . . I took the style and glitter of New York even above its own valuation."[21]

In nearly every line of the book there is a certain divided quality, not yet a "crack-up" but a slight fissure that yields a pervasive emotional tension, a tension where someday strain would tell. "I had no girl whose disembodied face floated along the dark cornices and blinding signs" (81), says Nick; and lacking Gatsby's obsession, he is left simply with dark cornices

20. "The Crack-Up," in *The Crack-Up*, ed. Edmund Wilson (New York: New Directions Publishing, 1945), 69: this article originally appeared in *Esquire*, Feb. 1936.

21. Letter to John Peale Bishop, Aug. 9, 1925, *Letters*, 358; "My Lost City," in *The Crack-Up*, 24.

and blinding signs for which his "interior rules" are sorry equipment. The world goes "glimmering" for Nick, but it lacks focus. This passage is representative of such a tension, I think: "Again at eight o'clock, when the dark lanes of the Forties were five deep with throbbing taxicabs bound for the theater district, I felt a sinking in my heart. Forms leaned together in the taxis as they waited, and voices sang, and there was laughter from unheard jokes, and lighted cigarettes outlined unintelligible gestures inside. Imagining that I, too, was hurrying toward gayety and sharing their intimate excitement, I wished them well" (57–58). Nick's despair and provincial magnanimity punctuate his description of this haunted scene of faceless forms—irregularly lighted and half heard—throbbing with excitement but stalled in traffic.

This is typical of the El Greco–like distortion that permeates the novel, "at once conventional and grotesque" (178). And we find it everywhere in the book. In the photograph of Myrtle Wilson's mother that "hovered like an ectoplasm on the wall" (30); in the invisible object Jordan Baker balances upon her chin; in Nick's simultaneous fascination and repulsion by the idea that one man could fix the World Series; in the tramp who sells dogs on the street and yet looks all the world like John D. Rockefeller; in the tragic eyes and short upper lips of eastern European faces in a funeral train; in the city itself, "rising up across the river in white heaps and sugar lumps all built with a wish" (69). And we find it in Nick's reaction to Gatsby himself, at once "gorgeous" and representative of "everything for which I have an unaffected scorn" (2).

How much of this was the result of sheer "craftsmanship" and how much represented a heavy investment of the author himself in his material is unknown. But we do know that Fitzgerald continued his inventory of losses in a sequel to "The Crack-Up," which looks back to that time: "For a check-up of my spiritual liabilities indicated that I had no particular head to be bowed or unbowed. Once I had had a heart but that was all I was sure of." His perception of the grotesqueries of life had once been tempered by sympathy and sustained by an enormous vitality. But these qualities had played out; he had developed a "sad attitude toward sadness, a melancholy attitude toward melancholy and a tragic attitude toward tragedy."[22] He had become identified with the objects of his "horror and compassion,"

22. "Pasting It Together," in *The Crack-Up*, 80–81; this article originally appeared in *Esquire*, April 1936.

and he was paralyzed by his own perceptions. "Life, ten years ago," he wrote, "was largely a personal matter. I must hold in balance the sense of the futility of effort and the sense of the necessity to struggle. . . . If I could do this through the common ills—domestic, professional and personal—then the ego would continue as an arrow shot from nothingness to nothingness with such force that only gravity would bring it to earth at last."[23] This passage has the ring of truth, but it stands as a statement of philosophical conviction rather than a felt reaction to life. But there seems to have been a time when life, indeed, was a "personal matter" for Fitzgerald, when Gatsby, when all vain human striving, "stuck in his heart."

The search for a lost vitality and a lost self that characterized the strivings of Bartley Alexander and Jay Gatsby was too familiar to Fitzgerald by the time he came to write "The Crack-Up." If at one time he had sympathized with their middle-aged dream of youth, now he shared it. In the end, Fitzgerald suffered from that very condition he had himself once so compassionately dramatized:

> It was back into the mind of the young man with cardboard soles who had walked the streets of New York. I was him again—for an instant I had the good fortune to share his dreams, I who had no more dreams of my own. And there are still times I creep up on him, surprise him on an autumn morning in New York or a spring night in Carolina when it is so quiet that you can hear a dog barking in the next county. But never again as during that all too short period when he and I were one person, when the fulfilled future and the wistful past were mingled in a single gorgeous moment—when life was literally a dream.[24]

23. "The Crack-Up," 70.
24. "Early Success," in *The Crack-Up,* 90; this article originally appeared in *American Cavalcade,* Oct. 1937.

XII

A Source for "Where Are You Going, Where Have You Been?"

One of Joyce Carol Oates's most familiar and most disturbing short stories—"Where Are You Going, Where Have You Been?"—is so richly symbolic and her characters are so improbably dressed and motivated that one is tempted to see it exclusively as a play of primal forces rather than as a fiction derived from and responsive to life itself. One critic, in fact, has argued that the story is an allegory.[1] And, indeed, the characters in the story seem larger than life. Her villains (and there is no mistaking that they are villains) are actuated by raw emotions, or none at all, outfitted in the most unlikely and sinister ways, and possessed of an unaccountable knowledge of the doings of the victim and her family. The victim herself is a freshly washed, blonde, blue-eyed picture of innocence. But however attractive a view it may be to imagine Ms. Oates conceiving of a modern "tale" in the tradition of Hawthorne and Poe that freely mingles the marvelous with the psychologically true, it is contrary to the overwhelming evidence that the author drew her inspiration for her story from a real event publicized in popular national magazines. This allegorical view also injures the story itself for it diverts our attention from the fact that the evil she portrays is all too real and renders ineffective the pointed criticism Oates makes of the American Dream, which is the larger purpose of her story. Rather, Oates modeled her story after real people and real events—though she did, as any gifted writer does, imaginatively transform the actual into a fiction of dramatic power. It is my purpose here, then, to identify the parallels between her story and the magazine reports of a real criminal and a real crime that seem to have had a germinal effect upon Oates's creative imagination and

---

1. Marie Mitchell Olesen Urbanski, "Existential Allegory: Joyce Carol Oates's 'Where Are You Going, Where Have You Been?'" *Studies in Short Fiction* 15 (spring 1978), 200–203.

to suggest how her theme of the death of the American Dream may have been prompted by these magazines.

The source of and inspiration for Oates's fiend, Arnold Friend, is not nearly so mysterious as the almost supernatural attributes of this character might suggest. Oates's character was derived from the exploits, widely publicized by *Time, Life,* and *Newsweek* magazines during the winter of 1965– 1966, of a real killer from Tucson, Arizona.[2] Moreover, the publication date of "Where Are You Going, Where Have You Been?" in *Epoch* (fall 1966) suggests this influence, though the more accessible appearance of the story later in her collection of short stories, *The Wheel of Love* (1970), tends to obscure the implication that she probably wrote the story soon after her acquaintance with the grisly details of the three murders committed by a young man named Charles Howard Schmid and nicknamed by the author of the *Life* piece about him as the "Pied Piper of Tucson."

Oddly enough, those very details which, by their peculiarity, tend to mark Arnold Friend as an inhuman, perhaps superhuman avatar of undiluted evil are derivative rather than invented. Charles Schmid, an extremely short and muscular man, was a mere five feet three inches tall but nevertheless had been a state champion in gymnastics during his high school years. After being suspended from high school for stealing tools from the auto shop, he continued to inhabit well beyond his teen years such high school haunts as drive-in restaurants, bowling alleys, and the public swimming pool. He was, in fact, twenty-three years old when he was arrested for the murders of Gretchen and Wendy Fritz, aged seventeen and thirteen, in the fall of 1965 and while an earlier third murder of Alleen Rowe, fifteen, was still being investigated. To compensate for his shortness and to disguise the fact that he was a good deal older than the teen-aged girls to whom he was attracted, Schmid went to bizarre and rather stagey extremes. As all the national magazines pointed out, Schmid stuffed rags and folded

2. "Secrets in the Sand," *Time,* November 26, 1965, 28; Dan Moser, "The Pied Piper of Tucson," *Life,* March 4, 1966, 18–21, 80C f; "Growing Up in Tucson: Death Sentence," *Time,* March 11, 1966, 28; and "Killing for Kicks" *Newsweek,* March 14, 1966, 35–36. Since some of the parallels between the Oates short story and the national magazine coverage of the Charles Schmid case occur only in the *Life* essay—for example, the fact that the real victim, Alleen Rowe, and Oates's fictional victim, Connie, both washed their hair shortly before the arrival of their assailant—it seems likely that this essay was the primary, if not the sole source of Oates's familiarity with the story. Therefore, all the information about the murder case has been taken from the *Life* piece unless otherwise indicated in the text or by footnote.

tin cans into his black leather boots to appear a few inches taller. And he dyed his hair raven black, often wore pancake makeup, pale cream lipstick, and mascara. He sometimes darkened his face to a "tan" with makeup and painted a beauty mark on his cheek.

His behavior was as audacious as his appearance. He drove a gold-colored car, in which he "cruised" Tucson's Speedway Boulevard. And he was known to tell tall tales about how he came into the money he habitually flourished—to his male admirers he suggested that he trafficked in drugs; to the females he bragged that he had been paid by women whom he had taught "100 ways to make love." He was also inclined to introduce himself by a number of aliases, his favorite being "Angel Rodriguez."

The parallels in "Where Are You Going?" to the reports of the Schmid case are too clear-cut to have been accidental. The young victim of Arnold Friend's attention, Connie, notices that he, like Schmid, is quite short: "He wasn't tall, only an inch or so taller than she would be if she came down to him." But he, like the gymnast Schmid, is muscular as well. He wore a "belt that pulled his waist in and showed how lean he was, and a white pull-over shirt that was a little soiled and showed the hard, small muscles of his arms and shoulders. He looked as if he probably did hard work, lifting and carrying things. Even his neck looked muscular."[3] And Arnold Friend totters and wobbles on his black leather boots and eventually almost loses his balance. This draws Connie's attention to his feet: "He had to bend and adjust his boots. Evidently his feet did not go all the way down; the boots must have been stuffed with something so that he would seem taller" (49).

Oates's description of Friend's face was probably derived from the several photographs reprinted in national magazines. One photo in particular may have been influential for it showed Schmid, as Oates had described Friend, with "cheeks slightly darkened because he hadn't shaved for a day or two, and the nose long and hawklike" (42). Schmid's dark eyes in this photograph may well have impressed her as "chips of broken glass that catch the light in an amiable way" (43). But more concretely, Friend also wears makeup, as did Schmid. His eyelashes are extremely dark, "as if painted with a black tarlike material" (45), and he may even be wearing a

---

3. "Where Are You Going, Where Have You Been?" reprinted in *The Wheel of Love* (New York: Vanguard Press, 1970), 42. Subsequent citations will be to this edition and will be included parenthetically in the text.

wig (46). Connie notes Friend's fascinating but dangerous smile, "as if he were smiling from inside a mask." "His whole face was a mask, she thought wildly, tanned down to his throat but then running out as if he had plastered make-up on his face but had forgotten about his throat" (48).

In incidental ways, too, Arnold Friend recalls Charles Schmid. Friend also drives a gold car, apparently older than the gold car Schmid owned, but newly painted. He is older than the boys with whom Connie is familiar; though Oates makes his age a question, Connie thinks he may be thirty, even older. And Arnold Friend is characterized by the same sort of compensating braggadocio Schmid's friends remembered of him in the magazine articles: "He sounded like a hero in a movie, declaring something important. But he spoke too loudly and it was as if he were speaking to someone behind Connie" (50). Moreover, the shocking and confident sexual directness of Friend contrasts sharply with the "caresses of love" Connie dreamed of before Friend pulled into her drive, "sweet, gentle, the way it was in the movies and promised in songs" (39). Schmid's habitual brag to teenage girls that he knew "100 ways to make love" is only slightly less direct than Friend's brag to Connie: "I'll hold you so tight you won't think you have to get away or pretend anything because you'll know you can't. And I'll come inside you where it's all secret and you'll give in to me and you'll love me" (47). "People don't talk like that," says Connie, but of course some people do, and Charles Schmid apparently did. Finally, even the name of Oates's villain may have been suggested by the *Life* article. For, whatever other symbolic suggestion the name may have, the irony of a young man who had once tied a string to the tail of his pet cat and had beaten it against the wall until it was a bloody mass but nevertheless assumed the alias "Angel" could hardly have been lost upon Oates's artistic sensibility. Surely she intended the same sort of irony in naming her demoniac character "Friend."

For the violent crime implied in "Where Are You Going?"—the rape and subsequent murder of Connie—which is not dramatized but is a sure eventuality, Oates also seems to have drawn upon the story of Charles Schmid, but she made certain alterations in the details of it. Alleen Rowe was, like Connie, fifteen years old at the time of her assault, and she too had washed her hair just before her assailants arrived. Rowe's rape and murder also involved accomplices with an apparent knowledge of her parents' habits. Friend, it will be remembered, knows Connie's name, that her family is gone to a barbecue, and how long they will be gone. Arnold Friend is accompanied by Ellie, a rather passive if not oblivious accomplice to be sure, but Schmid's violent crime involved a young man, John Saunders, and a young woman, Mary French. Apparently on the spur of the moment, these three wondered whether they might kill someone and get away with it.[4] Because she had once "stood up" John Saunders, they decided upon Alleen Rowe and went to her house the same evening. Perhaps by a "fortunate" coincidence, or perhaps aware that Alleen's mother worked nights, they found Alleen home alone. Mary French tapped on Alleen's window and eventually persuaded her to go for a drive with them. In the desert, the two men raped her and then beat her to death, and the three buried her in the sand.

The rape of the Rowe girl was, according to the *Newsweek* account of the murder, an afterthought. The *Newsweek* article is entitled "Killing for Kicks" and it portrays the real criminal act as very nearly motiveless and unaccountable. In fact, *Life, Time,* and *Newsweek* all preferred to lay the blame on a generation of indulgent, cruising teenagers and their unmindful parents. But Oates modified the details of the actual event in significant ways. For one thing, she has Connie's seduction conducted in broad daylight while her family is away at a family barbecue and has Arnold Friend display intimate, even satanic knowledge of her family's doings. Also, she chose to downplay Saunders's part in the murder and eliminated the role of Mary French altogether. It is Friend, rather than his accomplice, who is apparently offended by the casual snub he receives at a drive-in restaurant and says to Connie, "Gonna get you, baby" (37). And she seems to have combined Schmid's reputation as a "pied piper" with Mary French's inducements to Alleen to leave her house in the character of Arnold Friend. Thus, she gave to her story an unsettling tension by locating the evil in a single character whose motive was even slighter than John Saunders's and who was not afraid to tempt her in the daytime.

Oates also seems to have combined Schmid's three victims into one, or perhaps two characters. The murder of Wendy Fritz had been the result of her having accompanied her older sister Gretchen to the desert with Schmid. Oates suggests at least the unintentional complicity of Connie's older sister June, whom Connie resents because her mother continually reminds Connie what a model daughter June is. But Connie's parents allow her to go out at night with her friends because June does the same; and it

4. "Killing for Kicks," *Newsweek,* March 14, 1966, 35–36.

is this freedom that brings Connie into the orbit of Arnold Friend. But Connie also resembles Alleen Rowe in her age, her freshly washed hair, her love for rock and roll music, and, as *Life* described it, a susceptible, romantic mentality.

Thus far our discussion of Oates's reaction to an actual incident has focused upon the particular ways she took suggestions from the documented reports of Schmid's violent crimes and dramatized them in her story. But, more significantly, she seems also to have taken her cues from these magazine reports in more general ways, which may account for the related thematic elements of seductive rock and roll and violently extinguished innocence that permeate her story.

One cannot help but pause and ponder Oates's dedication of this story to Bob Dylan. However, it is a mistake, I think, to conclude with Marie Urbanski that the dedication is pejorative because Dylan made music "almost religious in dimension among youth."[5] Rather, it is honorific because the history and effect of Bob Dylan's music had been to draw youth away from the romantic promises and frantic strains of a brand of music sung by Buddy Holly, Chuck Berry, Elvis Presley, and others. It was Bob Dylan, after all, who told us that the "times they are a changin'," and one of Oates's aims in her short story is to show that they have already changed. It is the gyrating, hip-grinding music of people like Elvis Presley, whom Schmid identified as his "idol," which emanates from Ellie's transistor radio, the "hard, fast, shrieking" songs played by the disc jockey "Bobby King," rather than the cryptic, atonal folk music of Bob Dylan.

Both Connie and Arnold Friend are enthusiastic about "Bobby King" and psychologically linked to one another by an appreciation of the rhythmic beat of the music he plays. Connie observes that Ellie's radio is tuned to the same station as her radio in the house, and when Arnold Friend says that King is "great," Connie concedes, "He's kind of great." Arnold counters, "Listen, that guy is great. He knows where the action is" (41). Friend's statement of enthusiasm recalls the quotation that introduces the *Life* essay on Charles Schmid:

> "Hey, c'mon babe, follow me,
> I'm the Pied Piper, follow me,

5. Urbanski, "Existential Allegory," 202.

I'm the Pied Piper
And I'll show you where it's at."
—Popular song,
Tucson, winter 1965

Arnold Friend does, indeed, show Connie "where it's at," and he draws her from the house with his alternating blandishments and threats much as a pied piper. Moreover, Connie's ultimate, mindless decision to go with Friend is meant to recall the beckoning tempo of rock and roll: "She cried out, she cried for her mother, she felt her breath start jerking back and forth in her lungs as if it were something Arnold Friend was stabbing her with again and again with no tenderness. A noisy, sorrowful wailing rose all about her and she was locked inside the way she was locked inside the house" (52).

When Connie kicks the telephone away and opens the screen door to go with Friend, there can be little question where she is going or where she has been. She is going to her death, and her fate is largely the result of a consciousness shaped by the frantic life of cruising in fast cars, sipping Cokes out of sweating paper cups with anonymous boys, a consciousness epitomized by the frantic music she listens to.

But it is naive to suppose that this story is about the dangerous effects of rock and roll; rather, the music is emblematic of the tempo of American life generally. And the questions in the title—where are you going, where have you been?—are addressed to America itself. The author of the *Life* article asked sarcastically, "Isn't Tucson—out there in the Golden West, in the grand setting where the skies are not cloudy all day—supposed to be a flowering of the American Dream?" Oates's short story is her withering, disturbing reply, and her story is very nearly a suspenseful parody of the mythic promises of the West and "Home on the Range." For Connie's house is distant from any others and the "encouraging words" Arnold Friend speaks are hypnotic enough to lure her out of doors beneath a perfectly blue, cloudless sky.

Insofar as this story has a setting, it is set in the West. Connie's parents leave for a family barbecue, and their daughter daydreams in the summer heat ("It was too hot," she thinks), under the sky "perfectly blue and still" (39). She stares from her "asbestos 'ranch house'" to the limitless expanse of land outside it. Her house seems small to her, and Arnold reminds her that the walls of her house do not provide a citadel: "The place where you came from ain't there any more, and where you had in mind to go is cancelled out. This place you are now—inside your daddy's house—is nothing but a cardboard box I can knock down any time. You know that and always did know it. You hear me?" (52). Her "asbestos" house is no protection from the devilish forces embodied in Arnold Friend, nor from his fiery passion, and never has been. If there were a fire inside, Friend tells her, "If the place got lit up with a fire, honey, you'd come runnin' out into my arms an' safe at home" (49).

Of course there is a fire inside, a fire inside Connie's brain. The pounding of her heart is simply "a pounding, living thing inside this body that really wasn't really her either." Arnold's "incantation" (53) draws her out, but those values generally associated with the American Dream, of hearth and home and innocent youth, are by this time a dim flicker in her mind. Thoughts of "Aunt Tillie's" barbecue, hot dogs and corn on the cob, tender flirtations, the lovely promises of songs are now remote, almost as though they had never been. As she steps out to Arnold Friend, she sees the land: "the vast sunlit reaches of the land behind him and on all sides of him—so much land that Connie had never seen before and did not recognize except to know that she was going to it" (54). When one knows that Charles Schmid buried his victims in the desert, the dictum of the American Dream that one ought to return to the land, that nature speaks to us in lasting and benevolent ways, takes on a singularly sinister connotation. The American Dream is quite extinct here, and Connie's parents and sister are as much dreamers as she. Ultimately, the questions that Oates chose as a title for her story might be asked about America itself as well as about Connie's life, and asked more effectively in the slang idiom of Connie's generation: "Where *are you* going? Where *have you* been?" For they address a society that, by tradition, has preferred its agrarian dreams and promises to harsher realities and aggressive evils and is therefore dangerously blind to them. Our antique values, says Oates, are not proof against the seductions of the piper's song.

XIII

Justice on the Reservation

Tony Hillerman's Novels and the Conflict between Federal and Tribal Jurisdiction

Early in Tony Hillerman's detective novel *The Dance Hall of the Dead* (1975), the chief of the Zuni police, Ed Pasquaanti, discusses the problem of jurisdiction among state, county, and Navajo tribal officers. He does so because he wants it clearly understood that, on the Zuni reservation, the Zuni police will be directing the investigation of the suspected murder of a Zuni boy, Ernesto Cata. The various law enforcement agents defer to Pasquaanti's assertion of authority, but behind their acknowledgment is the tacit recognition of and familiarity with the fact that almost any major crime committed on an Indian reservation may involve problems of jurisdiction. According to William C. Canby, Professor of Indian Law at Arizona State University, almost all crimes committed on an Indian reservation have a jurisdiction problem at bottom, and a great many cases are dismissed on that basis.[1] Such problems are generally complicated, if not bewildering, and typify the bureaucratic, legalistic blend of complex, sometimes paradoxical, sometimes absurd relations of state and federal governments to Indian tribes. In Hillerman's detective novel, however, this jurisdiction problem implicitly provides a bureaucratic background against which his main character, Lt. Joe Leaphorn, a Navajo tribal policeman, emerges as a genuinely heroic figure. For a cultural sense of justice and communal harmony, at once more ancient and more pure than the legal fictions that constrain him, claims his attention and motivates him.

Briefly, the novel concerns the ritual-like slaying of a young Zuni boy. Leaphorn is called into the investigation to locate George Bowlegs, a young

---

1. Professor Canby patiently answered several questions of jurisdiction that I put to him and was most helpful in many other ways as well.

Navajo friend of the slain Zuni. Bowlegs is a suspect in the murder case and Leaphorn's job is to bring the boy in for questioning. His search for the youth takes him back and forth between the Zuni and Ramah reservations and eventually onto private land in Arizona. In attempting to obtain information that might help him find the boy, Leaphorn travels to a hippie commune, which may or may not be on Navajo land, where Bowlegs was a frequent visitor. He questions a graduate student in archaeology, Ted Isaacs, and Professor Chester Reynolds, a noted anthropologist, at the site of an archaeological dig on the Zuni reservation. He visits the Bowlegs hogan on Navajo land in Ramah, where on one occasion he sees a figure wearing a Zuni mask and later finds the boy's father murdered. And he travels to a lake sacred to the Zunis but located in Arizona and therefore not part of the Zuni reservation.

It soon becomes apparent to Leaphorn that the masked figure he had seen in the darkness is probably the real murderer, who is also looking for the Navajo boy. His quest for Bowlegs then becomes a race to find the boy before the mysterious figure does. He finally finds Bowlegs in Zuni during the celebration of Shalako, but too late. Bowlegs is murdered, and Leaphorn glimpses the masked figure as he is being dragged away by Zunis, who will surely kill him for profaning this holy event. If Leaphorn is unsuccessful in bringing in the Bowlegs boy, he nevertheless does solve the crime: Professor Reynolds has been salting the dig site and allowing his unsuspecting graduate student to find and document information that will support Reynolds's theories about Folsom man. The young friends, Cata and Bowlegs, mischievously picked up samples of the fake artifacts. Discovery of Reynolds's deception would destroy his professional reputation, so the anthropologist has murdered three men, including Cata, in his efforts to retrieve the damning evidence.

Such an oversimplification of Hillerman's ingenious plot is a disservice to his novel, but it is sufficient for an examination of the jurisdictional problems in question. Quite apart from these strict legal considerations, however, the responsibilities of the Navajo police are awesome. Approximately 230 officers cover an area roughly three times the size of New Jersey and operate on an annual budget somewhat smaller than Newark's.[2] But added

2. The information about the number of police officers comes from an article by John Orr of the Dine Bureau entitled "Navajo Police Go with Times," *Gallup (New Mexico) Independent,* May 25, 1979, sec. C, p. 2.

to these severe limitations are the general federal restraints under which tribal law enforcement operates.

It is generally agreed that the powers of Indian jurisdiction in criminal and civil cases occurring on land known as "Indian country"[3] is historically derived from the Supreme Court decision in the case of *Worcester vs. Georgia* (1832).[4] In that case, the state imprisoned with tribal consent a white man living among the Cherokees, but the court ruled that states had no power to infringe upon the rights of the federal government to regulate intercourse with Indian tribes. In the words of Chief Justice Marshall: "The Indian nations had always been considered as distinct, independent, political communities. . . . The Cherokee nation, then, is a distinct community, occupying its own territory, with boundaries accurately described, in which the laws of Georgia can have no force. . . . The whole intercourse between the United States and this nation, is, by our constitution and laws, vested in the government of the United States."[5]

So complete was the sovereignty of Indian nations and the authority of the federal government above state powers that the Supreme Court later ruled (*Ex parte Crow Dog,* 1883) that the criminal jurisdiction of a tribe extended even to capital punishment, where no express limitation for those powers existed. Congress found this ruling obnoxious, however, and less than two years later enacted a law which made the crimes of homicide, manslaughter, rape, assault with intent to kill, arson, burglary, and larceny committed on reservation land federal crimes and therefore subject to federal jurisdiction. Later, notorious cases of robbery, incest, assault with a dangerous weapon,[6] and embezzlement[7] were added to the list, making

3. The term "Indian country" is defined in *U.S. Code,* vol. 18, sec. 1151, and is meant to include rights of way and patent land within the exterior boundaries of a reservation.

4. See Monroe E. Price, *Law and the American Indian: Readings, Notes, and Cases* (Indianapolis: Bobbs-Merrill, 1973), 40–43; Brend H. Gubler, "A Constitutional Analysis of the Criminal Jurisdiction and Procedural Guarantees of the American Indian" (Ph.D. diss., Syracuse University, 1963), 57–63; and *Felix Cohen's Handbook of Federal Indian Law* (1942; reprint, Albuquerque: University of New Mexico Press, 1971), 116ff and 122ff.

5. Quoted in *Cohen's Handbook,* 123.

6. *Cohen's Handbook,* 124–25, 147.

7. Murray L. Crosse, "Criminal and Civil Jurisdiction in Indian Country," paper presented to Southwest Indian Tribal Courts Conference, University of Arizona, June 22, 23, 24, 1960, reprinted in *Program and Proceedings* and published by the Bureau of Indian Affairs, Branch of Law and Order, Phoenix Area Office. Crosse notes that embezzlement was added to the list in 1956.

these eleven major offenses areas in which federal jurisdiction displaced tribal jurisdiction. In all other criminal and civil cases committed by Indians on Indian land, tribal laws have force so long as they do not conflict with the U.S. Constitution or are not restricted by individual treaty agreements. The relation of an Indian nation to federal and state governments is much like that of a territory: Except where limited by federal act, it has concurrent powers of investigation, prosecution, and punishment. And an offender who has been punished under tribal law is exempt from additional federal punishment.

Federal limitations of tribal jurisdiction are fragmentary at best, however, and perhaps ill-conceived. A man may beat another with his hands near death, for example, but, if it cannot be established that his hands are "dangerous weapons" or that he assaulted the person with the clear "intent to kill," the offense does not come under federal jurisdiction. And the list of federal offenses does not include kidnapping, blackmail, or poisoning (if the victim does not die). Moreover, even among the so-called major offenses, federal jurisdiction is sometimes limited or arguable. There are no federal provisions for statutory rape, for instance; and a case of embezzlement might be tried in either a federal or tribal court, depending on the severity of the crime. The question of jurisdiction, from the point of view of the offender, is not merely one of legal technicalities, however; it may mean substantial differences in penalties and punishment. As jurist Felix Cohen has pointed out: "The maximum punishment specified in the Indian penal codes is generally more humane, seldom exceeding imprisonment for 6 months, even for offenses like kidnapping, for which state penal codes impose imprisonment for 20 years or more."[8]

Apart from strict legal jurisdiction considerations, there exist geographical considerations as well. Mark Twain noted the whimsicality of such legal fictions as borders in *Life on the Mississippi* when he observed that the ever-shifting course of the Mississippi River might alter the state boundaries of Missouri and Illinois in the days before the Civil War and, thus, overnight, make a slave of a free man while he was asleep in his bed. The same sort of complications are often present with reservations. The boundary lines of Indian country are often ill-defined and disputed. (Hillerman hints at this problem when he locates the hippie commune on disputed ter-

8. *Cohen's Handbook,* 147, 149.

ritory; the hippies claim they are living on Bureau of Land Management land, but Leaphorn says that Navajo maps show the land to be on the reservation.) And in the case of the so-called "checkerboard" area of the Navajo reservation, in northwest New Mexico, there exists a constantly shifting mosaic of Indian and non-Indian lands that come under separate jurisdiction.

In a lecture some years ago, Roland Dart, then chief of the Navajo Tribal Police, remarked that it was not uncommon to call in a surveyor to determine the exact location of a criminal act in order to ascertain jurisdiction in the case. More recently, in a conversation with a B.I.A. investigator, I learned of a statutory rape case that occurred in the "checkerboard" area. It appears that the rape took place in an automobile parked across the boundary separating state and Navajo lands, and it had to be determined whether the criminal act took place in the front or the back seat of the car. The distinction was an important one, for statutory rape in New Mexico may be a first-degree felony and carry a maximum penalty of life imprisonment;[9] whereas the *Navajo Tribal Code* provides a maximum penalty of six months' hard labor and a fine of five hundred dollars. It was decided that the sexual act occurred in the back seat and therefore was subject to New Mexico jurisdiction, but one wonders what legalistic metaphysics would have been involved if the car, rather than crossing the line, had been straddling it.

Hillerman betrays his familiarity with the special jurisdictional complications in the "checkerboard" area in *People of Darkness* (1980). The Valencia County sheriff warns a Navajo tribal policeman, Jimmy Chee, that problems of this sort are especially knotty on this part of the reservation. "You're driving along and one minute you're on the Navajo Reservation and the next minute you're in Valencia County jurisdiction and usually there's no way in God's world to know the difference." Jurisdictional problems are pervasive everywhere on the sprawling reservation, the narrator observes, "But here on the southwestern fringe of the reservation, checkerboarding complicates the problem. In the 1880s, the government deeded every other square mile in a sixty-mile strip to the Atlantic and Pacific Railroad to subsidize extension of its trunk line westward. The A & P had become the Santa Fe generations ago, and the Navajo Nation had gradually

9. *New Mexico Statutes*, 31–18–3.

bought back part of this looted portion of its Dinetah, its homeland, but in many places this checkerboard pattern of ownership persisted."

The author never fully integrates his self-evident awareness of jurisdictional difficulties into the texture of his plot in *People of Darkness,* but Jimmy Chee emerges, as does Leaphorn, as someone more mindful of native tradition than bureaucratic restraint. Hillerman provides a concrete example of jurisdictional problems in *Dance Hall of the Dead,* however, when he identifies Leaphorn's involvement in an embezzlement case, a case that in all probability would never go to court.

A Navajo man has given a Navajo woman eight hundred dollars to take into Gallup, New Mexico, to make a down payment on a pickup truck. The woman, however, uses the money to get her jewelry out of pawn. The man claims the money changed hands on nonreservation lands, but the woman maintains that they were standing on the reservation when he gave her the money. If it could be established that the man is correct, the case will be tried under New Mexico embezzlement laws, where the crime will constitute a fourth-degree felony, carrying a penalty of not less than one year nor more than five years' imprisonment and/or a five-thousand-dollar fine. But if the woman is correct, the maximum penalty will be six months at hard labor, provided the federal courts decline jurisdiction in the case.[10] Since the exact location can probably never be determined, however, and since it is simply a matter of one person's word against another's, the case will in all likelihood be dismissed.

It is amidst this dizzying complexity of jurisdiction and the sometimes absurd discrepancies in laws and penalties that the Navajo tribal policeman works on a day-to-day basis. And the *Navajo Tribal Code* plainly recognizes these special circumstances. In outlining the functions of the Navajo Law Enforcement Agency, the code specifies that:

> Due to the peculiar nature of the land ownership pattern on or near the Reservation and due to the multiplicity of the agencies having jurisdiction over these lands, the Department must establish satisfactory working relationships with other law enforcement organizations in order that crimes may be expeditiously investigated and crime prevention programs established.[11]

10. *New Mexico Statutes,* 30–16–8; 31–18–3D; *Navajo Tribal Code,* title 17–391.
11. *Navajo Tribal Code,* rev. 1978, title 2–1114.

And Hillerman, of course, is aware of this multiplicity: "At the moment," says the narrator of *Dance Hall of the Dead,*

> six law-enforcement agencies were interested in the affair at Zuni (if one counted the Bureau of Indian Affairs Law and Order Division, which was watching passively). Each would function as its interests dictated that it must. Leaphorn himself, without conscious thought, would influence his actions to the benefit of the Dinée if Navajo interests were at stake. Orange Naranjo, he knew, would do his work honestly and faithfully with full awareness that his good friend and employer, the sheriff of McKinley County, was seeking reelection. Pasquaanti was responsible first to laws centuries older than the whiteman's written codes. Highsmith, whose real job was traffic safety, would do as little as possible. And O'Malley would make his decisions with that ingrained FBI awareness that the rewards lay in good publicity, and the sensible attitude that other agencies were competitors for that publicity.

Moreover, the author also expresses here the probable feelings of frustration and anger that a tribal policeman might feel in an investigation of this sort. Leaphorn's task of finding George Bowlegs takes him over several hundred miles of inhospitable territory, and the evidence he acquires in his dogged pursuit, as any tribal policeman knows, will and must be turned over to the FBI. And Hillerman is probably right, too, that these "proper authorities" will seldom acknowledge the efforts of a mere Indian policeman, or for that matter even inform him of the progress or eventual prosecution of a case:

> If the case broke, and the Albuquerque FBI office issued a statement explaining how the arrest had been made, Leaphorn wouldn't be told. He'd read about it in the *Albuquerque Journal* or the *Gallup Independent.* Leaphorn considered this fact without rancor as something natural as the turn of the seasons.

Whether or not Leaphorn feels any resentment toward the FBI, one wonders if Hillerman is not voicing the opinions of many Navajo policemen when he has his hero distinguish Agent Baker, actually an investigator for the Bureau of Narcotics, from the run-of-the-mill FBI man:

It had occurred to Leaphorn earlier that Baker was not, in fact, an agent of the Federal Bureau of Investigation. He didn't look like one. He had bad teeth, irregular and discolored, and an air of casual sloppiness, and something about him which suggested a quick, inquisitive, impatient intelligence. Leaphorn's extensive experience with the FBI suggested that any of these three characteristics would prevent employment. The FBI people always seemed to be O'Malleys—trimmed, scrubbed, tidy, able to work untroubled by any special measure of intelligence.

While Leaphorn may accept his working conditions as "natural," he is hardly complacent nor does he act passively or according to political expediency, as do the other law enforcement agents. Rather, he is motivated by simple curiosity and a personal impulse to see a pattern in the perplexing circumstances of this case. This is not to say, however, that Leaphorn acts illegally or disregards his proper duties.

Strictly speaking, he never exceeds the bounds of his authority in his pursuit of Bowlegs, but this is due to the special arrangements that govern the actions of tribal policemen. Leaphorn's several trips into Zuni fall within his proper jurisdiction, as does the visit made by the Zuni police to the Bowlegs hogan, because with contiguous reservations, as are Ramah and Zuni, a tribal policeman may pursue and apprehend a suspected Indian felon without violating his authority. In the case of noncontiguous reservations, however, an arrest warrant is no longer valid when the officer steps onto nonreservation land and then enters another reservation.[12] And, since Navajo policemen are cross-deputized in Arizona, New Mexico, and Utah,[13] Leaphorn's excursions onto state land are proper as well, though he would have been acting as a state deputy rather than as a tribal policeman had he apprehended Bowlegs. Thus, when Leaphorn threatens to run the hippie Halsey into the McKinley County sheriff's office for a violation of state game laws, he is acting as a sheriff's deputy. When he tracks George Bowlegs into Arizona, however, his authority is questionable. As an Arizona deputy, he may pursue a suspected felon onto private property, but had he found Bowlegs there it is doubtful that he could have arrested him, since

12. William Truswell, "Extradition," speech presented to the Second Southwest Indian Tribal Courts Conference, University of Arizona, March 21, 22, 1962. Highlights of the speech reprinted in *Program and Proceedings*, n.d., published by the B.I.A. Branch of Law and Order, Gallup Area Office.

13. Orr, "Navajo Police Go with Times."

no warrant existed in Arizona. Rather than powers of arrest, Leaphorn would merely have the power to detain the boy and deliver him to other authorities.

While Leaphorn appears to be aware of the special circumstances of his position and the limits of his authority, he is hardly a company man. His impulses are governed more by a native, traditional sense of values. As a Navajo Division of Public Safety paper states, "the traditional religious system [of the Navajos] placed a great value on the maintenance of a harmonious relationship between man and his environment. . . . A system of taboos and informal laws governed human behaviour." Rather than statute and code, crime and punishment, Leaphorn seeks a pattern to the puzzling case, and he is, at first, frustrated:

> Leaphorn studied the sky, his face dour. He was finding no order in his thoughts, none of that mild and abstract pleasure which the precise application of logic always brought to him. Instead there was only the discordant clash of improbable against unlikely, effect without cause, action without motive, patternless chaos. Leaphorn's orderly mind found this painful.

Hillerman describes Leaphorn's motivation quite simply. Navajo tradition taught

> that the only goal for man was beauty, and that beauty was found only in harmony, and that this harmony of nature was a matter of dazzling complexity. . . . Every cause has its effect. Every action its reaction. Thus one learned to live with evil by understanding it, by reading its cause. And thus one learned, gradually and methodically, if one was lucky, to always "go in beauty," to always look for the pattern, and to find it.

By temperament and tradition, Leaphorn is perfectly suited to his role as detective. More than allegiance to duty, his native values spur Leaphorn's search for Bowlegs and an explanation to the mystery. And he is angry and resentful, not because he must answer to and suffer abuse from the bungling FBI agent O'Malley, but because he can't see a pattern to the evidence he uncovers. He tracks the Navajo boy into Arizona simply because his curiosity demands it. And when the pieces begin to fall into place, Leaphorn is relieved: "For the first time since he had heard of George Bowlegs, some-

thing seemed to be working out with that rational harmony Leaphorn's or-
derly soul demanded." If he fails in the job assigned to him by a federal
agency, Leaphorn is nevertheless successful in the more important task of
discerning a pattern in complexity. He reads the cause of evil and attains,
through understanding, the beauty that comes with harmony.

Though he cannot appreciate the motives of a man who kills to protect
his professional reputation, he does understand them. And there is a certain satisfaction in the fact that Reynolds dies, not simply because he has
killed three men, but because he violated a Zuni taboo. By wearing a kachi-
na mask in which the spirit of the god does not live, Reynolds had committed the vilest sacrilege, and "the penalty for sacrilege is death."

"There is an old law," Leaphorn explains to Ted Isaacs, "that takes
precedence over the white man's penal code. It says 'Thou shall not pro-
fane the Sacred Ways of Zuni.'" The Zunis restore the sacred harmony of
their village by exacting that penalty which religious tradition demands.
They achieve communally what Leaphorn achieves individually, a harmony that is the goal of life. Both Leaphorn and the Zunis transcend the narrow bounds of temporal law and the complications of jurisdiction by adherence to their respective primitive and pure cultural codes. And the
background of jurisdiction questions and petty legal distinctions, by contrast, emphasizes the dignity of older laws and simpler personal satisfac-
tions.

Though *The Dance Hall of the Dead* is a conventional detective novel,
supplied with a hero whose devotion to seeing a pattern in the apparently
patternless any devotee of that genre may readily identify, and full of adventure and intrigue, it is nevertheless strangely reminiscent of Arthur
Miller's *A View from the Bridge*. In that play, too, community taboos are
dramatically poised against federal laws, and as the lawyer Alfieri says in
the play: "Nowadays we settle for half. And it is better." But he senses the
glory and majesty of the days in ancient Sicily when justice was pure and
uncomplicated. The Zunis do not settle for half in Hillerman's novel, nor
does Leaphorn. Though the conditions of his occupation urge complacency, compromise, and halfhearted endeavor, he nevertheless emerges as one
untainted by the technical constraints under which he labors, one quietly
loyal to the primitive, tribal claims upon him.

In Hillerman's three Joe Leaphorn novels—*The Blessing Way* (1970),
Dance Hall of the Dead (1975), and *Listening Woman* (1979)—the author
has moved his hero all over the Navajo reservation: into the secret recess-

es of Canyon de Chelly, as far north as Lake Powell on the Utah border, and as far south as Ramah. With *People of Darkness,* Hillerman promoted Leaphorn to captain and stationed him in Chinle, Arizona, and made Jimmy Chee his new hero. Thus far, Chee has worked on and off the reservation in the checkerboard area of New Mexico and, in *The Dark Wind* (1982), on the "Joint Use Area" of the Hopi and Navajo reservations. Chee differs from Leaphorn only in incidental ways, though he may have a bit more pep and a little less patience than his predecessor. But Chee, too, displays a devotion to seeing a pattern in mysterious events and a capacity to rise above bureaucratic technicalities. But then, Chee's heroic proportions had already been established in the character of Joe Leaphorn.

A Postscript

XIV

The Trying Out of Genetic Inquiry

I had contemplated providing this essay with the whimsical title: "On Not Being French." The whimsy involved would no doubt have been obscure to those unfamiliar with a special issue of the *Yale French Review* on geneticism of two or three years ago. I was surprised to discover there that geneticism dates from around 1979 and is actually a French creation. This disclosure would perhaps have surprised such scholars as Jonathan Livingston Lowes, Leon Howard, Walter Blair, Howard Vincent, and many others; it might well dismay all those involved in preparing CEAA or, later, CSE editions; it would have irritated W. W. Greg, R. B. McKerrow, and others whose thinking about genetic matters antedates the French discovery by forty or fifty years; and it likely would annoy the textual critics who followed them, Fredson Bowers and Thomas Tanselle, or those who called their position into deep question—I am thinking here of Hershel Parker on the one hand and Jerome McGann on the other.

That is the subject of the paper I did not write. But, as my present title suggests, I have decided instead to speculate a bit on the practical consequences of the genetic method. For those engaged in teaching American literature, it may be that what I have to suggest is a familiar part of your actual practice, in which case these speculations may be taken as an exercise in self-accusation. Nevertheless, I want to try to imagine what pedagogical implications, if any, there might be if we took geneticism into the classroom. I offer the following observations almost at random.

John Bryant has coined a wonderfully suggestive phrase to convey the genetic quality of literary works—"fluid texts." I myself tend to think of texts as somewhat gelatinous rather than fluid, but I don't want to quibble over a matter of viscosity. It is enough to say that the creation and persistence of a text is an unstable compound—a heterogeneous mix of the social, political, biographical, and linguistic circumstances of its composing alongside all manner of subsequent events that constitute a textual history.

And those subsequent events are likewise heterogeneous; they include, but are not limited to, the trivial (typesetter's errors, for example); the personal (authorial revisions, made, perhaps, on aesthetic grounds); the commercial (editorial decisions made in deference to publishing policy or current taste); the popular (such "readings" as are conveyed by contemporary reviews); and the institutional (the work of the academy, which brings about the sort of scholarly and critical additions to an understanding not only of the text in question but all those other circumstances just named).

A genetic approach to teaching literature would mean, among other things, making greater use of existing resources and perhaps creating others. From time to time, one sees evidence of increased interest in genetic matters—the new, revised Norton critical edition of *Walden*, for example, includes an essay on the writing of the book as well as a much more substantial selection from the *Journals*. The new Norton anthology of American literature includes both the 1855 and the 1881 versions of "Song of Myself"; this, I suspect, is primarily the work of one of its editors. Hershel Parker is passionately devoted to first intentions and has articulated in some detail his reasons for that devotion. The head note to the Whitman section, however, merely announces the editors' "confidence that teachers and students will welcome the chance to study Whitman's two principal versions of his masterpiece." (Either that confidence is misplaced, or I have been drawing the wrong breed of students, for whom one version is more than enough.) The new Bedford cultural editions historicize texts, but so far as I am aware there is little in the hundreds of pages of "cultural contexts" that would actively help the student to connect the compositional and textual history of the book to its historical context. Martha Nell Smith recently called for a new text of Emily Dickinson's poetry, one "liberated" from the constraints of the printed book and now made possible through the Internet and CD-ROM. However, she does not call for a new generation of readers who have even a rudimentary understanding of textual criticism; instead she wants a text that encourages "free play" and allows readers, as their fancy dictates, to instantly substitute alternate versions of passages or lines. Without some sort of rationale for emendations (however private and exhilarating the act might be), I do not see why the same free play might not as easily lead a reader to substitute lines, not from Dickinson at all but from, say, Edward Lear or Rod McKuen.

Evidently, texts are being liberated all over the province, though, so far as I am aware, little is being said about what we (or they) are to do with this new-won freedom in the classroom. Jerome McGann, in a deliberately self-conscious answer to Greg's 1949 essay "The Rationale of the Copy Text," posted on the Internet his own essay "The Rationale of HyperText." His rationale may serve as complementary to Smith's call for a liberated Dickinson text, since he too wishes to "secure freedom from the analytic limits of hardcopy text." (I must interrupt myself here, however, and note that I am citing a copy of McGann's essay last modified Saturday, May 6, 1995, at 5:55 and 14 seconds PM Eastern Daylight Time. The essay may have been modified a thousand times since then; I don't know. I do know that I don't want texts to become so very fluid that we must read the thoughts of one another like a ticker tape.) In any event, I have no quarrel with McGann's desire for hypertext archives in which nothing is privileged, nothing is hierarchical. Nevertheless his view of texts is more amenable to high-tech representation than more conventional means, I believe.

Existing resources for textual study have increased significantly in this the information age, but, from a pedagogical point of view, I wonder whether our students have the wherewithal (which is to say, the training) to distinguish information from form, authorial intent from readerly indulgence, problem solving from problematizing. The capacity to bring together diverse textual and contextual materials more rapidly and more universally constitutes a pedagogical opportunity. But textual liberation does not mean that students will know what to do with such anarchic freedom or that what they do do will be either coherent or satisfying, even to themselves. If I read McGann aright, the proliferation of textual resources brought together in innumerable combinations demolishes hierarchy, but what is left may be nothing more than a concatenation of textual shards indifferently vying for one's attention.

The new information highway may well be taking us to a better place. However, as William James once observed, one can imagine many different kinds of relations. One can imagine the things of this world hooked together in many different ways. But of all those vitalizing possibilities of all possible universes, says James, the "lowest grade" universe would be one of mere "withness." Without some training in editorial procedure and critical judgment, our students may well be condemned to just this sort of low-grade verbal withness.

Of course, survey and period courses present themselves (at least to the undergraduate) as predominantly possessing this same quality—one reads Emerson with Poe with Whitman with Fuller with Hawthorne with Melville, and so on. But the cross connections between and among these several writers are real enough. Hawthorne, for example, influenced the creation of *Moby-Dick;* and Melville likely influenced the creation of *The Blithedale Romance.* Critical editions often include a section on backgrounds and sources, but few books fashioned along the lines of Merton Sealts and Alfred Ferguson's *Emerson's Nature: Origin, Growth, Meaning* are in print these days, and perhaps they would have trouble getting published now. And I wonder whether St. Martin's or some other press might be persuaded to publish volumes that supplied biographical and genetic contexts? I, at any rate, would like an edition of *Moby-Dick* that included telling excerpts from Thomas Beale's *Natural History of the Sperm Whale,* J. Ross Browne's *Etchings of a Whaling Cruise,* Thomas Carlyle's *Sartor Resartus,* William Ellis's *Polynesian Researches,* and so forth. These at least were books Melville read and responded to in the writing of his novel. However, the current critical climate more often encourages one to read Melville with someone he obviously never read (Sigmund Freud, for example) than with someone he did.

But let me return to more immediate pedagogical concerns. Am I the only teacher who conscientiously orders authoritative texts that list textual variants and editorial emendations and then never directs the attention of his students to such back matter? Is my department the only one in the country in which our graduate students can converse knowingly about chiasmus, apodictic certainty, or "the gaze" but would be absolutely stymied if you asked them what a copy text is? Am I the only teacher who, in survey or period courses, dutifully lectures at some length on political, social, and biographical contexts and describes, if it is known, the compositional history of a given text and then turns right around and assigns a paper on character analysis—or some rather ordinary thematic subject—topics that in no way call upon the student to make use of the contextual or textual information I have emphasized? Am I the only teacher who is tired of having students interpret texts, is even tired of my own interpretations? Is mine the only English department in the country that justifies itself to the powers that be principally on the grounds that we teach "critical thinking" and, in turn, takes that justification as warrant to disencumber the activity of critical analysis from anything so messy as scholarly evidence, much less textual variants? Chemistry and mathematics departments teach critical thinking as well, but I rather suspect that when they start their students on that path they don't at the same time jettison the periodic table or the quadratic formula.

What is more, if the scholarly process influenced our teaching methods, it might so happen that there would be positive effects on student writing. I know from teaching a class in writing historical narrative that students write better prose when they are motivated by intellectual curiosity instead of personal predilection and when they write out of a base of information instead of abstract sentiment. Because of my biographical biases, in literature classes I tend to treat authors first and foremost as writers, and thus to stress matters of technique, conception, revision, and so forth. But until recently it never even occurred to me to ask my students if they did as well. More specifically, I asked them if they read the work of professional writers (a Virginia Woolf or a Henry Adams) with an eye toward emulating them in their own prose. Their unanimous answer, by the way, was that that idea had never entered their heads. Yet am I sure that if I could get students to at least try to write as well as Virginia Woolf that the critical thinking business would take care of itself easily enough.

Perhaps a genetic approach to literary study might enable those of us who teach literature to establish links between our discipline and those of our colleagues who teach creative writing or rhetoric and composition. For what, after all, is genetic study, finally, but a study of imaginative technique? And whatever else a fluid text may be, it impresses us first and foremost as a specimen of writing. Yet if your department is like mine, there is a strict separation of powers, and the relations between and among these three groups may be cordial or cool but are seldom collegial in a pedagogical sense.

Apparently it is a vexed question among compositionists whether literature should be taught at all in writing classes, and if taught, most insist it should be done only sparingly. Recently I heard a professor of rhetoric lecture on the process of revision and about how little attention is paid in composition studies to this process. The speaker offered a case study in the sequential publication of one of Adrienne Rich's essays and probably went to some trouble in determining the revisions. The paper was interesting, but the man had probably never heard of the Hinman collator, and he appeared totally unaware of the reservoir of case studies in the back matter of innumerable CSE or other editions. But if he is right in saying that composition studies have paid little attention to the activity of revision, then I suppose the whole revising process, in the minds of many compositionists, is a rather primitive notion, something akin to the third grader playing jacks and who, failing at first, shouts "Do overs!" At all events, I don't think one could properly describe James's New York edition as mere do-overs. The pedagogical point to be made, however, is that the student writer stands to learn a great deal from the professional, all the more so if the student thinks of authors as writers and texts as specimens of writing that have their own compositional history.

If texts are "fluid," then interpretation is no longer a self-sufficient enterprise. Instead, might the emphasis in the classroom be placed not on interpretation at all but on intelligibility? The first activity is one of making meaning, the second one of making sense. Many textual anomalies are rendered intelligible by bringing extratextual facts into play, whereas interpretation typically seeks to reconcile discrepancies by any number of possible and possibly tortured readings to account for a simple error. In fact, genetic inquiry, in some instances, might effectively place the accent on problem solving instead of problematizing. And to illustrate the difference one has only to note the perennial problem of the ending of *Huckleberry Finn.* So basic a critical issue is the evasion episode that Gerald Graf and James Phelan in preparing their edition of the novel named it as one of the three interpretive controversies that served to organize their casebook. And most all of us who teach that novel probably set aside at least some time to discuss this very problem if for no other reason than it has a distinguished critical history—starting with Leo Marx and moving forward to the day before yesterday.

However, a few years ago Gary Henrickson rather systematically explored the persistence of this critical issue in an essay. He noted that between 1950 and 1991 some eighty publications appeared defending the ending of the book. Of those eighty works, however, only nine made any use whatsoever of the wealth of scholarly material prepared and published by the Mark Twain Project or by others during the same period. Henrickson was too discreet, or perhaps too polite, to draw the same conclusions I did when I reviewed his essay for *American Literary Scholarship*: "No one to my knowledge," I wrote, "has established whether the evasion episode is in fact a problem (that is, an interpretive issue that may be framed in a way that makes it susceptible of solution or consensual understanding). It may be merely a conundrum that provides the opportunity to show off one's own critical acrobatics." Besides, from a genetic point of view, the evasion is not the conclusion of the book anyway. Twain wrote and interpolated two and a half chapters into the book after he had written the narrative conclusion.

Why shouldn't students learn to grapple with actual textual problems? What if the student thought seriously about compositional matters: about whether there were two or three *Moby-Dicks* or seven *Waldens*, or whether Emerson's *Nature* really has two introductions; about which alternate conclusion to Dickinson's "Safe in their Alabaster Chambers" or John Barth's *The Floating Opera* is better and why; about how a short story might be absorbed into a novel, as, in very different ways, happened in *The Sun Also Rises, The Professor's House,* and *The Sound and the Fury?* What if a student dealt with textual problems that might actually have a solution? What if the student read Carlyle in order to see how deeply and how differently he influenced Emerson or Thoreau or Melville; or tried to decide whether the new and much longer editions of *Sister Carrie* and *Native Son* are really better or even very different; or how great a stylistic distance there is between the juvenile and adult versions of "To Build a Fire," or between Crane's journalistic and imaginative accounts of his experience in a lifeboat? These are merely instances, and the prospect of chopping up texts this way may strike the fastidious reader as distinctly unliterary, even crude. Herman Melville, too, knew that it was devilishly hard to get poetry out of whale blubber, but he believed that it might be worth trying out nonetheless.

A CHECKLIST OF PUBLICATIONS

BOOKS

Mark Twain: A Study of the Short Fiction. Twayne Studies in Short Fiction. New York: Twayne Publishers, 1997.

Coming to Grips with "Huckleberry Finn": Essays on a Book, a Boy, and a Man. Columbia: University of Missouri Press, 1993.

Bergson in American Culture: The Worlds of Willa Cather and Wallace Stevens. Chapel Hill: University of North Carolina Press, 1990.

Melville's Confidence-Man: From Knave to Knight. Columbia: University of Missouri Press, 1982.

EDITIONS AND COLLECTIONS

Cather, Willa. *Alexander's Bridge.* Willa Cather Scholarly Editions Project. Lincoln: University of Nebraska Press, forthcoming.

Dictionary of Literary Biography, Documentary Series: Adventures of Huckleberry Finn. Detroit: Gale Research, Bruccoli, Clark, Layman, forthcoming.

Twain, Mark. *The Innocents Abroad.* New York: Penguin/Putnam, forthcoming.

Bierce, Ambrose. *Tales of Soldiers and Civilians and Other Stories.* New York: Penguin Publishers, 2000.

The Viking Portable American Realism Reader, 1865–1918. Ed. with James Nagel. New York: Penguin Publishers, 1997.

Biographies of Books: The Backgrounds, Genesis, and Composition of Notable American Writings. Ed. with James Barbour. Columbia: University of Missouri Press, 1996.

American Realism and the Canon: A Collection of Essays. Ed. with Gary Scharnhorst. Newark: University of Delaware Press, 1994.

Selected Tales, Essays, Speeches, and Sketches of Mark Twain. New York: Penguin Publishers, 1994.

Melville, Herman. *Moby-Dick.* Ed. with Andrew Delbanco. New York: Penguin Publishers, 1992.

Writing the American Classics. Ed. with James Barbour. Chapel Hill: University of North Carolina Press, 1990.

Howard, Leon. *Essays on the Puritans.* Ed. with James Barbour. Historical introduction by Leo Lemay. Albuquerque: University of New Mexico Press, 1986.

Romanticism: Critical Essays in American Literature. Ed. with James Barbour. New York: Garland Publishing, 1986.

EDITED MONOGRAPHS OR JOURNAL ISSUES

Editing the Literary Imagination. Ed. with Robert D. Sattelmeyer. *Studies in the Literary Imagination* 29, no. 2 (fall 1996).

American Literary Realism 23, no. 3 (spring 1991). Guest editor. Introduction reprinted with alterations in *Realism and the Canon,* pp. 13–20.

Howard, Leon. *The Unfolding of "Moby-Dick": Seven Essays in Evidence.* Ed. with James Barbour. Glassboro, N.J.: Melville Society, 1987.

ESSAYS AND CHAPTERS

"Cather and Twain, Once Again." In *Willa Cather, Mesa Verde, and the Southwest,* ed. Joseph Urgo and John Swift. Lincoln: University of Nebraska Press, forthcoming.

"Teaching the Isms of the Realist Era." In *Teaching American Realism and Naturalism,* ed. Thomas Dean and Louis J. Budd. New York: Publications of the Modern Language Association, forthcoming.

"Mark Twain in Large and Small: The Infinite and the Infinitesimal in Twain's Late Writing." In *Constructing Mark Twain: New Directions in Scholarship,* ed. Laura E. Skandera Trombley and Michael J. Kiskis. Columbia: University of Missouri Press, 2001.

"Authors, Intentions, and Texts." *Essays in Arts and Sciences* 28 (October 1999): 1–15.

"Samuel Langhorne Clemens." In *Dictionary of Missouri Biography,* ed. Lawrence O. Christensen et al. Columbia: University of Missouri Press, 1999.

"'In the Shallow Light of the Present': The Moral Geography of *Death Comes for the Archbishop.*" *Essays in Arts and Sciences* 24 (October 1995): 1–20.

"Sources, Influences, and Intertexts." *Resources for American Literary Study* 21, no. 2 (1995): 65–82.

"What If Poe's Humorous Tales Were Funny?: Poe's 'X-ing a Paragrab' and Twain's 'Journalism in Tennessee.'" *Studies in American Humor,* n.s. 3, no. 2 (1995): 36–48.

"Determinism" and "Jim." In *The Mark Twain Encyclopedia,* ed. J. R. LeMaster and James D. Wilson. New York: Garland Publishing, 1993.

"Is *Huckleberry Finn* Politically Correct?" In *Coming to Grips with "Huckleberry Finn,"* pp. 147–62. Reprinted in *Realism and the Canon,* pp. 190–200.

"A Pragmatic Defense of Source Study: Melville's 'Borrowings' from Judge James Hall." *MOSAIC: A Journal for the Comparative Study of Literature and Ideas* 26, no. 4 (fall 1993): 21–35.

"The Realism of *Huckleberry Finn.*" In *Coming to Grips with "Huckleberry Finn,"* pp. 83–105. Reprinted in *The Cambridge Companion to American Realism and Naturalism,* ed. Donald Pizer, 138–53. Cambridge: Cambridge University Press, 1995.

"The Judge Dragged to the Bar: Lemuel Shaw, Herman Melville, and the Webster Murder Case." *Melville Society Extracts* no. 84 (February 1991): 1–8.

"Nobility out of Tatters: The Writing of *Huckleberry Finn.*" In *Writing the American Classics,* pp. 79–105. Reprinted in *Coming to Grips with "Huckleberry Finn,"* pp. 10–41.

"Realism, the 'Real,' and the Poet of Reality: Some Reflections on American Realists and the Poetry of Wallace Stevens." *American Literary Realism* 21, no. 2 (winter 1989): 34–53.

"My Ántonia in a Survey of the American Novel." In *Approaches to Teaching Cather's "My Ántonia,"* ed. Susan J. Rosowski. New York: Modern Language Association, 1989.

"'Learning a Nigger to Argue': Quitting *Huckleberry Finn*." *American Literary Realism* 20, no. 1 (fall 1987): 18–33. Reprinted in *Coming to Grips with "Huckleberry Finn,"* pp. 63–82.

"Bergson in America." In *Prospects: An Annual Journal of American Cultural Studies,* vol. 11, *Essays,* 453–90. Cambridge: Cambridge University Press, 1987.

"Justice on the Reservation: Hillerman's Novels and the Conflict between Federal and Tribal Jurisdiction." *The Arm-Chair Detective* 18, no. 4 (fall 1985): 364–70.

"Life Imitating Art: *Huckleberry Finn* and Twain's Autobiographical Writings." In *One Hundred Years of "Huckleberry Finn": A Centennial Collection of Essays,* ed. Robert Sattelmeyer and J. Donald Crowley. Columbia: University of Missouri Press, 1985. Reprinted in *Coming to Grips with "Huckleberry Finn,"* pp. 42–61.

"Hawthorne's Last Tales and 'The Custom House.'" *ESQ: A Journal of the American Renaissance* 30, no. 4 (4th quarter, 1984): 183–94.

"Cather and Fitzgerald: *The Great Gatsby*." *American Literature,* 54, no. 4 (December 1982): 576–91.

"The Legend of Noah and the Voyage of Huckleberry Finn." *Mark Twain Journal* 21, no. 2 (summer 1982): 21–23.

"The Afro-American Journal," "Amistad," and "The Brown American" [magazine profiles]. In *Black Journals of the United States* ed. Walter Daniel. Westport, Conn.: Greenwood Press, 1982.

"More on the Composition of *Moby-Dick*." *Melville Society Extracts* no. 46 (May 1981): 6–7.

"A Source for *Where Are You Going, Where Have You Been?*" *Studies in Short Fiction* 18, no. 4 (fall 1981): 413–19. Reprinted in Joyce Carol Oates, *Where Are You Going, Where Have You Been?* ed. Elaine Showalter. New Brunswick, N.J.: Rutgers University Press, 1994.

"Melville and Man Traps." *Melville Society Extracts* no. 44 (November 1980): 11–12.

"Two Sources in Melville's *The Confidence-Man*." *Melville Society Extracts* no. 39 (September 1979): 12–13.

"Jean Toomer's Contributions to the *New Mexico Sentinel*." With Robert E. Fleming. *CLA Journal* 19, no. 4 (June 1976): 524–32. Reprinted in *Jean Toomer: A Critical Evaluation,* ed. Therman B. O'Daniel. Washington, D.C.: Howard University Press, 1988.

"Saint Paul's Types of the Faithful and Melville's Confidence Man." *Nineteenth-Century Fiction* 28, no. 4 (March 1974): 472–77.

MISCELLANEOUS

"Mark Twain." In *American Literary Scholarship, 1992, 1993,* and *1994.* Durham, N.C.: Duke University Press, 1992–1994.

Howard, Leon. "Artificial Sensitivity and Artful Rationality: Basic Elements in the Creative Imagination of Edgar Allan Poe." Ed. with James Barbour. *Poe Studies* 20, no. 1 (June 1987): 18–33.

Occasional reviews in *African American Review, American Literary Realism, Nineteenth-Century Literature, Modernism/Modernity,* and *American Literature.*

"Gateway to the West: Exploring Editorial Terrain" [proceedings report]. *Documentary Editing* 21, no. 1 (March 1999): 19.

"Dream On" [imaginary dialogue]. Published by Elmira College Center for Mark Twain Studies at Quarry Farm, October 1992.

Selected poems and aphorisms. Published in *Studies in American Humor* n.s. 3, no. 5 (1998): 97–99.

INDEX